Ric Pimentel
Terry Wall

Cambridge

checkpoint

ENDORSED BY

CAMBRIDGE
International Examinations

NEW EDITION

checkpoint
Maths

3

HODDER
EDUCATION
AN HACHETTE UK COMPANY

Acknowledgements

The authors and publishers would like to thank Adrian Metcalf for his help during the production of this book. The publishers would like to thank the following for permission to reproduce copyright material.

Photo credits

p.1 © SEF-Pics/Alamy; **p.2** © Robert Pernell – Fotolia; **p.72** © Jeremy Woodhouse/Photodisc/Getty Images; **p.102** http://en.wikipedia.org/wiki/File:Plimpton_322; **p.109** © Tan Kian Khoon – Fotolia; **p.142** M.C. Escher's "Symmetry Drawing E110" © 2011 The M.C. Escher Company-Holland. All rights reserved. www.mcescher.com; **p.149** © Sinopix/Rex Features; **p.159** © Stephen Bradley/Alamy; **p.176** © WestEnd61/Rex Features; **p.199** © Johnny Lye – Fotolia; **p.226** © barneyboogles – Fotolia.

Computer hardware and software brand names mentioned in this book are protected by their respective trademarks and are acknowledged.

Every effort has been made to trace all copyright holders, but if any have been inadvertently overlooked the publishers will be pleased to make the necessary arrangements at the first opportunity.

Hachette UK's policy is to use papers that are natural, renewable and recyclable products and made from wood grown in sustainable forests. The logging and manufacturing processes are expected to conform to the environmental regulations of the country of origin.

Orders: please contact Bookpoint Ltd, 130 Milton Park, Abingdon, Oxon OX14 4SB. Telephone: (44) 01235 827720. Fax: (44) 01235 400454. Lines are open 9.00–5.00, Monday to Saturday, with a 24-hour message answering service. Visit our website at www.hoddereducation.com

© Ric Pimentel and Terry Wall 2011

First published in 2011 by
Hodder Education, an Hachette UK Company,
Carmelite House, 50 Victoria Embankment
London EC4Y 0DZ

Impression number   9
Year   2017

Cover photo © Travelscape Images/Alamy
Illustrations by Barking Dog Art and Pantek Media
Typeset in 11pt Palatino light by Pantek Media, Maidstone, Kent
Printed in India

A catalogue record for this title is available from the British Library

ISBN 978 1444 143 997

Contents

The chapters in this book have been arranged to match the Cambridge Secondary 1 Mathematics Curriculum Framework for stage 9 as follows:
● Number
● Algebra
● Geometry
● Measure
● Handling data
● Calculation and mental strategies
● Problem solving

Introduction

This series of books follows the Cambridge Secondary 1 Mathematics Curriculum Framework drawn up by University of Cambridge International Examinations. It has been written by two experienced teachers who have lived or worked in schools in many countries, and worked with teachers from other countries, including England, Spain, Germany, France, Turkey, South Africa, Malaysia and the USA.

Students and teachers in these countries come from a variety of cultures and speak many different languages as well as English. Sometimes cultural and language differences make understanding difficult. However, mathematics is largely free from these problems. Even a maths book written in Japanese will include algebra equations with x and y.

We should also all be very aware that much of the mathematics you will learn in these books was first discovered, and then built upon, by mathematicians from all over the world, including China, India, Arabia, Greece and Western countries.

Most early mathematics was simply game play and problem solving. Later this maths was applied to building, engineering and sciences of all kinds. Mathematicians study maths because they enjoy it.

We hope that you will enjoy the work you do, and the maths you learn in this series of books. Sometimes the ideas will not be easy to understand at first. That should be part of the fun. Ask for help if you need it, but try hard first. Write down what you are thinking so that others can understand what you have done and help to correct your mistakes. Most students think that maths is about answers, and so it is, but it is also a way to exercise our brains, whether we find the solution or not. Some questions throughout this book are starred (✪). This means that these questions go slightly beyond the content of the curriculum at this level and will be an enjoyable challenge for those of you who try them.

Ric Pimentel and Terry Wall

SECTION 1

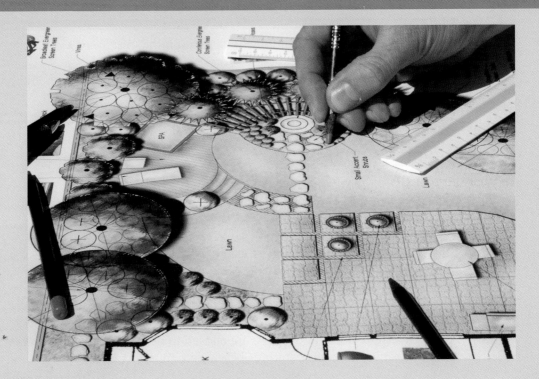

1 Integers, powers and roots

◆ Add, subtract, multiply and divide directed numbers.
◆ Estimate square roots and cube roots.
◆ Use positive, negative and zero indices and the index laws for multiplication and division of positive integer powers.

Directed numbers

A child learning to count says 'one, two, three, four …'. This set of numbers is called the counting numbers. If we include zero, we have the set of numbers called the **natural numbers**, 0, 1, 2, 3, 4, 5, … .

Numbers which have direction as well as size are called **directed numbers**. If one direction is chosen to be positive, then the opposite direction must be negative. For example,

  if north is chosen to be positive, then south must be negative

  if temperatures above zero are chosen to be positive, then temperatures below zero must be negative

  if a profit is chosen to be positive, then a loss must be negative.

Directed numbers can be positive, negative or zero. Examples of directed numbers are +7, −15, +3.5, −6.7, +13 and −0.75. Sometimes brackets are used to clarify calculations which involve directed numbers.

A directed number which is a whole number is called an **integer**. In the list of directed numbers above, +7, −15 and +13 are integers.

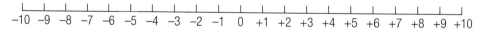

Directed numbers can be shown on a number line. Left to right is the positive direction. Right to left is the negative direction.

Adding and subtracting directed numbers

Worked examples

a) Use a number line to add (+4.5) and (−2.5).

Start at (+4.5) and move 2.5 in the negative direction.

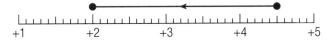

So (+4.5) + (−2.5) = (+2)   or 2

b) Use a number line to add (−5.1) and (+7.3).

Start at (−5.1) and move 7.3 in the positive direction.

So (−5.1) + (+7.3) = (+2.2)   or 2.2

c) Use a number line to calculate (+6.4) − (+2.8).

Start at (+6.4) and move 2.8 in the negative direction.

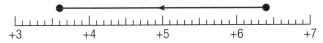

So (+6.4) − (+2.8) = (+3.6)   or 3.6

d) Use a number line to calculate (−2.9) − (+3.7).

Start at (−2.9) and move 3.7 in the negative direction.

So (−2.9) − (+3.7) = (−6.6)   or −6.6

e) Use a number line to calculate (−3.7) − (−6.4).

Start at (−3.7) and move 6.4 in the *positive* direction.

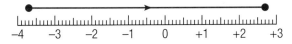

So (−3.7) − (−6.4) = (+2.7)   or 2.7

EXERCISE 1.1A

Work out the following additions. You may need to use a number line.

1 **a)** $(+5.3) + (−3.5)$
    b) $(+1.7) + (−1.4)$
    c) $(+1.0) + (−3.6)$

2 **a)** $(−3.4) + (+1.5)$
    b) $(−7.5) + (+5.1)$
    c) $(−1.8) + (−1.7)$

3 **a)** $(−5.5) + (−4.5)$
    b) $(−1.7) + (−1.1)$
    c) $(−7.1) + (−1.5)$

4 **a)** $(−5.3) + (+4.3) + (−1.6)$
    b) $(−8.3) + (−3.5) + (+1.6)$
    c) $(+1.7) + (−2.6) + (−2.3)$

Work out the following subtractions. You may need to use a number line.

5 **a)** $(+9.33) − (+4.3)$
    b) $(+5.43) − (+3.45)$
    c) $(+11) − (+4.55)$

6 **a)** $(+13) − (+4.56)$
    b) $(+4.5) − (+6.25)$
    c) $(+12) − (+5.37)$

7 **a)** $(−6) − (+3.87)$
    b) $(−14) − (+14.5)$
    c) $(−22.5) − (+22.5)$

8 **a)** $(−9.3) − (−15.7)$
    b) $(−3.67) − (−12.33)$
    c) $(−4.18) − (−11.56)$

Multiplying and dividing directed numbers

$+3 \times +2.3$ means 3 lots of $(+2.3)$ or $(+2.3) + (+2.3) + (+2.3) = (+6.9)$
$+3 \times −2.3$ means 3 lots of $(−2.3)$ or $(−2.3) + (−2.3) + (−2.3) = (−6.9)$
$−3 \times +2.3$ means $−3$ lots of $(+2.3)$ or $−((+2.3) + (+2.3) + (+2.3)) = −(6.9) = (−6.9)$
$−3 \times −2.3$ means $−3$ lots of $(−2.3)$ or $−((−2.3) + (−2.3) + (−2.3)) = −(−6.9) = (+6.9)$

EXERCISE 1.1B

Use a calculator where necessary.

1 Work out the following.
    a) $+8 \times −6.1$
    b) $+6 \times −5.2$
    c) $+4 \times −7.3$

2 Work out the following.
    a) $−5 \times +4.4$
    b) $−7 \times +9.5$
    c) $−7 \times +7.6$

3 Work out the following.
    a) $+4.5 \times +2.5$ **b)** $−3.8 \times +1.3$
    c) $+3.3 \times −4.6$ **d)** $−2.7 \times −5.25$
    e) $−5.5 \times −1.75$ **f)** $−3.3 \times −3.33$

4 Copy and complete this multiplication grid.

×	−3.25	−2.3	−1.4	0	+1.5	+2.6	+3.75
+3			−4.2			+7.8	
+2.5							
+2						+5.2	
0		0			0		
−1							−3.75
−2.3							
−3.7							

The rules for **division** of integers are the same as those for multiplication. When both quantities are positive or both are negative, the result is positive. When one is positive and the other is negative, the result is negative.

Worked examples

a) $+12.9 \div -3 = -4.3$

b) $-12.9 \div -3 = 4.3$

EXERCISE 1.1C

Use a calculator where necessary.

1 Calculate the following.
   a) $+29.25 \div +6.5$
   b) $+29.25 \div -6.5$
   c) $-29.25 \div +13$
   d) $-29.25 \div -3.25$
   e) $-58.5 \div -6.5$
   f) $-58.5 \div +13$

2 Copy and complete the following, writing in the missing numbers to make the calculations correct.
   a) _____ $\times +5.2 = +18.2$
   b) _____ $\times -3.8 = -17.1$
   c) _____ $\times -7.5 = -43.5$
   d) $-7 \times$ _____ $= 2.8$
   e) $+6 \times$ _____ $= -6.42$
   f) $-8 \times$ _____ $= +2.4$

➜

3 The table gives pairs of numbers x and y which add together to make 8.75. That is,

$$x + y = 8.75$$

Copy and complete the table.

x	+5	+4	+3	+2	+1	0	−1	−2	−3	−4	−5
y											

4 If $p + q = -3.25$, copy and complete this table.

p	+5	+4	+3	+2	+1	0	−1	−2	−3	−4	−5
q											

5 If $xy = +62$, copy and complete this table.

x	+8	+4	+2	+1	−1	−2	−4	−8
y								

> *xy means x multiplied by y.*

Powers and roots

Squares and square roots

The numbers 1, 4, 9, 16, 25, 36, 49, 64, 81, 100, ... are **square numbers**, and are made by multiplying an integer (whole number) by itself. For example,

$$7 \times 7 = 49 \quad \text{and} \quad 8 \times 8 = 64$$

Therefore 49 and 64 are square numbers.
    But

$$7.3 \times 7.3 = 53.29$$

53.29 is *not* a square number as 7.3 is not an integer.
Squaring a number is multiplying a number by itself. For example,

8 squared is $8 \times 8 = 64$
7.3 squared is $7.3 \times 7.3 = 53.29$

Using indices, 8 squared is written as 8^2 and 7.3 squared is written as 7.3^2.
The inverse operation of squaring is finding the **square root**. For example,

From what you learned about the multiplication of directed numbers earlier in this chapter, you know that $+9 \times +9 = +81$ and $-9 \times -9 = +81$.

So $(+9)^2$ and $(-9)^2$ are both $+81$. Therefore $+9$ and -9 are both square roots of $+81$. Every positive number has a positive and a negative square root.

Estimating square roots

To estimate the square root of a number which is not a square number, use the square numbers that it falls between as indicators.

Worked example

Estimate the square root of 53.

$7 \times 7 = 49$ and $8 \times 8 = 64$, so the square root of 53 is between 7 and 8.
53 is closer to 49 than to 64.
The square root of 53 is about $+7.3$ or -7.3.

EXERCISE 1.2A

Without using a calculator, work out the square roots in parts **a)** and **b)** in questions 1–10. Then estimate the square root in part **c)**. Give positive and negative roots.

1   **a)** $\sqrt{25}$ **b)** $\sqrt{36}$ **c)** $\sqrt{30}$

2   **a)** $\sqrt{49}$ **b)** $\sqrt{64}$ **c)** $\sqrt{60}$

3   **a)** $\sqrt{121}$ **b)** $\sqrt{144}$ **c)** $\sqrt{130}$

4   **a)** $\sqrt{81}$ **b)** $\sqrt{100}$ **c)** $\sqrt{90}$

5   **a)** $\sqrt{64}$ **b)** $\sqrt{81}$ **c)** $\sqrt{66}$

6   **a)** $\sqrt{25}$ **b)** $\sqrt{36}$ **c)** $\sqrt{33}$

7   **a)** $\sqrt{4}$ **b)** $\sqrt{9}$ **c)** $\sqrt{7}$

8   **a)** $\sqrt{0.01}$ **b)** $\sqrt{0.04}$ **c)** $\sqrt{0.02}$

9   **a)** $\sqrt{0.36}$ **b)** $\sqrt{0.49}$ **c)** $\sqrt{0.40}$

10   **a)** $\sqrt{0.25}$ **b)** $\sqrt{0.36}$ **c)** $\sqrt{0.33}$

11   Estimate each of these square roots.

    a) $\sqrt{80}$ **b)** $\sqrt{27}$ **c)** $\sqrt{110}$

    d) $\sqrt{0.03}$ **e)** $\sqrt{0.12}$

12   Check your answers to question 11 using a calculator.

Cubes and cube roots

This pattern sequence is made up of 1 cm cubes.

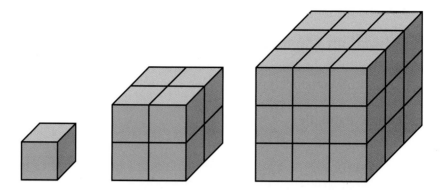

The 1 cm × 1 cm × 1 cm cube contains *one* 1 cm × 1 cm × 1 cm cube.
The 2 cm × 2 cm × 2 cm cube contains *eight* 1 cm × 1 cm × 1 cm cubes.
The 3 cm × 3 cm × 3 cm cube contains *twenty seven* 1 cm × 1 cm × 1 cm cubes.

The numbers 1, 8, 27, 64, 125, 216, 343, 512, 729, 1000, ... are **cube numbers**, and are made by multiplying an integer by itself three times. For example,

$$5 \times 5 \times 5 = 125$$

Therefore 125 is a cube number.

Cubing a number is multiplying a number by itself three times. As with squaring, there is a short way to write a number cubed using indices. For example,

$$5 \times 5 \times 5 = 5^3 \quad \text{and} \quad -5 \times -5 \times -5 = (-5)^3$$

The inverse of cubing a number is finding its **cube root**, written as $\sqrt[3]{}$.

So $\sqrt[3]{125}$ is 5 and $\sqrt[3]{343}$ is 7 (since $7 \times 7 \times 7 = 343$).

Similarly, $\sqrt[3]{-125}$ is −5 and $\sqrt[3]{-343}$ is −7.

Estimating cube roots

To estimate the cube root of a number which is not a cube number, use the cube numbers that it falls between as indicators.

Worked example

Estimate the cube root of 300.

$6^3 = 216$ and $7^3 = 343$, so the cube root of 300 is between 6 and 7.
300 is closer to 343 than to 216.
The cube root of 300 is about 6.7.

EXERCISE 1.2B

Without using a calculator, work out the cube roots of the numbers in parts **a)** and **b)** in questions 1–4. Then estimate the cube root of the number in part **c)**.

1 **a)** 8   **b)** 27   **c)** 20

2 **a)** 125   **b)** 216   **c)** 150

3 **a)** −27   **b)** −64   **c)** −50

4 **a)** 729   **b)** 1000   **c)** −800

Without using a calculator, work out the cube roots in parts **a)** and **b)** in questions 5–8. Then estimate the cube root in part **c)**.

5 **a)** $\sqrt[3]{64}$ **b)** $\sqrt[3]{125}$ **c)** $\sqrt[3]{100}$

6 **a)** $\sqrt[3]{343}$ **b)** $\sqrt[3]{512}$ **c)** $\sqrt[3]{400}$

7 **a)** $\sqrt[3]{216}$ **b)** $\sqrt[3]{125}$ **c)** $\sqrt[3]{-150}$

8 **a)** $\sqrt[3]{8000}$ **b)** $\sqrt[3]{1000}$ **c)** $\sqrt[3]{-5000}$

9 Check your answers to questions 1–8 using a calculator.

Indices

Al-Karaji was one of the greatest Arab mathematicians. He lived in the 11th century. He wrote many books on algebra and developed a theory of indices and a method of finding square roots.

In the expressions $ax^4 + bx^3 + cx^2 + dx + e$, the small numbers 4, 3 and 2 are called **indices**. Indices is the plural of **index**. So

x^4 has index 4
x^3 has index 3
x^2 has index 2

Although x does not appear to have an index, in fact it has index 1 but this is not usually written. So

$x = x^1$ has index 1

The **index** is the power to which a number is raised. In 5^3, the number 5 is raised to the power of 3, which means $5 \times 5 \times 5$. The 3 is known as the index and the 5 is known as the **base**. Here are some examples.

$5^3 = 5 \times 5 \times 5 = 125$
$7^4 = 7 \times 7 \times 7 \times 7 = 2401$
$3^1 = 3$

Laws of indices

When working with numbers involving indices there are three basic laws that can be applied. These are shown below.

- $4^2 \times 4^4 = 4 \times 4 \times 4 \times 4 \times 4 \times 4$
  $\qquad = 4^6 \quad$ (i.e. 4^{2+4})

  This can be written in a general form as:

  $$a^m \times a^n = a^{m+n}$$

  > *Notice that the base numbers must be the same for this rule to be true.*

- $3^6 \div 3^2 = \dfrac{3 \times 3 \times 3 \times 3 \times 3 \times 3}{3 \times 3}$
  $\qquad\quad = 3^4 \quad$ (i.e. 3^{6-2})

  This can be written in a general form as:

  $$a^m \div a^n = a^{m-n}$$

  > *Again, the base numbers must be the same for this rule to be true.*

- $(5^2)^3 = (5 \times 5) \times (5 \times 5) \times (5 \times 5)$
  $\qquad = 5^6 \quad$ (i.e. $5^{2\times3}$)

  This can be written in a general form as:

  $$(a^m)^n = a^{mn}$$

Worked examples

a) Simplify $4^3 \times 4^2$.

$4^3 \times 4^2 = 4^{(3+2)}$
$\qquad\quad = 4^5$

b) Evaluate $(4^2)^3$.

$(4^2)^3 = 4^{(2\times3)}$
$\qquad = 4^6$
$\qquad = 4096$

c) Simplify $2 \times 2 \times 2 \times 5 \times 5$ using indices.

$2 \times 2 \times 2 \times 5 \times 5 = 2^3 \times 5^2$

EXERCISE 1.3A

Simplify the following using indices.

1 $4 \times 4 \times 4$	**2** $3 \times 3 \times 3 \times 3 \times 3$	**3** $7 \times 7 \times 7 \times 7 \times 7 \times 7$
4 6×6	**5** $12 \times 12 \times 12$	

Write out the following in full.

6 7^4	**7** 3^3	**8** 9^4
9 6^5	**10** 11^2	

EXERCISE 1.3B

Simplify the following using indices.

1 $2^3 \times 2^2$ **2** $3^4 \times 3^5$ **3** $4^2 \times 4^3 \times 4^4$

4 5×5^2 **5** $8^3 \times 8^2 \times 8$ **6** $6^3 \div 6^2$

7 $8^5 \div 8^2$ **8** $2^7 \div 2^6$ **9** $10^5 \div 10^3$

10 $3^9 \div 3$

EXERCISE 1.3C

Simplify the following.

1 $(4^3)^2$ **2** $(3^2)^3$ **3** $(2^5)^2$

4 $(4^3)^4$ **5** $(3^7)^2$ **6** $(2^4)^4$

7 $(5^2)^2$ **8** $(6^3)^2$ **9** $(7^2)^4$

10 $(8^4)^4$

EXERCISE 1.3D

Simplify the following.

1 $2^3 \times 2^4$ **2** $3^5 \div 3^2$ **3** $2^4 \times 2^2 \div 2^3$

4 $3^8 \times 3^2 \div 3^4$ **5** $5^2 \times 5^3 \div 5$ **6** $6^3 \times 6 \div 6^2$

7 $(3^4)^2 \div 3^3$ **8** $(5^5)^2 \div 5^3$ **9** $(6^2)^3 \div 6^3$

10 $(7^3)^4 \div 7^5$

If the base numbers are not the same, only parts of the expression can be simplified. For example,

$$5 \times 5 \times 5 \times 5 \times 5 \times 3 \times 3 = 5^5 \times 3^2$$

EXERCISE 1.3E

Simplify the following. Leave your answers in index form.

1 $3 \times 3 \times 2 \times 2$ **2** $4 \times 4 \times 5 \times 5 \times 5$ **3** $2 \times 2 \times 3 \times 3 \times 3$

4 $3 \times 1 \times 4 \times 5 \times 5$ **5** $5 \times 5 \times 5 \times 5 \times 6 \times 6$ **6** $7 \times 7 \times 4 \times 4 \times 4$

7 $2 \times 2 \times 3 \times 3 \times 5 \times 5$ **8** $2 \times 3 \times 3 \times 5 \times 5 \times 5$

The zero index

The **zero index** means that a number has been raised to the power of 0. Any number raised to the power of 0 is equal to 1. For example,

$$4^0 = 1 \qquad 10^0 = 1 \qquad a^0 = 1$$

This can be explained by applying the laws of indices.

$$a^m \div a^n = a^{m-n}$$

Therefore

$$\frac{a^m}{a^m} = a^{m-m}$$
$$= a^0$$

But

$$\frac{a^m}{a^m} = 1$$

Therefore

$$a^0 = 1$$

This can also be demonstrated using numbers:

$$5^3 = 5 \times 5 \times 5$$
$$5^2 = 5 \times 5 \qquad \div 5$$
$$5^1 = 5 \qquad \div 5$$
$$5^0 = 1 \qquad \div 5$$

Worked examples

Using indices, find the value of each of these.

a) $3^6 \div 3^4$

$$3^6 \div 3^4 = 3^2 = 9$$

b) $4^5 \div 4^3$

$$4^5 \div 4^3 = 4^2 = 16$$

EXERCISE 1.3F

Using indices, find the value of each of these.

1   $5^3 \div 5^2$

2   $3^8 \div 3^6$

3   $4^2 \times 4^3 \div 4^4$

4   $2^4 \times 2^2 \div 2^6$

5   $3^3 \times 3^4 \div 3^7$

6   $2^4 \div 2^2$

7   $3^4 \div 3^3$

8   $4^4 \div 4^4$

9   $5^2 \times 5^5 \div 5^6$

10   $(6^2)^3 \div (6^3)^2$

Negative indices

A negative index means that a number has been raised to a negative power, for example 4^{-3}.

There are other ways of writing negative powers. For example, 4^{-3} can also be written as $\frac{1}{4^3}$ and in general a^{-m} can be written as $\frac{1}{a^m}$. This can be explained by applying the laws of indices.

$$a^{-m} = a^{0-m}$$
$$= \frac{a^0}{a^m}$$

But
$$a^0 = 1$$

Therefore
$$\frac{a^0}{a^m} = \frac{1}{a^m}$$

So

$$a^{-m} = \frac{1}{a^m}$$

This can also be demonstrated using numbers:

$5^2 = 5 \times 5$ ⎞ ÷5
$5^1 = 5$ ⎟ ÷5
$5^0 = 1$ ⎟ ÷5
$5^{-1} = \frac{1}{5}$ ⎟ ÷5
$5^{-2} = \frac{1}{25}$ ⎠

Worked examples

a) Write 4^{-2} as a fraction.

$$4^{-2} = \frac{1}{4^2}$$
$$= \frac{1}{16}$$

b) Simplify the following. Give your answer as a fraction.

$$7^{-4} \times 7^5 \times 7^{-3}$$
$$7^{-4} \times 7^5 \times 7^{-3} = 7^{-2}$$
$$= \frac{1}{7^2}$$
$$= \frac{1}{49}$$

To multiply, add the indices.
$-4 + 5 + -3 = -2$

EXERCISE 1.3G

Without using a calculator, write each of these as an integer or a fraction.

1 **a)** 2^{-3} **b)** 5^{-2} **c)** 3^{-2}

d) 4^{-3} **e)** 2^{-5}

2 **a)** 4×4^{-1} **b)** 9×3^{-2} **c)** 10×10^{-2}

d) 500×10^{-3} **e)** 1000×10^{-2}

3 **a)** 27×3^{-2} **b)** 16×2^{-3} **c)** 64×2^{-3}

d) 4×2^{-3} **e)** 36×6^{-3}

4 **a)** 27×3^{-4} **b)** 16×2^{-5} **c)** 4×2^{-3}

d) 4×2^{-4} **e)** 6×6^{-3}

5 **a)** $2^{-3} \times 2^{5}$ **b)** $5^{-2} \times 5^{3}$ **c)** $2^{7} \times 2^{-5}$

d) $4^{3} \times 4^{-5}$ **e)** $2^{-3} \times 2^{8} \times 2^{-4}$

EXERCISE 1.3H

Simplify the following. Give your answers as integers.

1 **a)** 4^{2} **b)** 11^{2} **c)** 3^{3}

2 **a)** 3^{4} **b)** 10^{6} **c)** 5^{3}

Using indices, find the value of each of these. Leave your answers in index form.

3 **a)** $5^{2} \times 5^{3}$ **b)** $3^{5} \times 3^{4}$ **c)** $6^{2} \times 6^{3} \times 6^{4}$

4 **a)** $10^{8} \div 10^{3}$ **b)** $5^{6} \div 5^{4}$ **c)** $8^{3} \div 8^{3}$

5 **a)** $10^{4} \times 10^{3} \div 10^{6}$ **b)** $3^{8} \times 3 \div 3^{7}$ **c)** $4^{3} \times 4^{5} \div 4^{8}$

6 **a)** $(3^{4} \times 3^{5}) \div (3^{3} \times 3^{4})$ **b)** $(5^{4} \times 5^{3}) \div (5^{2} \times 5)$ **c)** $(8^{8} \times 8^{7}) \div (8^{3} \times 8^{5})$

7 **a)** $4 \times 4 \times 4 \times 5 \times 5$ **b)** $7 \times 7 \times 8 \times 8 \times 2 \times 2 \times 2$ **c)** $5 \times 3 \times 5 \times 3 \times 5$

8 **a)** $2^{8} \div 4^{2}$ **b)** $2^{4} \div 4^{2}$ **c)** $9^{2} \div 3^{3}$

2 Expressions and formulae

- ◆ Know the origins of the word algebra and its links to the work of the Arab mathematician Al'Khwarizmi.
- ◆ Use index notation for positive integer powers; apply the index laws for multiplication and division to simple algebraic expressions.
- ◆ Construct algebraic expressions.
- ◆ Simplify or transform algebraic expressions by taking out single-term common factors.
- ◆ Add and subtract simple algebraic fractions.
- ◆ Derive formulae and, in simple cases, change the subject; use formulae from mathematics and other subjects.
- ◆ Substitute positive and negative numbers into expressions and formulae.

The Arabs and the Moors brought mathematics from India to Arabia and then to south western Europe, where they lived in Al Andaluce in what is now Spain.

Mathematics was studied in great universities in Baghdad, Alexandria and in Granada in Spain. Among the many great mathematicians were Al-Karaji who worked on indices, square roots and equations and Abu Al-Wafa' Buzjani who worked on geometry. Possibly the greatest was Muhammad ibn Musa Al'Khwarizmi, who is called 'the father of algebra'. He was born in Baghdad in 790 CE and wrote the book *Hisab al-jabr w'al-muqabala* in about 830 CE. The word algebra (*al-jabr*) comes from the title, which means *The Compendious Book on Calculation by Completion and Balancing*.

He found solutions to quadratic equations and also wrote about Hindu-Arabic numbers.

Index notation and algebra

In Chapter 1 you used indices to work with numbers. The same laws of indices that you met there also apply to algebra.

Laws of indices

- $4^2 \times 4^4 = 4 \times 4 \times 4 \times 4 \times 4 \times 4$
  $= 4^6$ (i.e. 4^{2+4})

  This can be written in a general form as:

  $$a^m \times a^n = a^{m+n}$$

  Notice that the base numbers must be the same for this rule to be true.

- $3^6 \div 3^2 = \dfrac{3 \times 3 \times 3 \times 3 \times 3 \times 3}{3 \times 3}$

  $= 3^4$ (i.e. 3^{6-2})

  This can be written in a general form as:

  $$a^m \div a^n = a^{m-n}$$

  Again, the base numbers must be the same for this rule to be true.

- $(5^2)^3 = (5 \times 5) \times (5 \times 5) \times (5 \times 5)$
  $= 5^6$ (i.e. $5^{2\times3}$)

  This can be written in a general form as:

  $$(a^m)^n = a^{mn}$$

Worked examples

a) Simplify $p^3 \times p^2$.

$p^3 \times p^2 = p^{(3+2)}$
$= p^5$

b) Simplify $w^5 \div w^3$.

$w^5 \div w^3 = w^{5-3}$
$= w^2$

c) Simplify $(m^2)^3$.

$(m^2)^3 = m^{(2\times3)}$
$= m^6$

d) Simplify $g \times g \times g \times h \times h$ using indices.

$g \times g \times g \times h \times h = g^3 \times h^2$

EXERCISE 2.1A

Simplify the following using indices.

1 $a \times a \times a$ **2** $b \times b \times b \times b \times b$ **3** $c \times c \times c \times c \times c \times c$

4 $d \times d$ **5** $e \times e \times e$

Write out the following in full.

6 p^4 **7** q^3 **8** r^4

9 s^5 **10** t^2

EXERCISE 2.1B

Simplify the following using indices.

1 $a^3 \times a^2$ **2** $b^4 \times b^5$ **3** $c^2 \times c^3 \times c^4$

4 $d \times d^2$ **5** $d^3 \times d^2 \times d$ **6** $e^3 \div e^2$

7 $g^7 \div g^6$ **8** $h^5 \div h^4$

EXERCISE 2.1C

Simplify the following.

1 $(m^3)^2$ **2** $(p^5)^2$ **3** $(r^3)^4$

4 $(s^7)^2$ **5** $(t^4)^4$ **6** $(m^3)^2$

7 $(p^2)^4$ **8** $(x^4)^4$

EXERCISE 2.1D

Simplify the following.

1 $a^3 \times a^4$ **2** $b^5 \div b^2$ **3** $c^4 \times c^2 \div c^3$

4 $d^2 \times d^3 \div d$ **5** $(e^4)^2 \div e^3$ **6** $(t^5)^2 \div t^3$

7 $(m^2)^3 \div m^3$ **8** $(r^3)^4 \div r^5$

If the base numbers are not the same, only parts of the expression can be simplified. For example,

$$p \times p \times p \times q \times q \times r \times r \times r \times r = p^3 \times q^2 \times r^4$$

$p^3 \times q^2 \times r^4$ can also be written as $p^3q^2r^4$.

EXERCISE 2.1E

Simplify the following. Do not write multiplication signs in your answers.

1 $a \times a \times b \times b$ **2** $p \times q \times q \times r \times r \times r$

3 $t \times t \times t \times t \times u \times u$ **4** $m \times m \times n \times n \times n$

5 $a \times a \times b \times b \times c \times c$ **6** $p \times r \times r \times s \times s \times s$

7 $u^2 \times uv$ **8** $s^2 \times s^3 \times t^2 \times t$

The zero index

The **zero index** means that a letter has been raised to the power of 0. Any letter (or number) raised to the power of 0 is equal to 1. For example,

$a^0 = 1$

This can be explained by applying the laws of indices.

$a^m \div a^n = a^{m-n}$

Therefore

$\frac{a^m}{a^m} = a^{m-m}$

$= a^0$

However

$\frac{a^m}{a^m} = 1$

Therefore

$a^0 = 1$

EXERCISE 2.1F

Using the laws of indices, simplify the following.

1 $a^8 \div a^7$ **2** $b^2 \times b^3 \div b^4$ **3** $c^4 \times c^2 \div c^6$

4 $a^3 \div a^2$ **5** $x^4 \div x^3$ **6** $x^4 \div x^4$

7 $p^2 \times p^5 \div p^6$ **8** $(p^2)^3 \div (p^3)^2$

EXERCISE 2.1G

Simplify the following.

1 $(m^3 \times m^5) \div (m^2 \times m^4)$ **2** $n^5 \times n^7 \times n \div n^6 \times n^2$ **3** $p^2 \times p^3 \times p^8 \div p^5 \times p^4$

4 $(a^3)^2 \div a^2$ **5** $(b^4)^2 \div (b^2)^4$ **6** $(c^2)^3 \times (c^3)^2 \div (c^5)^2$

7 $u \times w \times u \times w \times u$ **8** $u^2 \times w^3 \times u^3 \times w$ **9** $uv^2 \times u^2v \times u^2v^2$

10 $k^8 \div k^2$

Expressions

You already know that an **expression** is used to represent a value in algebraic form. For example,

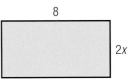

The length of the line is given by the expression $5x + 3$.

The perimeter of the rectangle is given by the expression $2(2x + 8)$. This can be simplified to $4x + 16$.

The area of the rectangle is given by the expression $8 \times 2x$, or $16x$.

Constructing expressions

The boxes below are full of counters.

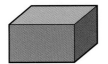 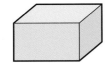  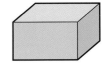

The boxes contain red, yellow, blue and green counters. We can use the letter r to stand for the number of counters in a full box of red counters, y for a full box of yellow counters, and b and g for full boxes of blue and green counters respectively.

If there are 4 full boxes of red counters, 3 full boxes of yellow, 5 of blue, 6 of green and 25 extra counters, we can write the total number of counters as:

$$4r + 3y + 5b + 6g + 25$$

EXERCISE 2.2A

Write an expression for the total number of counters in each of these cases. Use brackets in the expression where possible.

1. 6 full boxes of red counters, 2 of blue and 8 of green

2. 1 full box of red counters, 12 of green and 15 of yellow

3. 4 full boxes of blue counters, 7 of green and 23 extra counters

4. 3 boxes of yellow from which 25 counters have been removed in total

5. 4 boxes of blue from which 2 counters have been removed from each box

6. 5 boxes of red and 1 of yellow from which 12 counters have been removed from each box and then the remaining number has been doubled

7. 2 boxes of blue and 3 boxes of green from which 2 counters have been removed from each box and then the remaining amount is multiplied by 5

8. 1 box of yellow, 4 boxes of blue and 3 boxes of red from which 2 counters have been removed from each box and then the remaining number has been doubled

9. 7 boxes of each colour and 5 extra counters for each box

10. a half box of each colour

EXERCISE 2.2B

For each of the rectangles in questions 1–7 write an expression for:
  a) the area
  b) the perimeter.

Use brackets in the expression where possible.

1
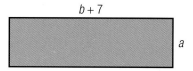

2
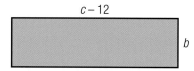

3

4
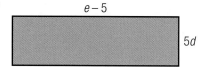

5
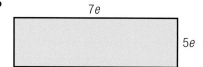

6
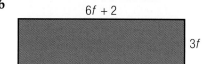

7
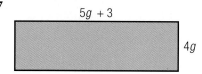

For each of the shapes in questions 8–10 write an expression for the perimeter.

8
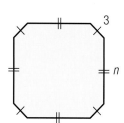

9
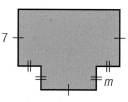

10
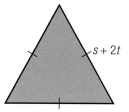

Expansion and factorisation

Changing $2(x + 3)$ to $2x + 6$ is called **expansion**. The opposite of expansion, changing $2x + 6$ to $2(x + 3)$ is called **factorisation**.

To factorise an expression, we first need to find the highest common factor (HCF) of all the terms. We write this factor outside the brackets. We then divide each term by this factor to find what goes inside the brackets.

Worked examples

a) Factorise $6x + 8$.

$6x + 8 = 2(3x + 4)$

The HCF of 6x and 8 is 2. So this goes outside the brackets.

b) Factorise $9a + 6b + 12$.

$9a + 6b + 12 = 3(3a + 2b + 4)$

The HCF of 9a, 6b and 12 is 3. So this goes outside the brackets.

EXERCISE 2.2C

Factorise the following.

1 a) $4a + 10$ b) $10a + 15$ c) $9a + 21$

2 a) $6b + 3$ b) $10b + 5$ c) $25b + 10$

3 a) $15c - 25$ b) $12c - 8$ c) $8a - 24$

4 a) $8 - 4d$ b) $6 - 4d$ c) $18 - 12d$

5 a) $6a + 4b$ b) $7c + 14d$ c) $12a - 16b$

Sometimes the highest common factor is a letter rather than a number.

Worked examples

a) Factorise $2ab + 3bc + 4bd$.

$2ab + 3bc + 4bd = b(2a + 3c + 4d)$

The HCF is b, so this goes outside the brackets.

b) Factorise $ax + bx + x^2$.

$ax + bx + x^2 = x(a + b + x)$

The HCF is x, so this goes outside the brackets.

EXERCISE 2.2D

Factorise the following.

1 **a)** $2ax + 3bx + 4cx$ **b)** $7ab - 8bc$

2 **a)** $3pq - 4q + 5qs$ **b)** $2mn - 3nr + 5np$

3 **a)** $4ax + 3x^2$ **b)** $4ab - 3b^2$

4 **a)** $6p^2 - 5pq$ **b)** $7mn - 2m^2$

5 **a)** $x^2 - ax$ **b)** $pqr - p^2$

Sometimes the highest common factor is a combination of numbers and letters.

Worked examples

a) Factorise $8x^2 - 4ax + 6bx$.

$8x^2 - 4ax + 6bx = 2x(4x - 2a + 3b)$

> The HCF is $2x$, so this goes outside the brackets.

b) Factorise $30abc - 24abd - 12a^2b$.

$30abc - 24abd - 12a^2b = 6ab(5c - 4d - 2a)$

> The HCF is $6ab$, so this goes outside the brackets.

EXERCISE 2.2E

Factorise the following expressions fully.

1 **a)** $4xy - 6yz$ **b)** $9pq - 12qr$

2 **a)** $15mn - 10pm$ **b)** $14bc - 21c^2$

3 **a)** $6pq - 30p^2$ **b)** $15x^2 - 10xy$

4 **a)** $12x^2y - 8xy^2$ **b)** $10ab^2 - 25a^2b$

5 **a)** $7ax - 14ay + 21az$ **b)** $30ax^2 - 6bx^2 + 9cx^2$

EXERCISE 2.2F

Factorise the following:

1 **a)** $9m - 15$ **b)** $16 - 6p$

2 **a)** $4p - 6$ **b)** $18 - 12b$

3 a) $6y - 3$ b) $4a - 6b$

4 a) $3a - 3b$ b) $8a + 12b + 20c$

5 a) $3ab + 4ac + 5ad$ b) $8pq + 6pr + 4ps$

6 a) $b^2 - bc$ b) $4a^2 - 10ab$

7 a) $abc - abd - abe$ b) $2m^2 - 3m$

8 a) $3abc - 9abd$ b) $5a^2 - 10ab$

9 a) $8a^2b - 6ab^2$ b) $2p^2q^2 - 3p^2r^2$

10 a) $12a - 24$ b) $42a - 63$

✪ Factorisation by grouping

Some expressions do not have a factor that is common to all their terms. For example, there does not seem to be a common factor in the expression $2xy + 4x + 3y + 6$.

Sometimes these expressions can be factorised by grouping. For example, we can split the expression above into two parts (groups) and factorise each part separately:

$$2xy + 4x + 3y + 6 = 2x(y + 2) + 3(y + 2)$$

We can see that $(y + 2)$ is a common factor of both parts, so the expression can now be written as:

$$(y + 2)(2x + 3)$$

Worked examples

a) Factorise $6x + 3 + 2xy + y$ by grouping.

$6x + 3 + 2xy + y$
$= 3(2x + 1) + y(2x + 1)$
$= (3 + y)(2x + 1)$

b) Factorise $ax + ay - bx - by$ by grouping.

$ax + ay - bx - by$
$= a(x + y) - b(x + y)$
$= (a - b)(x + y)$

c) Factorise $2x^2 - 3x + 2xy - 3y$ by grouping.

$2x^2 - 3x + 2xy - 3y$
$= x(2x - 3) + y(2x - 3)$
$= (x + y)(2x - 3)$

EXERCISE 2.2G

Factorise the following expressions by grouping.

1 **a)** $ac + ad + bc + bd$ **b)** $pr + ps + qr + qs$

2 **a)** $mp + mq + np + nq$ **b)** $ab + cd + ad + bc$

3 **a)** $ab + ac + 2b + 2c$ **b)** $ab + ac - 3b - 3c$

4 **a)** $ab - ac + 4b - 4c$ **b)** $ab - ac - 3b + 3c$

5 **a)** $pm - pn - qm + qn$ **b)** $pn - pm - qn + qm$

EXERCISE 2.2H

Factorise the following expressions by grouping.

1 **a)** $3ab + 3ac + b^2 + bc$ **b)** $6pr + 2ps + 3qr + qs$

2 **a)** $xz + xy - yz - y^2$ **b)** $8ac - 4ab - 2bc + b^2$

3 **a)** $3rt + r^2 - 6st - 2rs$ **b)** $2mq + 4m^2 + 3nq + 6mn$

4 **a)** $5f^3 + 5fh + gf^2 + gh$ **b)** $abd + abc + cd + c^2$

5 **a)** $2ghjk - 2ghi + ijk - i^2$ **b)** $ac - ab + bc - b^2$

Changing the subject of a formula

The formula $e = mc^2$ is one of the most well known formulae.

The formula $e = mc^2$ was worked out by the German theoretical physicist, Albert Einstein. His work in physics and mathematics made him a major figure of the twentieth century.

Einstein's formula is very simple. It states that the energy (e) which can be released from matter, is equal to the mass (m), multiplied by the square of the speed of light (c).

Other mathematical formulae you may have encountered are:

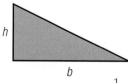

area of a triangle $= \frac{1}{2}bh$ circumference of a circle $= \pi D$

In the formula $a = 2b + c$, the letter a is on its own on one side of the formula. It is called the **subject** of the formula.

Sometimes a formula needs to be rearranged to make another letter the subject.

Worked examples

Rearrange the following formulae to make the letter in **red** the subject.

a) $a = 2b + c$ **b)** $m = 3n - r$ **c)** $p = 2w + 5$

d) $r = 2m + \dfrac{w}{3}$ **e)** $p = \dfrac{2t - m}{3}$

a)
$$a = 2b + c$$
$$a - 2b = 2b + c - 2b \quad \text{(subtract } 2b \text{ from both sides)}$$
$$a - 2b = c$$

> The subject must be positive and on its own but it can be on either side of the formula.

b)
$$m = 3n - r$$
$$m + r = 3n - r + r \quad \text{(add } r \text{ to both sides)}$$
$$m + r = 3n$$
$$m + r - m = 3n - m \quad \text{(subtract } m \text{ from both sides)}$$
$$r = 3n - m$$

c)
$$p = 2w + 5$$
$$p - 5 = 2w - 5 + 5 \quad \text{(subtract 5 from both sides)}$$
$$p - 5 = 2w$$
$$\frac{p - 5}{2} = w \quad \text{(divide both sides by 2)}$$

d)
$$r = 2m + \frac{w}{3}$$
$$r - 2m = 2m + \frac{w}{3} - 2m \quad \text{(subtract } 2m \text{ from both sides)}$$
$$r - 2m = \frac{w}{3}$$
$$3(r - 2m) = \frac{w}{3} \times 3 \quad \text{(multiply both sides by 3)}$$
$$3(r - 2m) = w$$

e)
$$p = \frac{2t - m}{3}$$
$$3p = \frac{2t - m}{3} \times 3 \quad \text{(multiply both sides by 3)}$$
$$3p = 2t - m$$
$$3p + m = 2t - m + m \quad \text{(add } m \text{ to both sides)}$$
$$3p + m = 2t$$
$$3p + m - 3p = 2t - 3p \quad \text{(subtract } 3p \text{ from both sides)}$$
$$m = 2t - 3p$$

EXERCISE 2.3A

Rearrange the following formulae to make the letter in **red** the subject.

1 **a)** $m = p + q$ **b)** $m = p + q$

2 **a)** $d = m - p$ **b)** $d = m - p$

3 **a)** $r = s + 3t$ **b)** $r = s + 3t$

4 **a)** $x = 2d - c$ **b)** $x = 2d - c$

5 a) $d = 2a + 3b$ b) $d = 2a + 3b$

6 a) $p = 3r - 5s$ b) $p = 3r - 5s$

7 a) $m = 2(r - p)$ b) $m = 2(r - p)$

8 a) $w = 5(r - 2p)$ b) $w = 5(r - 2p)$

9 a) $d = \dfrac{w - r}{t}$ b) $d = \dfrac{w - r}{t}$

10 a) $y = mx + c$ b) $y = x + \dfrac{c}{m}$

EXERCISE 2.3B

Rearrange the following formulae to make the letter in **red** the subject.

1 a) $a + b = c$ b) $a + b = c$

2 a) $a - c = b$ b) $a - c = b$

3 a) $pqr = s$ b) $pqr = s$

4 a) $3p + q = r$ b) $3p + q = r$

5 a) $mn + p = t$ b) $mn + p = t$

6 a) $2p + 3q = r$ b) $2p + 3q = r$

7 a) $\dfrac{m}{n} = r$ b) $\dfrac{m}{n} = r$

8 a) $\dfrac{d}{v} = \dfrac{w}{s}$ b) $\dfrac{d}{v} = \dfrac{w}{s}$

9 a) $\dfrac{mn}{w} = t$ b) $\dfrac{mn}{w} = t$

10 a) $mn + \dfrac{1}{w} = t$ b) $mn + \dfrac{1}{w} = t$

EXERCISE 2.3C

1 The area of a triangle is given by the
   formula $A = \frac{1}{2}bh$.
   Rearrange the formula to make h the subject.

2 The volume of a cuboid is given by the
   formula $V = lwh$.
   Rearrange the formula to make w the subject.

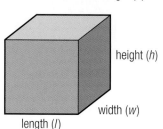

3 The area of a parallelogram is given by
   the formula $A = bh$.
   Rearrange the formula to make b
   the subject.

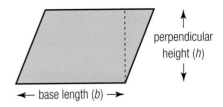

perpendicular
height (h)

← base length (b) →

4 The formula for calculating the area
   of a trapezium is $A = \frac{1}{2}(a + b)h$.
   Rearrange the formula to make:

   a) h the subject
   b) b the subject.

← length (b) →

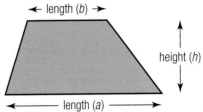

height (h)

← length (a) →

5 Newton's second law of motion can
   be expressed in the formula
   $F = ma$, where F stands for the force, m for the mass of an object and a
   stands for acceleration.
   Rearrange the formula to make a the subject.

6 Another equation of motion is $v = u + at$, where v is the final velocity, u is
   the initial (starting) velocity, a is acceleration and t is time.
   Rearrange the formula to make:

   a) u the subject   **b)** a the subject   **c)** t the subject.

Substitution

Substitution into an expression

You already know that $a + b$ is an **expression**. If you are told that $a = 3.5$ and
$b = 2.7$, then you can **substitute** 3.5 for a and 2.7 for b into the expression to give
$3.5 + 2.7$. So the value of the expression $a + b$ when $a = 3.5$ and $b = 2.7$ is 6.2.
   When $a = 4\frac{1}{2}$ and $b = 5\frac{1}{4}$, the value of $a + b =$ is $9\frac{3}{4}$.

Worked example

Calculate the value of the expression $4a + 2b + 3c - d$ when $a = 0.5$, $b = 0.3$,
$c = -0.5$ and $d = -0.3$.

$4a + 2b + 3c - d$
$= (4 \times 0.5) + (2 \times 0.3) + (3 \times -0.5) - (-0.3)$
$= 2 + 0.6 - 1.5 + 0.3$
$= 1.4$

EXERCISE 2.4A

Calculate the value of each of the following expressions when $a = 0.5$, $b = 0.3$, $c = -0.5$ and $d = -0.3$. Use a calculator if necessary.

1 $a + b$	2 $a - b$	3 $a + b - c$
4 $a + b - c - d$	5 $3a$	6 $4b$
7 $6c$	8 $3d$	9 $a + b + c + d$
10 $a - b + c - d$	11 $-a - b - c - d$	12 $a + b + (c - d)$
13 $a + b - (c - d)$	14 a^2	15 b^2
16 c^2	17 d^2	18 $a^2 - b^2$
19 $c^2 - d^2$	20 $a^2 - b^2 + c^2 - d^2$	

Substitution into a formula

You can substitute known values into a formula to find an unknown value.

For example, if we know the mass of an object (in kg) and its acceleration (in m/s²), we can use the formula for Newton's second law of motion, $F = ma$, to find the force (in newtons, N).

Worked examples

a) Use the formula $F = ma$ to calculate the force on a object when $m = 10\,\text{kg}$ and $a = 3.2\,\text{m/s}^2$.

$F = ma$
$F = 10 \times 3.2$
$F = 32$
The force is 32 newtons.

b) An equation of motion is $v = u + at$, where
$\quad\quad v$ is the final velocity (in m/s)
$\quad\quad u$ is the initial (starting) velocity (in m/s)
$\quad\quad a$ is acceleration (in m/s²)
$\quad\quad t$ is time (in seconds).

Calculate the final velocity when $u = 4\,\text{m/s}$, $a = 5.8\,\text{m/s}^2$ and $t = 40$ seconds.

$v = u + at$
$v = 4 + 5.8 \times 40$
$v = 4 + 232$
$v = 236$
The final velocity is 236 m/s.

EXERCISE 2.4B

1 Given the formula $v = u + at$, find the value of v when:
  a) $u = 8.5\,\text{m/s}$, $a = 6.1\,\text{m/s}^2$ and $t = 10\,\text{s}$
  b) $u = 15.2\,\text{m/s}$, $a = 4.5\,\text{m/s}^2$ and $t = 18\,\text{s}$
  c) $u = 1\,\text{m/s}$, $a = 1.5\,\text{m/s}^2$ and $t = 110\,\text{s}$
  d) $u = 25\,\text{m/s}$, $a = -2.8\,\text{m/s}^2$ and $t = 48\,\text{s}$
  e) $u = 0\,\text{m/s}$, $a = 6.25\,\text{m/s}^2$ and $t = 50\,\text{s}$.

2 Given the formula $s = ut + \frac{1}{2}at^2$, where

  s = distance (in metres)
  u = initial velocity (in m/s)
  a = acceleration (in m/s^2)
  t = time (in seconds).

Find the value of s when:

  a) $u = 500\,\text{m/s}$, $t = 10\,\text{s}$ and $a = -4\,\text{m/s}^2$
  b) $u = 300\,\text{m/s}$, $t = 5.8\,\text{s}$ and $a = -25\,\text{m/s}^2$
  c) $u = 1000\,\text{m/s}$, $t = 52\,\text{s}$ and $a = -12.6\,\text{m/s}^2$
  d) $u = 80\,\text{m/s}$, $t = 5\,\text{s}$ and $a = -12.5\,\text{m/s}^2$
  e) $u = 0\,\text{m/s}$, $t = 10\,\text{s}$ and $a = 0\,\text{m/s}^2$

Adding and subtracting algebraic fractions

In arithmetic it is straightforward to add or subtract fractions with the same denominator. The same method can be used to add or subtract algebraic fractions.

Worked examples

a) $\dfrac{4}{11} + \dfrac{3}{11} = \dfrac{7}{11}$ **b)** $\dfrac{a}{11} + \dfrac{b}{11} = \dfrac{a+b}{11}$ **c)** $\dfrac{4}{x} + \dfrac{3}{x} = \dfrac{7}{x}$

If the denominators are not the same, the fractions must be changed to equivalent fractions with the same denominator.

Worked examples

a) $\dfrac{2}{9} + \dfrac{1}{3} = \dfrac{2}{9} + \dfrac{3}{9} = \dfrac{5}{9}$

b) $\dfrac{a}{9} + \dfrac{b}{3} = \dfrac{a}{9} + \dfrac{3b}{9} = \dfrac{a+3b}{9}$

c) $\dfrac{4}{5a} + \dfrac{7}{10a} = \dfrac{8}{10a} + \dfrac{7}{10a} = \dfrac{15}{10a} = \dfrac{3}{2a}$

Similarly, with subtraction, the denominators must be the same.

Worked examples

a) $\dfrac{7}{a} - \dfrac{1}{2a} = \dfrac{14}{2a} - \dfrac{1}{2a}$

$\qquad\qquad = \dfrac{13}{2a}$

b) $\dfrac{p}{3} - \dfrac{q}{15} = \dfrac{5p}{15} - \dfrac{q}{15}$

$\qquad\qquad = \dfrac{5p - q}{15}$

c) $\dfrac{5}{3b} - \dfrac{8}{9b} = \dfrac{15}{9b} - \dfrac{8}{9b}$

$\qquad\qquad = \dfrac{7}{9b}$

EXERCISE 2.5A

Simplify the following.

1 $\dfrac{1}{8} + \dfrac{3}{8}$

2 $\dfrac{a}{8} + \dfrac{b}{8}$

3 $\dfrac{5}{11} + \dfrac{3}{11}$

4 $\dfrac{p}{11} + \dfrac{q}{11}$

5 $\dfrac{p}{5} + \dfrac{q}{5} + \dfrac{r}{5}$

6 $\dfrac{m}{7} + \dfrac{n}{7} + \dfrac{p}{7}$

7 $\dfrac{9}{11} - \dfrac{5}{11}$

8 $\dfrac{c}{9} - \dfrac{d}{9}$

9 $\dfrac{3a}{5} - \dfrac{9}{5}$

10 $\dfrac{2p}{3} + \dfrac{q}{3} - \dfrac{3r}{3}$

11 $\dfrac{2}{3} - \dfrac{1}{6}$

12 $\dfrac{2a}{3} - \dfrac{a}{6}$

13 $\dfrac{x}{12} + \dfrac{x}{6}$

14 $\dfrac{3a}{5} + \dfrac{4a}{15}$

15 $\dfrac{3a}{5b} + \dfrac{4a}{15b}$

16 $\dfrac{7x}{y} - \dfrac{2x}{3y}$

17 $\dfrac{a}{b} + \dfrac{c}{2b} - \dfrac{d}{6b}$

18 $\dfrac{x}{y} - \dfrac{x}{2y}$

19 $\dfrac{3ab}{mn} + \dfrac{2ab}{3mn}$

20 $\dfrac{3b}{5x} + \dfrac{2b}{10x} - \dfrac{b}{20x}$

If one denominator is not a multiple of the other, the fractions must be changed to equivalent fractions with the same denominator.

Worked examples

a) Simplify $x + \dfrac{3x}{8}$

$$x + \frac{3x}{8} = \frac{8x}{8} + \frac{3x}{8}$$

$$= \frac{11x}{8}$$

Write x as a fraction with 8 as the denominator.

b) Simplify $2m - \dfrac{m}{3}$

$$2m - \frac{m}{3} = \frac{6m}{3} - \frac{m}{3}$$

$$= \frac{5m}{3}$$

Write 2m as a fraction with 3 as the denominator.

EXERCISE 2.5B

Simplify the following.

1 $a + \dfrac{a}{2}$

2 $b - \dfrac{b}{3}$

3 $c + \dfrac{2c}{3}$

4 $d - \dfrac{2d}{5}$

5 $m + \dfrac{m}{3}$

6 $p - \dfrac{p}{5}$

7 $r + \dfrac{2r}{7}$

8 $w - \dfrac{3w}{5}$

9 $2x + \dfrac{x}{3}$

10 $3m - \dfrac{5m}{2}$

3 Shapes and geometric reasoning

♦ Calculate the interior or exterior angle of any regular polygon; prove and use the formula for the sum of the interior angles of any polygon; prove that the sum of the exterior angles of any polygon is 360°.
♦ Solve problems using properties of angles, of parallel and intersecting lines, and of triangles, other polygons and circles, justifying inferences and explaining reasoning with diagrams and text.
♦ Analyse three-dimensional shapes through plans and elevations.
♦ Draw three-dimensional shapes on isometric paper.
♦ Identify reflection symmetry in three-dimensional shapes.
♦ Use a straight edge and compasses to:
 – construct the perpendicular from a point to a line and the perpendicular from a point on a line
 – inscribe squares, equilateral triangles, and regular hexagons and octagons by constructing equal divisions of a circle.

Polygons

A polygon is a two-dimensional closed shape with straight sides. Examples of polygons include triangles, quadrilaterals, pentagons and hexagons.

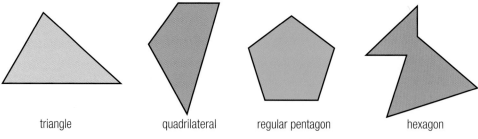

triangle   quadrilateral   regular pentagon   hexagon

You already know that angles on a straight line add up to 180°. We can use this information to work out the sum of the three angles of any triangle.
 In this triangle, the **interior angles** are labelled a, b and c and the **exterior angles** are labelled d, e and f.

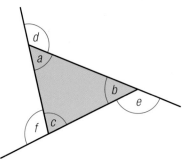

Imagine a person standing at one of the **vertices** (corners) and walking along the edges of the triangle until they are at the start again. At each vertex they would have turned through an angle the same size as the exterior angle at that point. During the complete journey, they would have turned through an angle equivalent to one complete turn, i.e. 360°. Therefore

$$d + e + f = 360°$$

We know that $a + d = 180°$ (angles on a straight line), also $b + e = 180°$ and $c + f = 180°$. Therefore

$$a + b + c + d + e + f = 180° + 180° + 180° = 540°$$
$$a + b + c + 360° = 540°$$
$$a + b + c = 540° - 360° = 180°$$

These findings lead us to two important rules.

The exterior angles of a triangle (in fact of any polygon) add up to 360°.

The interior angles of a triangle add up to 180°.

EXERCISE 3.1A

Calculate the size of the unknown angles in these diagrams.

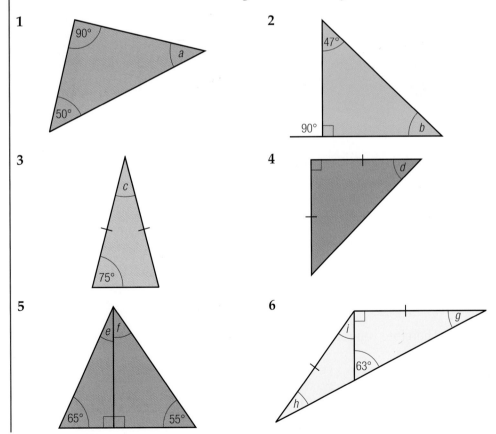

1

90°
a
50°

2

47°
90°
b

3

c
75°

4

d

5

e *f*
65° 55°

6

g
i
63°
h

Interior angles of polygons

We have seen that the three interior angles of any triangle always add up to 180°. This result can be used to calculate the sum of the interior angles for *any* polygon.

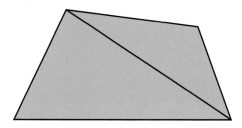

This diagram shows a quadrilateral split into two triangles. As the sum of the interior angles of each triangle is 180°, then the sum of the four angles of any quadrilateral must be 2 × 180° = 360°.

Other polygons can also be split into triangles, as shown.

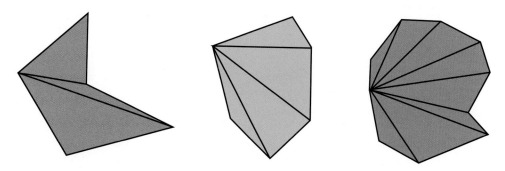

A **regular polygon** is one in which all the sides are the same length and all the angles are equal in size.

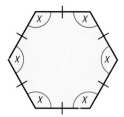

Therefore you can calculate the size of each interior angle of a regular polygon as follows:

$$\text{Size of each interior angle} = \frac{\text{sum of interior angles}}{\text{number of sides}}$$

Similarly, all the exterior angles of a regular polygon are the same size.

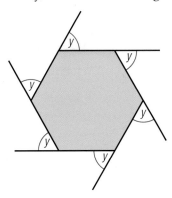

$$\text{Size of each exterior angle} = \frac{360°}{\text{number of sides}}$$

EXERCISE 3.1B

1 By drawing polygons and splitting them into triangles, copy and complete this table.

Number of sides	Name of polygon	Number of triangles	Total sum of interior angles
3	triangle	1	180°
4	quadrilateral	2	2 × 180° = 360°
5	pentagon		
6			
8			
9			
10			
12			

2 From your table of results for question 1, describe any pattern linking the number of sides of a polygon and the number of triangles it can be split into.

3 Copy and complete this table for *regular* polygons.

Number of sides	3	4	5	6	8	9	10	12
Sum of the interior angles	180°	360°						
Size of each interior angle	60°							
Size of each exterior angle	120°							

Parallel lines

In Student's Books 1 and 2 you studied the relationships between angles within parallel and intersecting lines. You know that:

- **Alternate** angles are equal. They can be found by looking for a 'Z' formation in a diagram.

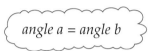

angle a = angle b

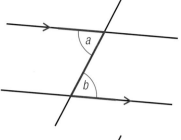

- **Corresponding** angles are equal. They can be found by looking for an 'F' formation in a diagram.

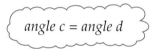

angle c = angle d

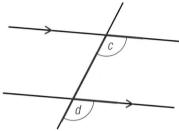

EXERCISE 3.1C

Calculate the size of the unknown angles in these polygons.
Give reasons for your answers.

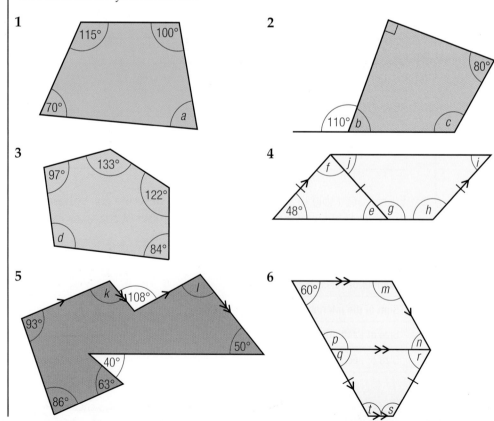

Circle geometry

EXERCISE 3.2

1 This diagram shows a triangle *ABC* drawn inside a circle. The line *AB* passes through the centre of the circle, *O*.

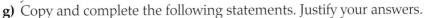

   a) What is the name given to each of the lines *OA* and *OC*?
   b) What is the name given to the line *AB*?
   c) What type of triangle is triangle *OAC*?
   d) Are angles *p* and *r* equal in size? Justify your answer.
   e) What is the sum of the angles *p*, *q* and *r*? Justify your answer.
   f) What is the sum of angles *q* and *t*? Justify your answer.
   g) Copy and complete the following statements. Justify your answers.
   (i) $p + r + s + u =$ _____
   (ii) $r + s =$ _____
   h) Look at the diagrams below. Thinking about your answers to part **g)**, what conclusion can you make about the size of each of the angles labelled *C*?

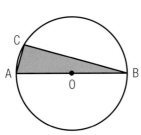 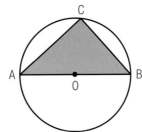 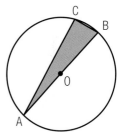

If a triangle *ABC* is drawn in a circle such that all three vertices lie on the circumference and *AB* is the diameter of the circle, then the angle at *C* is always 90°.

Drawing three-dimensional shapes

Plans

All views of objects are either two-dimensional (2D) or three-dimensional (3D). However, it is possible to draw a three-dimensional object using two-dimensional techniques.

   One way is by drawing a **net** of the object. You are already familiar with drawing nets of simple three-dimensional shapes.

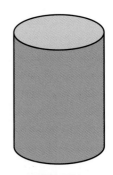

The diagram on page 37 shows a cylinder. It is drawn in such a way as to look three-dimensional.

The diagrams below show how a cylinder can be drawn using **plans** or **elevations**. These are two-dimensional views of an object from different angles.

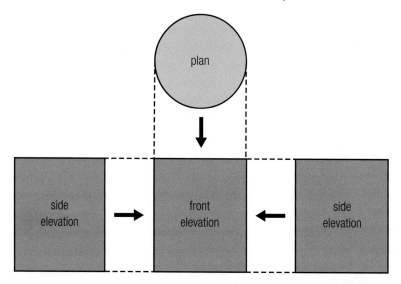

As the name suggests, the front elevation is the view from the front; the side elevations are the views from the left and right sides; the top elevation is the view from above and is more commonly known as the plan view.

Notice that the dimensions of all the views must be consistent with each other. This is shown in the diagrams above by the dotted lines.

EXERCISE 3.3A

For each of the three-dimensional shapes below, draw front, side and plan elevations.

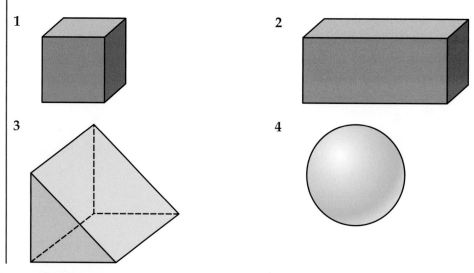

1

2

3

4

EXERCISE 3.3B

You will need Multi-link cubes for this exercise.

The following diagrams shows shapes made of small cubes. For each of them, draw the front, side and plan elevations. In each case, an arrow shows the direction of the front elevation. Assume that there are no hidden cubes.

> *You may find the drawings easier to do if you are able to build each of the shapes first using Multi-link cubes.*

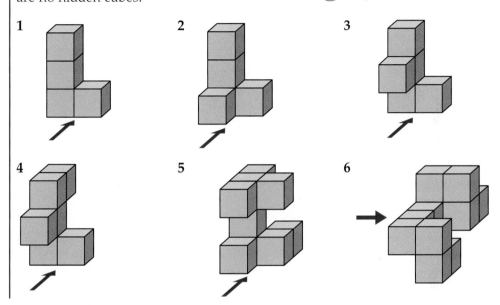

1   2   3

4   5   6

EXERCISE 3.3C

For each of the following sets of elevations, sketch the three-dimensional object.

1

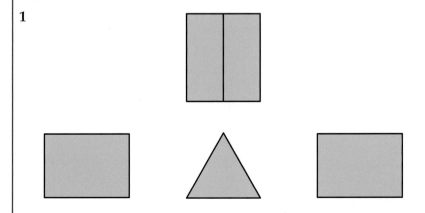

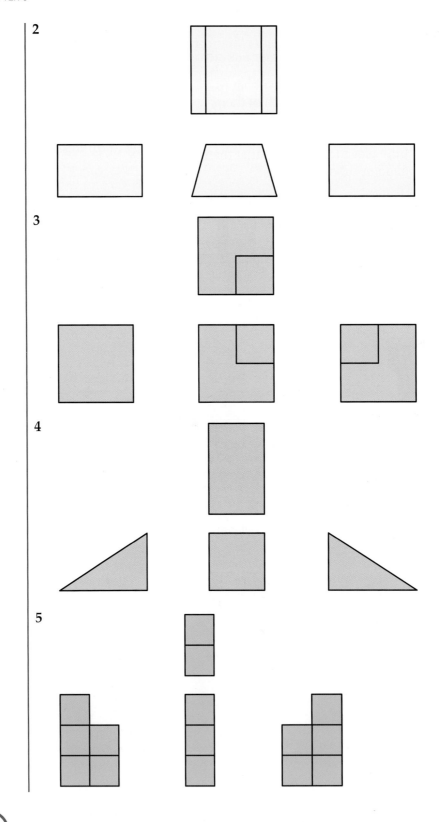

6

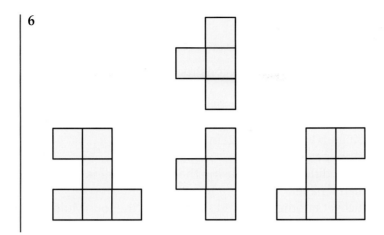

Isometric drawings

All the methods used for drawing three-dimensional objects so far have involved two-dimensional views of the object. However, views that look three-dimensional can also be used. There are many different types of three-dimensional drawings. One of the most common is called an **isometric drawing**.

In an isometric drawing, the object is shown aligned on a grid with three axes at 120° to each other. The axes are shown in **a)** drawn on 'isometric dot' paper. The dots act as a guide for the lines.

Horizontal and vertical lines on the three-dimensional object are drawn so that they are parallel to the three axes. The vertical lines on the object are drawn vertically on the paper.

Diagram **b)** shows a cube drawn on isometric dot paper. The vertical and horizontal faces have been shaded differently to make the diagram clearer. This is often useful, but it is not essential. When drawing more complex shapes, care needs to be taken.

Diagram **c)** shows three cubes joined together to form an L-shape. Notice how only the faces and edges that can be *seen* are drawn, and how the shading has helped to show the direction of the faces.

To avoid having to rub out hidden lines and faces, it is helpful to draw from top to bottom and from the front to the back.

a)　　　　　　　　　　　b)　　　　　　　　　　　c)

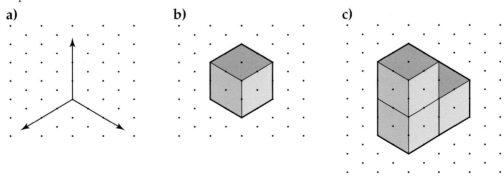

EXERCISE 3.3D

You will need Multi-link cubes for this exercise.

1 a) Use four Multi-link cubes to construct this shape.
   b) Draw the shape on isometric paper.
   c) Turn the Multi-link shape so that it is standing up and draw it again on isometric paper.
   d) Construct a different shape using the four Multi-link cubes and draw it on isometric paper.
   e) Construct yet another different shape using the four Multi-link and draw it on isometric paper.

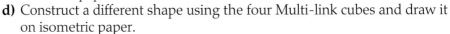

2 a) Use five Multi-link cubes to construct this shape.
   b) Draw the shape on isometric paper.
   c) Draw the same shape on isometric paper from a different viewpoint.
   d) Construct a different shape using the five Multi-link cubes and draw it on isometric paper.
   e) Construct as many different shapes using the five Multi-link cubes as you can and draw them on isometric paper.

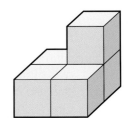

3 a) Use eight Multi-link cubes to construct a shape. Make it as complicated as you can.
   b) Draw the shape you have constructed on isometric paper from different viewpoints.

Reflection symmetry in three-dimensional shapes

A **plane of symmetry** divides a three-dimensional shape into two congruent (identical) shapes. The cuboid below has three planes of symmetry.

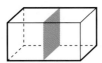 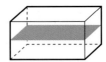 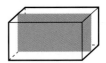

A three-dimensional shape has **reflection symmetry** if it has one or more planes of symmetry.

EXERCISE 3.4

For each of the following three-dimensional objects, make two copies of the diagram shown. Then:

    a) on each drawing show a different plane of symmetry

    b) work out how many planes of symmetry the shape has in total.

1

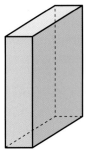

a rectangular cuboid

2

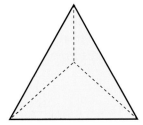

a triangular-based pyramid (tetrahedron)

3

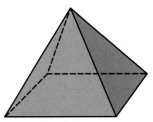

a square-based pyramid

4

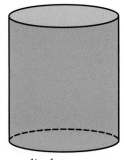

a cylinder

5

a cone

6

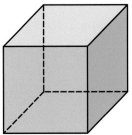

a cube

Geometric constructions

In Student's Book 2 you studied how to construct a line perpendicular to another line, and how to bisect an angle using a pair of compasses. Construction using a pair of compasses is at the heart of many geometric diagrams.

Constructing the perpendicular from a point to a line

Look at the diagram below of a point P and a line. The point does not lie on the line. The distance from P to the line depends on how it is measured. Five different distances from P to the line are shown on the diagram.

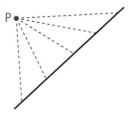

However, there is only one distance that can be the *shortest* distance from P to the line. This is represented by a line drawn through P which is perpendicular to the line, as shown.

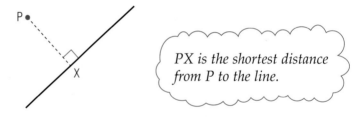

PX is the shortest distance from P to the line.

Worked example

Use a ruler and a pair of compasses to construct the line though *P* which is perpendicular to the line shown.

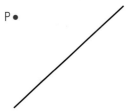

- Open the pair of compasses. Place the compass point on *P* and draw two arcs so that they intersect the line. Label the points of intersection *A* and *B*.

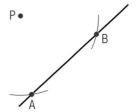

- Now construct the perpendicular bisector of the line segment *AB*.

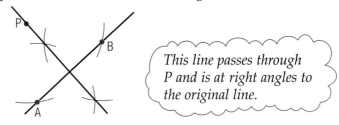

This line passes through P and is at right angles to the original line.

Constructing the perpendicular from a point on a line

Similarly, it is possible to construct a perpendicular line *from* a point on an existing line.

Worked example

Use a ruler and a pair of compasses to construct the perpendicular to the line *AB* which passes through the point *P*.

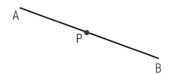

- Open the pair of compasses. Place the compass point on *P* and draw two arcs so that they intersect *AB*. Label the points of intersection *X* and *Y*.

- Now construct the perpendicular bisector of the line segment *XY*.

This line passes through P and is at right angles to AB.

EXERCISE 3.5A

1   Copy this diagram.

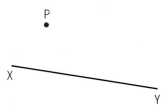

Construct a line which passes through *P* and is perpendicular to the line *XY*.

2   Construct a triangle *ABC* such that *AB* = 8 cm, *AC* = 5 cm and *BC* = 7 cm.

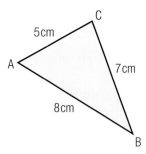

a) Construct a line which is perpendicular to *AB* and passes through *C*. Label its point of intersection with *AB* as *X*.
b) Measure the distance *CX*. Give your answer to the nearest millimetre.
c) Calculate the area of the triangle *ABC*.

3 Construct a triangle *PQR* such that *PQ* = *PR* = 6 cm and *QR* = 10 cm.

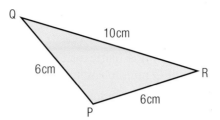

a) Extend the line *QP*. Draw a line which is perpendicular to *QP* and passes through *R*. Label the its point of intersection with the extension of *QP* as *S*.

b) Measure the distance *RS*. Give your answer to the nearest millimetre.

c) Calculate the area of triangle *PQR*.

4 a) Draw a sloping line 8 cm long. Label it *XY*.

b) Mark a point on the line *XY* 3 cm from *X*. Label the point *P*.

c) Construct a line which is perpendicular to *XY* and passes through *P*.

5 a) Draw a sloping line 8 cm long. Label it *XY*.

b) On the line mark two points 6 cm apart. Label them *P* and *Q*.

c) Construct a line which is perpendicular to *XY* and passes through *P*.

d) Mark a point 6 cm from *P* on this perpendicular line. Label it *R*.

e) Construct a line which is perpendicular to *XY* and passes through *Q*.

f) Mark a point 6 cm from *Q* on this perpendicular line, on the same side of *XY* as *P*, and label it *S*.

g) Join *R* and *S* with a straight line.

h) What is the name of the shape *PQRS* you have constructed?

Constructing geometric shapes

Regular polygons can be constructed such that all of their vertices lie on the circumference of a circle. They are called **inscribed polygons**. Examples of some are shown below.

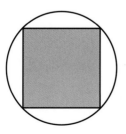 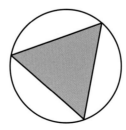 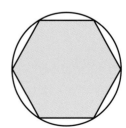

Worked example

Construct a square with all its vertices on
the circumference of a circle.

This is called an inscribed square.

- Draw a straight line using a ruler.
  Mark a point O near its centre.

———————•———————
               0

- Using a pair of compasses draw a circle with its centre at O. Label the points
  where the circle intersects the line as A and C.

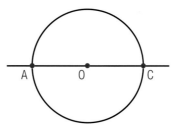

- Construct the perpendicular bisector of AC. Label the points where the
  perpendicular bisector intersects the circumference of the circle as B and D.

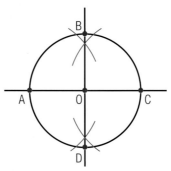

- Join up the points AB, BC, CD and DA with a ruler.

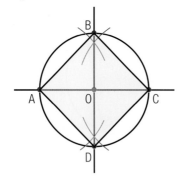

The shape ABCD is an inscribed square.

The construction used for an inscribed square can be extended to construct an
inscribed regular octagon.

Worked example

Construct an inscribed regular octagon.
- Follow the same steps as for the inscribed square until this stage.

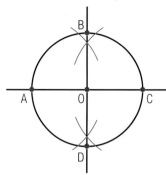

- Construct the perpendicular bisectors of *AB* and *BC*. Label the points of intersection with the circumference of the circle as *E*, *F*, *G* and *H*.

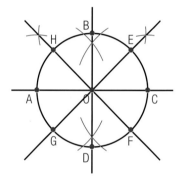

- Join up the points *A*, *H*, *B*, *E*, *C*, *F*, *D* and *G* with a ruler.

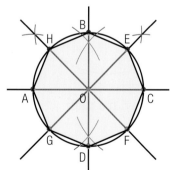

The resulting shape is an inscribed regular octagon.

Worked example

Construct an inscribed regular hexagon using a pair of compasses and a ruler.

- Open the pair of compasses and draw a circle.

- Keep the compasses open by the same amount. Put the compass point on the circumference of the circle and draw an arc. Make sure that the arc intersects the circumference.

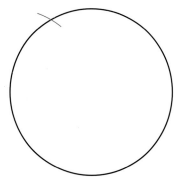

- Place the compass point on the point of intersection of the arc and the circumference and draw another arc. Repeat this procedure until you have drawn six arcs.

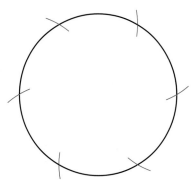

- Join up the points of intersection with a ruler.

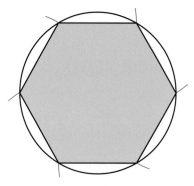

The resulting shape is an inscribed regular hexagon.

The same process can be used to construct an inscribed equilateral triangle. The only difference is that, rather than joining all six points of intersection in the final stage, only alternate points are joined, like this.

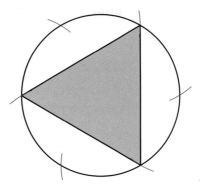

EXERCISE 3.5B

Construct the following geometric patterns using a ruler and a pair of compasses.

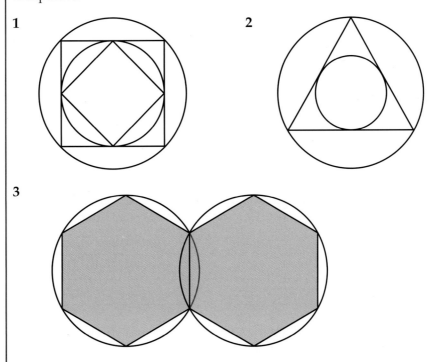

1   **2**

3

4 Design a geometric pattern of your own involving a regular octagon.

5 Design a geometric pattern of your own involving a regular hexagon and equilateral triangles.

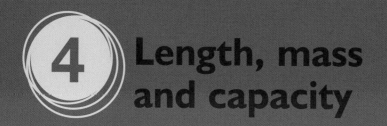

4 Length, mass and capacity

◆ Solve problems involving measurements in a variety of contexts.

The metric system of measures was developed by a group of French scientists during the French Revolution in the 18th century. They had been asked to create a unified and logical system to replace earlier measures.

The first metric unit to be adopted in France was the metre, for lengths, followed by the gram and kilogram, for masses. Use of the metric system has spread around the world, replacing many older measurement systems. Some countries, including the USA and the UK, also use the earlier **imperial system**.

Scientists and engineers throughout the world use an international system of measures which was developed from the metric system in the 20th century. This system includes extra units to cover the measurement of temperature and light, and mechanical, electromagnetic and chemical quantities. It is called the **SI system**, from the French name, *Le Système international d'unités*. Its seven base units are shown in the table.

Name	Unit symbol	Quantity
metre	m	length
kilogram	kg	mass
second	s	time
ampere	A	electric current
kelvin	K	thermodynamic temperature
candela	cd	luminous intensity
mole	mol	amount of substance

Different prefixes are added to the names of the base units to produce larger or smaller units, in multiples of ten and a thousand.

Multiples

Prefix		deca-	hecto-	kilo-	mega-	giga-	tera-	peta-	exa-	zetta-	yotta-
Symbol		da	h	k	M	G	T	P	E	Z	Y
Factor	10^0	10^1	10^2	10^3	10^6	10^9	10^{12}	10^{15}	10^{18}	10^{21}	10^{24}

Fractions

Prefix		deci-	centi-	milli-	micro-	nano-	pico-	femto-	atto-	zepto-	yocto-
Symbol		d	c	m	μ	n	p	f	a	z	y
Factor	10^0	10^{-1}	10^{-2}	10^{-3}	10^{-6}	10^{-9}	10^{-12}	10^{-15}	10^{-18}	10^{-21}	10^{-24}

For example, 'kilo-' is used for multiples of a thousand and 'milli-' for multiples of a thousandth. So there are 1000 millimetres in one metre and 1000 metres in one kilometre.

Because scientists and mathematicians use standard index form, which you will learn about later, the prefixes beyond micro- and mega- are rarely used.

The prefixes are never combined: a millionth of a kilogram is a milligram, not a microkilogram.

In addition to the SI units themselves, there is also a set of 'accepted units' for use with SI, which includes units such as the litre.

The metric system

The metric system uses a number of units for length. They are:
>   kilometre (km), metre (m), centimetre (cm) and millimetre (mm)

The units for mass are:
>   tonne (t), kilogram (kg), gram (g) and milligram (mg)

The units for capacity are:
>   litre (*l*) and millilitre (m*l*)

EXERCISE 4.1A

1 Copy and complete the sentences below.
   a) There are _____ centimetres in 3.45 metres.
   b) 25 centimetres is _____ part of 5 metres.
   c) There are _____ metres in 7.6 kilometres.
   d) 750 metres is _____ part of 3.75 kilometres.
   e) There are _____ grams in 4.25 kilograms.
   f) 800 grams is _____ part of 3.2 kilograms.
   g) 875 kilograms is _____ part of a tonne.
   h) There are _____ millilitres in 2.125 litres.
   i) One tenth of a litre is _____ millilitres.
   j) One ten-thousandth of a litre is _____ millilitre.

2 Give one example of a quantity which can be measured with each of the following units.
   >   mm   cm   m   km   mg   g   kg   tonne   m*l*   litre

Converting from one unit to another

Length

1 km is 1000 m, so

        to change from km to m, multiply by 1000
        to change from m to km, divide by 1000.

Worked examples

a) Change 3.54 km to metres.

    1 km = 1000 m, so multiply by 1000.
    $3.54 \times 1000 = 3540$ m

b) Change 8760 mm to metres.

    1 m = 1000 mm, so divide by 1000.
    $8760 \div 1000 = 8.76$ m

Mass

1 tonne is 1000 kg, so

        to change from tonnes to kg, multiply by 1000
        to change from kg to tonnes, divide by 1000.

Worked examples

a) Change 0.456 tonne to kilograms.

    1 tonne = 1000 kg, so multiply by 1000.
    $0.456 \times 1000 = 456$ kg

b) Change 7800 kg to tonnes.

    1 tonne = 1000 kg, so divide by 1000.
    $7800 \div 1000 = 7.8$ tonnes

Capacity

1 litre is 1000 ml, so

        to change from litres to ml, multiply by 1000
        to change from ml to litres, divide by 1000.

Worked examples

a) Change 9.8 litres to millilitres.

    1 litre is 1000 ml, so multiply by 1000.
    $9.8 \times 1000 = 9800$ ml

b) Change 7875 ml to litres.

    1 litre is 1000 ml, so divide by 1000.
    $7875 \div 1000 = 7.875$ litres

EXERCISE 4.1B

1   Copy and complete the sentences below.
    a) To change from cm to m _____.
    b) To change from m to mm _____.
    c) To change from mm to cm _____.

2   Convert these to kilograms.
    a) 0.1 tonne   b) 0.024 tonne
    c) 7650 g   d) 3 million grams

3   Convert these to litres.
    a) 1544 m*l*   b) 5789 m*l*
    c) 345 m*l*   d) 12 m*l*

4   How much water is left in a 2-litre bottle after 1650 m*l* is drunk?

5   How much water is left in a 25-litre bottle after 16550 m*l* is drunk?

6   A pile of bricks weighs 22 kg.
    18750 g of bricks are removed. What weight is left?

7   I am travelling to a city 380 km away.
    I take a break after 288 km. How many kilometres do I have left to travel?

8   A cyclist travels for five days, and covers 423 km in total.
    He covers 83 km, 88 km, 96 km, 79 km on the first four days.
    How far does he travel on day 5?

9   The mass of four containers loaded on a ship are 48 tonnes, 35 tonnes,
    29.8 tonnes and 56500 kg. What is the total mass in tonnes?

10 Three test tubes contain 0.03 litre, 0.77 litre and 185 m*l* of solution.
    a) What is the total volume of solution in millilitres?
    b) How many millilitres of water need to be added to make the volume of
       solution up to 0.995 litre?

EXERCISE 4.1C

Write an estimate for each of the following using a sensible unit.

1   How long would it take you to walk 1 km?

2   How thick is a nail?

3   What does a bag of sugar weigh?

4   How much medicine is one teaspoon?

5   How long is a paperclip?

6   What does a newborn baby weigh?

7   How much water is there in a normal bath?

8   How many days in summer?

9   How long is your bed?

10   How long does it take to complete this exercise?

5 Planning and collecting data

◆ Suggest a question to explore using statistical methods; identify the sets of data needed, how to collect them, sample sizes and degree of accuracy.
◆ Identify primary or secondary sources of suitable data.
◆ Design, trial and refine data collection sheets.
◆ Collect and tabulate discrete and continuous data, choosing suitable equal class intervals where appropriate.

You are already familiar with some methods for collecting data. You also know how to display the data in a clear way and how to analyse it by carrying out simple calculations.

This chapter will build on the methods for collecting data, in particular on the planning that needs to take place before any data is collected to ensure that it will be reliable and produce useful information.

For example, we might want to answer the following question:

'Are boys better at maths than girls?'

To begin to answer this question it is important to be precise about what it means. For example,

● What age (or ages) should be considered?
● What is meant by 'better at maths'?

Discuss in pairs or small groups.

Q How can this question be made more precise?

Once the question has been decided on, it is important to think about where your data will come from. For example,

● You may collect the data yourself. This is called **primary data**.
● You may use data collected by your teachers or from the internet. This is called **secondary data**.

Q What primary data could be collected to answer the question 'Are boys better at maths than girls?' Make a list of your suggestions.

Q What types of secondary data could be collected? Make a list of your suggestions.

Once the sources of data are decided on, you need to decide how it is going to be collected.

- Primary data is usually collected by questionnaire or by interview.
- Secondary data will often be in number form. How will this be collected?

> **Q** Make notes on how both the primary and secondary data will be collected.
>
> **Q** If you have decided on using a questionnaire for the primary data, design a first draft for the questionnaire.
>
> **Q** If the secondary data is in number form, design tables (or a spreadsheet) in which to collect the data.

You also need to make a decision about how much data is to be collected. For this investigation, it will clearly not be possible to collect data from every student in the country or region, or even in the whole school. You will need to decide on a **sample size**, in other words how many people will be included in the investigation. It is also important to discuss how you are going to select people within the sample. For example,

- If you are looking at students from Years 7–11, will you choose the same number from each year?
- Will you choose the same number of boys and girls?
- Will the students you choose be your friends or will they be picked randomly?

> **Q** Make notes about the sample sizes you will use for both the primary and the secondary data.
>
> **Q** Make notes on how the samples are to be chosen to ensure that students are picked randomly.

You also need to decide how accurate the data collection needs to be. This may seem an odd consideration: it seems obvious that the data collection should be as accurate as possible. However, this is not necessarily the case. For example,

- If exam results are being collected and the data is in percentages, is it sensible to count the number of students who got 1%, 2%, 3%, … ?
- Would it be better to group the data and count the number of students getting 1–10%, 11–20%, 21–30%, … ?

> **Q** Decide on the level of accuracy needed for your data.

Once all of these points have been carefully considered, it is likely that the data collected will be appropriate and that any conclusions made will be valid. However, it is always possible that something has been overlooked or that the data collection doesn't work out exactly as planned. Before starting the actual data collection, it is always sensible to do a trial of the whole process. For example,

- If you are using a questionnaire, test it with a few people first to make sure the questions are clear.
- If you are organising your data in a spreadsheet, make sure that it works with a small amount of data first.
- You may decide that the sample size is too big or too small.

Once you have carried out a trial on the different stages of your data collection process, you can make any improvements that you think are necessary.

> **Q** What improvements have you made, and why did you decide to make them?

EXERCISE 5.1

Choose *one* of the following suggested questions as an area for investigation and data collection. Then:

    a) plan your data collection following the steps outlined in this chapter
    b) carry out the data collection in full
    c) present your findings in a clear way.

1   Are teenagers affected by advertising?

2   Do teenagers have a good diet?

3   Is maths more important than art?

4   How do people's spending habits change as they get older?

5   How much do people recycle?

By completing a data collection exercise thoroughly you will have noticed that it is not an exact science. The planning decisions you make will affect what data is collected, how it is collected and how accurate it is. Therefore it is important to plan things thoroughly and be able to justify any decisions you make.

6 Calculations and mental strategies 1

◆ Solve word problems mentally.
◆ Divide by decimals by transforming to division by an integer.

Word problems

Word problems do not always use the simple mathematical words 'add', 'subtract', 'multiply' or 'divide'. They often use words like 'sum', 'difference', 'product' or 'share' instead.

For example, a word problem involving adding $1.50, $2, $3.50 and $5 might also be written as:

● Find the total bill for items costing … .
● Find the sum of the following amounts.
● What is $1.50 plus $2 plus … ?

When solving word problems mentally, the actual maths is usually easy once you have decided which process is needed.

EXERCISE 6.1A

1   Write each of the following calculations as a word problem in two different ways.
    a) $6.2 + 4.3 + 9.5$
    b) $20 - $11.50
    c) 8×12
    d) $64 \div 8$
    e) $2(3 + 1.5)$

2   Write each of the following as a simple maths calculation.
    a) Find the difference between 1.84 m and 1.62 m.
    b) What is the sum of the first five even numbers?
    c) What is the product of 20 and 5?
    d) Share $25 equally among four people.
    e) Add 5 to 15 and treble the total.

EXERCISE 6.1B

Solve the problems in Exercise 6.1A mentally.

EXERCISE 6.1C

Solve the following problems mentally.

1   What is the difference between 2.6 m and 108 cm?

2   What is the product of 8 and 25?

3   Share $250 equally between five people.

4   What is the total of all the factors of 6?

5   Add 5, 10 and 15 and double the total.

6   Find the area of a square of side 9 cm.

7   What is the volume of a cube of side 3 cm?

8   A clock reads 8.10 p.m. It is 20 minutes fast.
    What is the time using a 24-hour clock?

9   A train is travelling at an average speed of 160 km per hour.
    How far will it travel in 4 hours 30 minutes?

10 A wall is 150 bricks wide and 12 bricks high.
    How many bricks are used?

11 To make it safe, the wall from question 10 is 3 bricks deep.
    How many bricks are used now?

12 Add the factors of 12 together and double the result.

13 What is 30% of 200?

14 Increase 130 by one fifth.

15 Decrease 64 by one quarter.

16 What is the product of half of 16 and a quarter of 16?

17 A dress costs $42 and a coat costs twice as much.
    What do they cost in total?

18 Petrol costs $1.80 per litre.
    How much does it cost to fill a fuel tank of capacity 50 litres?

19 What is the perimeter of a square of side 15 m?

20 Increase half of 90 by one fifth.

Dividing by decimals

You already know from Student's Book 2 that the following division can be done either mentally or by short division.

$$5.82 \div 3 = 1.94$$

What about $5.82 \div 0.3$?

You can use place value to help you. The division can be re-written:

$$5.82 \div 0.3 = 5.82 \div \frac{3}{10}$$
$$= 5.82 \times \frac{10}{3}$$
$$= (5.82 \div 3) \times 10$$
$$= 1.94 \times 10$$
$$= 19.4$$

Similarly, $5.82 \div 0.03 = 194$.

EXERCISE 6.2A

Work out the following without using a calculator.

1	**a)** $8.31 \div 3$	**b)** $8.31 \div 0.3$	**c)** $8.31 \div 0.03$
2	**a)** $36.74 \div 2$	**b)** $36.74 \div 0.2$	**c)** $36.74 \div 0.02$
3	**a)** $69.66 \div 3$	**b)** $69.66 \div 0.3$	**c)** $69.66 \div 0.03$
4	**a)** $1.2848 \div 4$	**b)** $1.2848 \div 0.4$	**c)** $1.2848 \div 0.04$
5	**a)** $37.65 \div 5$	**b)** $37.65 \div 0.5$	**c)** $37.65 \div 0.05$
6	**a)** $6.72 \div 6$	**b)** $6.72 \div 0.6$	**c)** $6.72 \div 0.06$
7	**a)** $722.19 \div 7$	**b)** $722.19 \div 0.7$	**c)** $722.19 \div 0.07$
8	**a)** $44.568 \div 8$	**b)** $44.568 \div 0.8$	**c)** $44.568 \div 0.08$
9	**a)** $36.396 \div 9$	**b)** $36.396 \div 0.9$	**c)** $36.396 \div 0.09$
10	**a)** $0.036 \div 3$	**b)** $0.036 \div 0.3$	**c)** $0.036 \div 0.03$

Dividing by a decimal using long division

Worked example

Calculate $7184 \div 23$. Give your answer to one decimal place (d.p.).

```
        3 1 2 . 3 4
23 ) 7 1 8 4 . 0 0
     6 9
       2 8
       2 3
         5 4
         4 6
           8 0
           6 9
           1 1 0
             9 2
             1 8
```

Therefore $7184 \div 23 = 312.3$ (to one decimal place).

The calculation could be continued if the answer was required to more decimal places. For example,

$$7184 \div 23 = 312.348 \text{ (to three decimal places)}$$

This result can be used to deduce the answers to other divisions.

Worked examples

a) Calculate $7184 \div 2.3$.

$$7184 \div 2.3 = 71840 \div 23$$
$$= (7184 \div 23) \times 10$$
$$= 312.348 \times 10$$
$$= 3123.48 \text{ (to two decimal places)}$$

Multiply both numbers by 10 in order to eliminate the decimal in the divisor (the number we are dividing by).

b) Calculate $7.184 \div 0.23$.

$$7.184 \div 0.23 = 718.4 \div 23$$
$$= (7184 \div 23) \div 10$$
$$= 312.348 \div 10$$
$$= 31.2348 \text{ (to four decimal places)}$$

Multiply both numbers by 100 in order to eliminate the decimal in the divisor.

EXERCISE 6.2B

1   Use the fact that 23 949.3 ÷ 194 = 123.45 to work out these divisions.
   a) 23 949.3 ÷ 19.4
   b) 23 949.3 ÷ 1.94
   c) 239.493 ÷ 19.4
   d) 23.9493 ÷ 0.194
   e) 0.239 493 ÷ 0.0194

2   Use the fact that 4902.7293 ÷ 62.34 = 78.645 to work out these divisions.
   a) 490.272 93 ÷ 6.234
   b) 49.027 293 ÷ 62.34
   c) 4.902 729 3 ÷ 0.6234
   d) 490 272.93 ÷ 623.4
   e) 0.490 272 93 ÷ 0.062 34

Comparison of compound measures – value for money

Many electricity, gas and mobile phone companies offer customers a choice of tariffs. In other words, customers can choose the pricing plan that offers them the best deal for their usage. This type of comparison is called finding 'the best value for money'.

Worked example

A girl sends around 12 text messages each day. A mobile phone company offers two tariffs.

   Tariff A: The first 100 texts each month cost 3c each, the second 100 texts cost 2c each and after this the cost of each text is 1c

   Tariff B: All texts costs 2.2c

Which tariff offers her better value for money?

Assume she sends 300 texts each month, then

   Tariff A costs 100 × 3 + 100 × 2 + 100 × 1 = 600c = $6

   Tariff B costs 300 × 2.2 = 660c = $6.60

So, tariff A is better value for money.

Shops often sell 'multi-packs' of items which are usually cheaper than buying multiple individual items. These are said to be 'better value for money'. If you drink lots of cans of soft drink, it is often cheaper to buy a pack of six rather than buy six individual cans, but if you have to carry them a long way, you may decided that carrying the extra five cans around is not worth the saving.

Worked example

Dhiann uses lots of batteries in her camera and her mp3 player. Her local shop sells the batteries in packs of three for $4.50 or packs of five for $6.

a) Which is better value for money?

b) Why might she not take up the better offer?

a) Pack of 3 works out at 4.50 ÷ 3 = $1.50 each
Pack of 5 works out at 6 ÷ 5 = $1.20 each
So, the pack of five is better value for money.

b) She might choose not to buy the pack of five if, for example, she does not have that much money to spend or if she doesn't think the batteries are as good as the packet of three.

EXERCISE 6.3

1 Three electricity companies sell electricity as 'units of electricity'. Their charges are shown below.

Company A: 25 cents per unit
Company B: $20 per quarter plus 20 cents per unit
Company C: $40 per quarter plus 10 cents per unit

Work out what each company would charge and state which company offers the best value for money in each of these cases.

a) A 2 bedroomed house using an average of 400 units each quarter of a year

b) An apartment using 250 units per quarter

c) A larger family house using 800 units per quarter.

2 Three water companies offer the following tariffs.

Standard Water: unlimited use for $650 a year
Local Water: $135 plus 0.3 cents per litre
Environmental water: 0.8 cents per litre

Work out what each comany would charge and state which company offers the best value for money in each of these cases.

a) A single person using 60 000 litres a year

b) A married couple using 150 000 litres a year

c) A family using 370 000 litres a year

3 For parts **a)** to **d)**

i) find the quantity that offers the 'best' value

ii) give one reason (other than 'not enough money') why a customer might choose not to accept the 'best' offer.

a) A4 paper: 4 packs for $4.20 or 10 packs for $9.50

b) Pens: 3 for 50c or 10 for $1.50

c) Paving slabs: 10 for $22, 100 for $159, 500 for $550

d) Text messages: 100 for $1.20, 500 for $4 or unlimited texts for $20

The tariffs that we have looked at here have a 'break even point' when one becomes better value than another. It is easier to find this using a graph, as shown in Chapter 11.

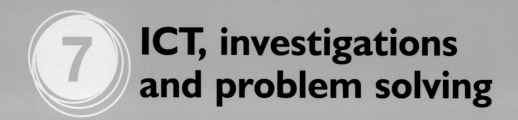

7 ICT, investigations and problem solving

1 Overlapping polygons

a) This diagram shows a regular pentagon overlapping a square.

An obtuse angle x is formed at the overlap of the two shapes.

  (i) What is the size of each of the internal angles of the square?

  (ii) What is the size of each of the internal angles of the pentagon?

  (iii) Calculate the size of angle x.

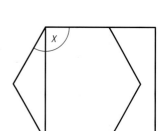

b) This diagram shows a regular hexagon overlapping a square.
Calculate the size of angle x.

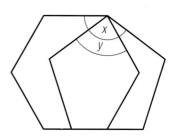

c) This diagram shows a regular hexagon overlapping a regular pentagon.

  (i) Calculate the size of angle x.

  (ii) Calculate the size of angle y.

d) Extend this investigation further by investigating the angles formed when other regular polygons overlap.

2 Circles and polygons

You already know that for any circle:

$$\frac{\text{circumference}}{\text{diameter}} = \pi$$

The screenshots on the next page are taken from the geometry package Cabri Géomètre II.

You are going to investigate the relationship between the perimeter and the 'diameter' of regular polygons and see how it compares with that for a circle.

a) Using Cabri, draw a four-sided regular polygon (i.e. a square).

b) By selecting the 'Segment' option, draw a line segment from one corner of the square to the opposite corner – this will produce a diagonal: the 'diameter'.

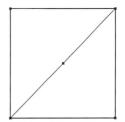

c) Select 'Distance and Length' then move the mouse over the perimeter and diagonal in turn and click.

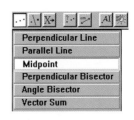

    The computer will then display the length of each on the screen.

      Record these results either in a table or on a spreadsheet.

d) Calculate also the value of perimeter length ÷ diagonal length.

e) Repeat steps **a)** to **d)** for all *even*-sided regular polygons up to 20 sides, i.e. hexagon, octagon, decagon, etc.

f) How do your results for perimeter length ÷ diagonal length change as the number of sides increases? How do the results compare with those for circumference ÷ diameter of a circle?

g) Repeat steps **a)** to **d)** and **f)** for *odd*-sided regular polygons, i.e. equilateral triangle, pentagon, heptagon, etc. For odd-sided polygons you cannot draw a diagonal to join two opposite corners. Therefore a corner is joined to the midpoint of the opposite side to form the 'diameter'.

To find the midpoint of a side of a regular polygon select 'Midpoint' on the toolbar. Move the mouse over one of the sides of the regular polygon and click. The midpoint will appear as a point on the side.

    An example of a regular pentagon, with a 'diagonal' drawn, is shown.

h) (i) How are the results for even and odd-sided regular polygons similar?

     (ii) How do the results for even and odd-sided regular polygons differ?

1 Without using a calculator, work out the cube roots of the numbers in parts **(i)** and **(ii)**. Then estimate the cube root of the number in part **(iii)**.

    a) **(i)** 64   **(ii)** 125   **(iii)** 100

    b) **(i)** 216   **(ii)** 343   **(iii)** 230

2 Simplify the following using indices:

    a) $3^2 \times 3^5 \times 3$

    b) $7^6 \div 7^2$

    c) $(4^3)^4$

    d) $(3^5)^3 \div 3^5 \times (3^3)^2 \div 3^5$

3 For each of the following rectangles, write an expression for:

    (i) the area

    (ii) the perimeter.

    Use brackets in the expression where possible.

    a) 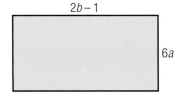   **b)**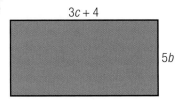

4 Factorise the following expressions fully.

    a) $16p - 36q$ **b)** $10a + 25b$ **c)** $56d - 42e$

    d) $6a - 18b + 12c$ **e)** $4ab^2 - 12b^3$ **f)** $a^4 - a^3 + a^2$

5 Rearrange the following formulae to make the letter in **red** the subject.

    a) $3q = 2p + 4$ **b)** $5q = 4p + 6$ **c)** $4x + 8y = 6z$

6 Calculate the size of the unknown angles in these polygons.

    Give reasons for your answers.

    a)    **b)**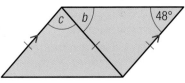

7 Draw the front, side and plan elevations of this three-dimensional shape.

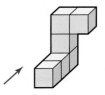

8 For each of the following three-dimensional objects, copy the diagram shown. Then:
  (i) draw a plane of symmetry on your copy
  (ii) work out how many planes of symmetry the object has in total.

a)

a cuboid

b)

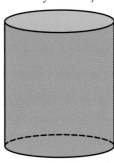

a cylinder

9 Draw a line *AB*, where *AB* = 6 cm and mark a point *M*, like this.

  a) Construct a line which passes through *M* and is perpendicular to *AB*.
  b) Mark a point *C* on the perpendicular line so that *MC* = 3 cm.
  c) Draw the lines *AC* and *BC*.
  d) Calculate the area of the triangle *ABC*.

10 a) A load of cement weighs 3.4 tonnes.
      2730 kg is removed. What weight is left?
   b) A driver travels for four days and covers 900 km in total.
      He covers 223 km, 188 km and 309 km on the first three days.
      How far does he travelled on day 4?

11 Data is to be collected in order to answer the following question:
      'Are children eating too much fast food?'
   a) Give an example of a type of primary data that could be collected to investigate this question.
   b) Give an example of a type of secondary data that could be collected.
   c) Design a questionnaire with five questions that could be used.

12 Use the fact that 4592.34 ÷ 37.2 = 123.45 to work out these divisions.
   a) 4592.34 ÷ 372
   b) 459 234 ÷ 123.45

1 If $xy = +18$, copy and complete this table.

x	+9	+6	+3	+2	+1	−1	−2	−3	−6	−9
y										

2 Simplify the following using indices.
  a) $a^3 \times a^7$
  b) $b^5 \times b^3 \div b^4$
  c) $(c^3)^4 \div c^9$
  d) $(d^4)^2 \div d^7$
  e) $(e^5)^3 \div (e^3)^5$

3 Factorise the following expressions by grouping.
  a) $af - ag - bf + bg$ **b)** $a^2 - ab^2 + ac - cb^2$

4 Calculate the value of each of the following expressions when $a = \frac{1}{4}$, $b = -\frac{1}{4}$, $c = 3$ and $d = -2$. Use a calculator if necessary.
  a) $a - b + (c - d)$ **b)** $a^2 + b^2$
  c) $c^2 - d^2$ **d)** $a + b + c - d$

5 Simplify the following.
  a) $\dfrac{3}{5} - \dfrac{3}{10}$ **b)** $\dfrac{2a}{10} + \dfrac{4a}{25}$

  c) $\dfrac{2ab}{xy} - \dfrac{ab}{4xy}$ **d)** $\dfrac{b}{5x} - \dfrac{b}{15x} + \dfrac{2b}{20x}$

6 Calculate the size of the unknown angles in this diagram.
Give reasons for your answers.

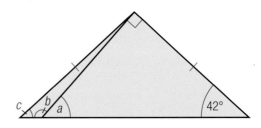

7 Sketch the three-dimensional object from the elevations given.

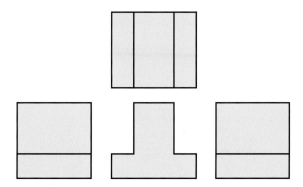

8 Using a ruler and a pair of compasses construct:
   a) a regular hexagon
   b) a regular octagon.

9 Write an estimate for each of the following using a sensible unit.
   a) What does a newborn baby elephant weigh?
   b) How long does an average film at the cinema last?
   c) How tall is an adult?

10 When collecting data, why should a trial be carried out before the actual data is collected?

11 Solve the following problems mentally.
   a) What is the perimeter of a square of side 15 cm?
   b) What is the area of the square in part **a)**?

12 **a)** A train is travelling at an average speed of 120 km/h.
      How far does it travel in $2\frac{1}{4}$ hours?

   b) If the journey takes $2\frac{1}{4}$ hours and the train arrives at 13 10, what time did it leave?

SECTION ②

8 Place value, ordering and rounding

◆ Recognise the equivalence of 0.1, $\frac{1}{10}$ and 10^{-1}; multiply and divide whole numbers and decimals by 10 to the power of any positive or negative integer.
◆ Round numbers to a given number of decimal places or significant figures.
◆ Use the order of operations, including brackets and powers.

Powers of 10

You already know that
$$10^3 = 10 \times 10 \times 10 = 1000 \quad \text{and} \quad 10^2 = 10 \times 10 = 100$$

and that 10 can be written as 10^1.

From work on indices in Chapter 1 you also know that
$$n^0 = 1 \quad \text{and} \quad n^{-1} = \frac{1}{n}$$

So
$$10^0 = 1 \quad \text{and} \quad 10^{-1} = \frac{1}{10} \quad \text{and} \quad 10^{-2} = \frac{1}{10^2} = \frac{1}{100}$$

So we can re-write the headings of the usual place value table like this:

Thousands	Hundreds	Tens	Units	•	Tenths	Hundredths	Thousandths
1000	100	10	1	•	$\frac{1}{10}$	$\frac{1}{100}$	$\frac{1}{1000}$
10^3	10^2	10^1	10^0	•	10^{-1}	10^{-2}	10^{-3}

Since 4000 is 4×1000 we can write
$$4000 \quad \text{as} \quad 4 \times 10^3$$

Similarly, we can write

200	as	2×10^2
60	as	6×10^1
5	as	5×10^0
0.3	as	3×10^{-1}
0.08	as	8×10^{-2}
0.007	as	7×10^{-3}

and so on.

Multiplying whole numbers and decimals by powers of 10

You already know how to multiply by 1000, 100, 10, 0.1 and 0.01. The following examples revise this work and show how you can use it to multiply by powers of 10.

Worked examples

7×10^3 $= 7 \times 1000$ $= 7000$
7.5×10^3 $= 7.5 \times 1000$ $= 7500$
7.58×10^3 $= 7.58 \times 1000$ $= 7580$

8×10^2 $= 8 \times 100$ $= 800$
8.3×10^2 $= 8.3 \times 100$ $= 830$
8.36×10^2 $= 8.36 \times 100$ $= 836$

9×10^1 $= 9 \times 10$ $= 90$
9.3×10^1 $= 9.3 \times 10$ $= 93$
9.35×10^1 $= 9.35 \times 10$ $= 93.5$

4×10^0 $= 4 \times 1$ $= 4$
4.8×10^0 $= 4.8 \times 1$ $= 4.8$
4.83×10^0 $= 4.83 \times 1$ $= 4.83$

5×10^{-1} $= 5 \times 0.1$ $= 0.5$
5.3×10^{-1} $= 5.3 \times 0.1$ $= 0.53$
5.364×10^{-1} $= 5.364 \times 0.1$ $= 0.5364$

6×10^{-2} $= 6 \times 0.01$ $= 0.06$
6.4×10^{-2} $= 6.4 \times 0.01$ $= 0.064$
6.45×10^{-2} $= 6.45 \times 0.01$ $= 0.0645$

EXERCISE 8.1A

Work out the following multiplications.

1 a) 5.0×10^3 b) 5.1×10^3 c) 5.17×10^3

2 a) 7.0×10^{-1} b) 7.3×10^{-1} c) 7.36×10^{-1}

3 a) 8.0×10^4 b) 8.4×10^4 c) 8.42×10^4

4 a) 6.0×10^{-3} b) 6.4×10^{-3} c) 6.49×10^{-3}

5 a) 4.19×10^2 b) 7.81×10^{-2}

6 a) 8.831×10^3 b) 5.728×10^{-3}

7 a) 8×10^5 b) 4.1×10^{-5}

Dividing whole numbers and decimals by powers of 10

You already know how to divide whole numbers and decimals by 1000, 100, 10, 0.1, 0.01. The following example revises this work and shows how you can use it to divide by powers of 10.

Worked example

$$4.31 \div 10^3 = 4.31 \div 1000 = 0.00431$$
$$4.31 \div 10^2 = 4.31 \div 100 \ \ = 0.0431$$
$$4.31 \div 10^1 = 4.31 \div 10 \ \ \ \ = 0.431$$
$$4.31 \div 10^0 = 4.31 \div 1 \ \ \ \ \ = 4.31$$
$$4.31 \div 10^{-1} = 4.31 \div 0.1 \ \ \ = 43.1$$
$$4.31 \div 10^{-2} = 4.31 \div 0.01 \ = 431$$

You can see that dividing by 0.1 or $\frac{1}{10}$ is the same as multiplying by 10, and that dividing by 0.01 or $\frac{1}{100}$ is the same as multiplying by 100.

EXERCISE 8.1B

Work out the following divisions.

1   **a)** $5.728 \div 10^2$ **b)** $5.728 \div 10^1$ **c)** $5.728 \div 10^0$
    d) $5.728 \div 10^{-1}$ **e)** $5.728 \div 10^{-2}$ **f)** $5.728 \div 10^{-3}$

2   **a)** $6.308 \div 10^2$ **b)** $6.308 \div 10^{-1}$ **c)** $6.308 \div 10^{-3}$

3   **a)** $7.92 \div 10^2$ **b)** $7.92 \div 10^{-2}$ **c)** $7.92 \div 10^{-4}$

4   **a)** $1.357 \div 10^2$ **b)** $1.357 \div 10^{-3}$

5   **a)** $8.63 \div 10^{-1}$ **b)** $8.63 \div 10^1$

6   **a)** $3.428 \div 10^0$ **b)** $3.428 \div 10^{-3}$

7   **a)** $8.1 \div 10^2$ **b)** $8.1 \div 10^{-4}$

Rounding

Significant figures

The use of **significant figures** (s.f.) is a way of *rounding* a number. The term 'significant' means important. So a significant figure is an important figure.

Worked example

6387 people went to see a basketball game. Write 6387 to:
a) one significant figure
b) two significant figures.

a) The most important figure is the 6 as it is worth 6000.
Therefore 6387 written to one significant figure is 6000.

The 6 is said to be the first significant figure.

b) The second most important figure is the 3 as it is worth 300.
Look at the number line.

Only write the two most important figures. Write the rest as zeros.

6387
6300   6400

The numbers 6300 and 6400 are the two numbers written to two significant figures either side of 6387. 6387 is closer to 6400, so 6387 written to two significant figures is 6400.

EXERCISE 8.2A

1 Write each of the following numbers to one significant figure.
   a) 6320 b) 785 c) 93 d) 4856
   e) 4.3 f) 6.7 g) 0.84 h) 0.076

2 Write each of the following numbers to two significant figures.
   a) 6834 b) 6874 c) 4.62 d) 7.38
   e) 52.84 f) 46.39 g) 0.8738 h) 0.8783

3 Write each of the following numbers to three significant figures.
   a) 87645 b) 476.93 c) 0.8756
   d) 82.43 e) 82.48

Decimal places

Another way of *rounding* a number, which you have already met, is to write it to a given number of **decimal places**. This refers to the number of digits written after the decimal point.

Worked example

The length of a model car is 7.864 cm.
Write 7.864 to one decimal place.
Draw a number line to help you.

A number written to one decimal place has one digit after the decimal point.

7.864

7.8   7.9

7.864 is closer to 7.9 than it is to 7.8, so 7.864 written to one decimal place is 7.9.

To round to a certain number of decimal places or significant figures, look at the next digit to the one in question. If that digit is 5 or more, round up. If it is 4 or less, round down.

EXERCISE 8.2B

1 Round each of the following numbers to one decimal place.
   a) 6.37   **b)** 4.13   **c)** 0.85
   d) 8.672   **e)** 1.093   **f)** 0.063

2 Round each of the following numbers to two decimal places.
   a) 4.383   **b)** 5.719   **c)** 5.803
   d) 1.477   **e)** 3.899   **f)** 6.273

3 Round each of the following numbers to three decimal places.
   a) 0.000 82   **b)** 0.007 65   **c)** 0.004 67
   d) 3.6543   **e)** 3.4567

Estimating answers to calculations

Even though calculators are a quick and easy way of solving arithmetical problems, an **estimate** can be a useful check.

Worked examples

a) Estimate the answer to 18×71.

To one significant figure 18 is 20 and 71 is 70.
So an easy estimate is
$$20 \times 70 = 1400.$$

b) Estimate the answer to $3568 \div 28$.

3568 is 3600 to two significant figures.
28 is 30 to one significant figure.
So a good estimate would be
$$3600 \div 30 = 120.$$

If 3568 was rounded to 4000 then $4000 \div 30 = 133$ is still a reasonable estimate.

EXERCISE 8.3

Estimate the answers to the calculations in questions 1 and 2.
State the number of significant figures in your answers.

1 **a)** 42×19 **b)** 63×27 **c)** 198×39
  d) 8.9×384 **e)** 55×77

2 **a)** $3984 \div 41$ **b)** $5872 \div 32$ **c)** $8.972 \div 2.8$
  d) $0.414 \div 2.1$ **e)** $0.414 \div 0.21$

3 Using estimation, write down which of these calculations are definitely wrong.
  a) $6357 \div 21 = 30.27$ **b)** $834 \times 7.9 = 6588$
  c) $189 \div 8.9 = 212$ **d)** $78.3 \times 11.2 = 8769$

Order of operations

You are already familiar with the order in which calculations must be carried out:

Brackets
Indices
Division and/or **M**ultiplication
Addition and/or **S**ubtraction

A useful way of remembering the order is with the shorthand **BIDMAS**.

Worked examples

a) Calculate $4 + 3^2 \times 2$.

$4 + 3^2 \times 2$

> *The index or power (3^2) is worked out first …*

$= 4 + 9 \times 2$

> *… then the multiplication …*

$= 4 + 18$

> *… then the addition.*

$= 22$

b) Calculate $3(4^3 - 7^2)$.

$3(4^3 - 7^2)$

> *The brackets are worked out first …*

$= 3(64 - 49)$

> *… then the multiplication.*

$= 3 \times 15$

$= 45$

c) Calculate $(5^2 - 4^2)^2$.

$(5^2 - 4^2)^2$

$= (25 - 16)^2$

$= 9^2$

$= 81$

EXERCISE 8.4

Work out the following.

1 $3^2 + 4^2$ **2** $5^2 + 12^2$

3 $5^2 - 4^2$ **4** $2(13^2 - 12^2)$

5 $2(4^2 + 5^2) - 4(2^2 + 2^2)$ **6** $5(1^2 + 2^2 + 3^2)$

7 $2 + 2(1^3 + 2^3) - 2(1 + 2 + 3 + 4)$ **8** $4(2^3 + 4^2) + 4$

9 $\dfrac{(5^2 - 3^2)}{4}$ **10** $5(9^2 - 3^4) - 3(2^4 - 4^2)$

11 $(4^2 + 3^2)^2$ **12** $(1^2 + 2^2 - 3^2)^3$

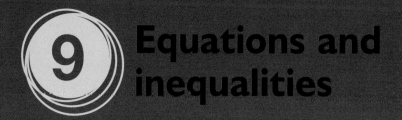

Equations and inequalities

◆ Construct and solve linear equations with integer coefficients (with and without brackets, negative signs anywhere in the equation, positive or negative solution); solve a number problem by constructing and solving a linear equation.

◆ Solve a simple pair of simultaneous linear equations by eliminating one variable.

◆ Expand the product of two linear expressions of the form $x \pm n$ and simplify the corresponding quadratic expression.

◆ Understand and use inequality signs ($<, >, \leqslant, \geqslant$); construct and solve linear inequalities in one variable; represent the solution set on a number line.

Equations

You already know that an equation represents two quantities which are equal to each other. To help see what an equation is and how it can be manipulated, you have seen that it can be thought of as a pair of balanced scales.

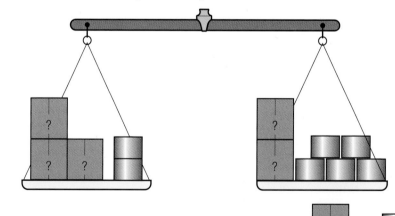

In the scales above there are two different types of object: 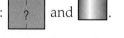 and ▨.

The left-hand side of the scales balances the right-hand side, i.e. the total masses on both sides are equal.

Worked example

For the scales on the previous page, find the mass of each 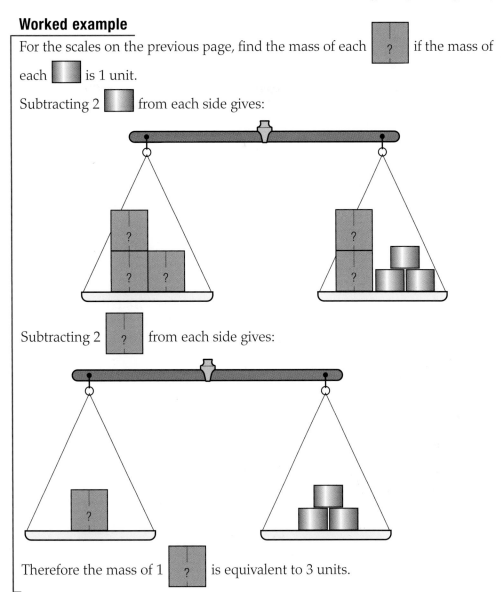 if the mass of

each ▨ is 1 unit.

Subtracting 2 ▨ from each side gives:

Subtracting 2 [?] from each side gives:

Therefore the mass of 1 [?] is equivalent to 3 units.

A more efficient way is to use algebra instead of diagrams. The problem above can be written as:

$$3x + 2 = 2x + 5 \quad \text{where } x \text{ is the mass of } 1 \; [?].$$

To solve the equation:

$$3x + 2 = 2x + 5$$
$$3x = 2x + 3 \qquad \text{(subtract 2 from both sides)}$$
$$x = 3 \qquad \text{(subtract } 2x \text{ from both sides)}$$

More complicated equations can be solved in the same way as long as the fundamental rule of equation solving is used, i.e. what is done to one side of the equation must also be done to the other side.

Worked examples

a) Solve the equation $5x - 3 = 2x + 12$.

$5x - 3 = 2x + 12$
$3x - 3 = 12$ (subtract $2x$ from both sides)
$3x = 15$ (add 3 to both sides)
$x = 5$ (divide both sides by 3)

b) Solve the equation $16 = 24 + 4x$.

$16 = 24 + 4x$
$-8 = 4x$ (subtract 24 from both sides)
$x = -2$ (divide both sides by 4)

c) Solve the equation $5(y - 2) = 5 + 2y$.

$5(y - 2) = 5 + 2y$
$5y - 10 = 5 + 2y$ (expand the brackets)
$3y - 10 = 5$ (subtract $2y$ from both sides)
$3y = 15$ (add 10 to both sides)
$y = 5$ (divide both sides by 3)

d) Solve the equation $3(x - 4) = 9(3x + 4)$.

$3(x - 4) = 9(3x + 4)$
$3x - 12 = 27x + 36$ (expand the brackets)
$-12 = 24x + 36$ (subtract $3x$ from both sides)
$-48 = 24x$ (subtract 36 from both sides)
$x = -2$ (divide both sides by 24)

EXERCISE 9.1

Solve the following linear equations.

1
  a) $a + 6 = 8$ **b)** $2a + 4 = 10$ **c)** $3a + 12 = 36$
  d) $4a + 8 = 28$ **e)** $5a + 3 = 33$

2
  a) $b - 5 = 10$ **b)** $2b - 4 = 10$ **c)** $3b - 9 = 9$
  d) $4b - 16 = 8$ **e)** $5b - 2 = 38$

3
  a) $5c = 4c + 2$ **b)** $8c + 2 = 7c$ **c)** $6c = 5c - 4$
  d) $3c + 4 = 4c$ **e)** $7c - 2 = 6c$

4
  a) $4d = d + 3$ **b)** $6d = 3d + 15$ **c)** $5d = 2d - 9$
  d) $4d = 7d + 12$ **e)** $9d = 13d - 16$

5
  a) $2(e - 3) = 2$ **b)** $3(3 + e) = 24$ **c)** $4(e - 6) = -8$
  d) $5(2 - e) = 15$ **e)** $3(4e + 1) = 39$

6
  a) $2(f - 1) = 4(f - 2)$ **b)** $3(2 + f) = 7(f - 2)$ **c)** $4(2f - 1) = 3(f + 2)$
  d) $4(3 - f) = 2(f + 12)$ **e)** $2(10 - 2f) = 8(4 - f)$

Constructing and solving equations

Sometimes you are asked to use some information you are given to construct (make) an equation and then use algebra to solve the equation.

Worked example

Ahmet says, 'I think of a number, add 7 and then multiply everything by 4. The answer is 12. What is my number?'

Using n to represent the number Ahmet chose:

$$4(n + 7) = 12$$
$$n + 7 = 3$$
$$n = 3 - 7$$
$$n = -4$$

So the number he chose is −4.

EXERCISE 9.2A

Construct an equation from the information given in each question and then solve it.

1 I think of a number, multiply it by 5 and add 6. The answer is 41. What is the number?

2 I think of a number, multiply it by 3 and add 7. The answer is 34. What is the number?

3 I think of a number, multiply it by 7 and subtract 4. The answer is 31. What is the number?

4 I think of a number, multiply it by 9 and subtract 10. The answer is 53. What is the number?

5 I think of a number, add 2 and multiply this all by 3. The answer is 12. What is the number?

6 I think of a number, add 7 and multiply this all by 5. The answer is 65. What is the number?

7 I have five full boxes of counters and eight counters left over. There are 68 counters altogether. How many are in each full box?

8 I have six full boxes of counters and one box with eight counters missing. There are 132 counters altogether. How many are in each full box?

9 I put the same number of chocolate buttons on each of seven cakes. I had 40 buttons at the start and now have five buttons left over. How many did I put on each cake?

10 Two children had the same amount of money. One bought four drinks and had 40 cents left. The other bought three drinks and had $1 left. How much was each drink?

Worked example

A number has 7 subtracted from it and the result is multiplied by 3. The answer is the same as doubling the number, subtracting 15 and then doubling again. What is the number?

Using n to represent the number:

$$3(n - 7) = 2(2n - 15)$$
$$3n - 21 = 4n - 30$$
$$3n - 4n = -30 + 21$$
$$-n = -9$$
$$n = 9$$

So the number is 9.

EXERCISE 9.2B

Construct an equation from the information given in each question and then solve it.

1 A number is subtracted from 10 and the answer is 3. What is the number?

2 A number is subtracted from 3. The result is multiplied by 4 and the answer is 8. What is the number?

3 A number is subtracted from 7. The result is multiplied by 3 and the answer is 6. What is the number?

4 A number is subtracted from 9. The result is multiplied by 10 and the answer is 40. What is the number?

5 A number is subtracted from 16. The result is multiplied by 33 and the answer is 66. What is the number?

6 6 is subtracted from a number and the result is multiplied by 4. The answer is the same if 3 is subtracted from the number and the result is multiplied by 2. What is the number?

7 If 5 is subtracted from a number and the result is multiplied by 3, the answer is the same as adding 1 to the number and doubling the result. What is the number?

8 Add 2 to a number and then multiply the result by 6. If this is the same as subtracting 4 and then multiplying the result by 10, what is the number?

9 Multiply a number by 4 and add 2, then multiply the result by 10. The answer is the same if you multiply the number by 6, add 10 and then multiply the result by 5. What is the number?

10 9 times a number has 1 subtracted from it. The result is trebled. The answer is the same if you add 7 to twice the number and multiply the result by 7. What is the number?

Simultaneous equations

Solving simultaneous equations by elimination

Here are three examples of linear equations.

$$p + 7 = 11 \qquad 2(m + 3) = 4(4 - 2m) \qquad \frac{2(r - 4)}{3} = 4$$

Each of these equations has only one unknown (p, m or r) and can be solved by applying simple rules. In each case there is only one solution ($p = 4$, $m = 1$, $r = 10$).

The equation below has two unknowns (sometimes called **variables**).

$$2a + 3b = 22$$

It has a number of possible solutions, for example

$$a = 2, b = 6 \qquad or \qquad a = 5, b = 4$$
$$2a + 3b = 22 \qquad\qquad 2a + 3b = 22$$
$$(2 \times 2) + (3 \times 6) = 4 + 18 \qquad (2 \times 5) + (3 \times 4) = 10 + 12$$
$$= 22 \checkmark \qquad\qquad = 22 \checkmark$$

We know these solutions are correct because in each case, when the values are substituted, the left-hand side of the equation equals the right-hand side.

However, if there are *two* equations, *both* involving the same two unknowns, they are called **simultaneous equations**. For example,

$$2a + 3b = 22 \qquad \text{equation 1}$$
$$2a + b = 14 \qquad \text{equation 2}$$

How can we find a solution which satisfies both equations?

Try $a = 2$, $b = 6$ in equation 1:
$$2a + 3b = 22$$
$$(2 \times 2) + (3 \times 6) = 22$$
$$4 + 18 = 22 \checkmark$$

Try $a = 2$, $b = 6$ in equation 2:
$$2a + b = 14$$
$$(2 \times 2) + 6 = 14$$
$$4 + 6 = 14$$
$$10 \neq 14 \text{ ✗}$$

The value of the left-hand side does not equal the right-hand side, so $a = 2$, $b = 6$ is not a solution that works for both equations.

Try $a = 5$, $b = 4$ in the two equations. What do you find?

In this case, there is only one solution that satisfies both equations simultaneously. The method of trying lots of different possible solutions is called **trial and improvement**. It works but it can take a long time, especially if the solutions are not whole numbers.

A better method is called the method of **elimination**.

Look at these two simultaneous equations.

$$3p + q = 17 \qquad \text{equation 1}$$
$$5p - q = 15 \qquad \text{equation 2}$$

If you *add* the two equations, you will find that one of the variables (q) is **eliminated**:

$$3p + q = 17$$
$$\underline{5p - q = 15}$$
$$8p = 32$$

Therefore $p = 4$.

To find the value of q, substitute $p = 4$ into equation 1:

$$3p + q = 17$$
$$(3 \times 4) + q = 17$$
$$12 + q = 17$$
$$q = 17 - 12$$
$$q = 5$$

So $p = 4$ and $q = 5$.

Check by substituting $p = 4$ and $q = 5$ in equation 2:

$$5p - q = 15$$
$$20 - 5 = 15 \checkmark$$

EXERCISE 9.3A

Solve each of these pairs of simultaneous equations by elimination.

1 $a + b = 8$
  $3a - b = 12$

2 $c + d = 7$
  $4c - d = 8$

3 $e + f = 5$
  $4e - f = 5$

4 $g + h = 6$
  $5g - h = 12$

5 $j + k = 7$
  $4j - k = 23$

6 $l + m = 9$
  $2l - m = 6$

7 $n + p = 9$
  $4n - p = 1$

8 $q + r = 9$
  $10q - r = 2$

9 $s + t = 8$
  $5s - t = 16$

10 $u + v = 15$
  $2u - v = 6$

11 $3a + 2b = 8$
  $2a - 2b = 2$

12 $c + 4d = 16$
  $5c - 4d = 8$

13 $e + 2f = 8$
  $5e - 2f = 4$

14 $3g + 4h = 21$
  $9g - 4h = 15$

15 $3j + 4k = 23$
  $2j - 4k = 2$

16 $3l + 2m = 14$
  $5l - 2m = 2$

17 $n + 4p = 13$
  $12 - 4p = 0$

18 $n + 6p = 19$
  $3n - 6p = -15$

19 $r + 6s = 11$
  $r - 6s = -1$

20 $t + 3u = 22$
  $7t - 3u = -14$

In Exercise 9.3A, in each case, one variable was eliminated by *addition*. In the next two examples one variable is eliminated by *subtraction*.

Worked examples

a) Solve these simultaneous equation by eliminating by subtraction.

$$5a + 2b = 16 \quad \text{equation 1}$$
$$3a + 2b = 12 \quad \text{equation 2}$$

Subtract equation 2 from equation 1:

$$\begin{array}{r} 5a + 2b = 16 \\ 3a + 2b = 12 \\ \hline 2a = 4 \end{array}$$

Therefore $a = 2$.

Substitute $a = 2$ in equation 1:

$$5a + 2b = 16$$
$$10 + 2b = 16$$
$$2b = 16 - 10$$
$$2b = 6$$
$$b = 3$$

Check by substituting $a = 2$, $b = 3$ in equation 2:

$$3a + 2b = 12$$
$$6 + 6 = 12 \checkmark$$

b) Solve these simultaneous equation by eliminating by subtraction.

$$4c - 3d = 14 \quad \text{equation 1}$$
$$c - 3d = -1 \quad \text{equation 2}$$

Subtract equation 2 from equation 1:

$$\begin{array}{r} 4c - 3d = 14 \\ c - 3d = -1 \\ \hline 3c = 15 \end{array}$$

Note: $14 - (-1) = 15$

Therefore $c = 5$.

Substitute $c = 5$ in equation 1:

$$4c - 3d = 14$$
$$20 - 3d = 14$$
$$-3d = 14 - 20$$
$$-3d = -6$$
$$d = 2$$

Check by substituting $c = 5$, $d = 2$ in equation 2:

$$c - 3d = -1$$
$$5 - 6 = -1 \checkmark$$

EXERCISE 9.3B

Solve each of these pairs of simultaneous equations by elimination.

1	$3a + 2b = 10$ $2a + 2b = 8$	**2**	$3c + 4d = 13$ $c + 4d = 7$	**3**	$5e - 2f = 4$ $2e - 2f = -2$
4	$4g - 2h = 8$ $g - 2h = -1$	**5**	$j - k = 1$ $2j - k = 3$	**6**	$l - 2m = -5$ $3l - 2m = -3$
7	$2n - p = 0$ $n - p = -2$	**8**	$3q + 2r = 14$ $q + 2r = 6$	**9**	$s + t = 8$ $5s + t = 28$
10	$2u + v = 6$ $3u + v = 7$	**11**	$3a + 2b = 10$ $3a - b = 4$	**12**	$2c - d = -1$ $2c + 3d = 11$
13	$4e - 2f = 8$ $4e + 3f = 18$	**14**	$g + h = 3$ $g + 3h = 7$	**15**	$j + 2k = 8$ $j - 3k = -7$
16	$4l + m = 20$ $4l + 2m = 24$	**17**	$2n + 3p = 11$ $2n - 2p = -4$	**18**	$3r - s = -1$ $3r - 2s = -8$
19	$t + u = 11$ $t + 3u = 29$	**20**	$4t + 5u = 49$ $4t + u = 29$		

Look at these two simultaneous equations.

$$x + 2y = 7 \qquad \text{equation 1}$$
$$3x + y = 11 \qquad \text{equation 2}$$

In this case, simply adding or subtracting the equations will not result in the elimination of either x or y. An extra process is needed.

Remember that if you multiply all the terms of an equation by the same number it will still balance. For example, if you multiply $y = x$ throughout by 2 you get the equation $2y = 2x$. This is equivalent to $y = x$.

Multiply equation 1 throughout by 3 and call the result equation 3:

$$x + 2y = 7 \qquad \text{equation 1}$$
$$\times 3 \qquad 3x + 6y = 21 \qquad \text{equation 3}$$

Now replace equation 1 in the pair of simultaneous equations by equation 3:

$$3x + 6y = 21 \qquad \text{equation 3}$$
$$3x + y = 11 \qquad \text{equation 2}$$

Subtract equation 2 from equation 3 to eliminate x:

$$\begin{aligned} 3x + 6y &= 21 \\ \underline{3x + y} &= \underline{11} \\ 5y &= 10 \end{aligned}$$

Therefore $y = 2$.

Substitute $y = 2$ in equation 1:

$$x + 2y = 7$$
$$x + 4 = 7$$
$$x = 7 - 4$$
$$x = 3$$

Check by substituting $x = 3$, $y = 2$ in equation 2:

$$3x + y = 11$$
$$9 + 2 = 11 \checkmark$$

EXERCISE 9.3C

Solve each of these pairs of simultaneous equations by elimination.

1 $a + 3b = 5$
$\quad 3a + 2b = 8$

2 $b + 3c = 7$
$\quad 2b + c = 4$

3 $2d + e = 7$
$\quad 3d + 2e = 12$

4 $3f + g = 11$
$\quad 2f + 3g = 12$

5 $2h - j = 3$
$\quad 3h + 2j = 8$

6 $2k - 2l = -2$
$\quad 3k + l = 5$

7 $3m - 4n = -14$
$\quad 2m + 2n = 14$

8 $p + q = 7$
$\quad 2p - 3q = -6$

9 $r + 2s = 0$
$\quad 3r - s = -7$

10 $2t + u = 1$
$\quad 3t - 2u = 0$

EXERCISE 9.3D

Form a pair of simultaneous equations for each of these solutions.

1 $a = 2, b = 1$

2 $c = 3, d = 2$

3 $e = 2, f = 3$

4 $g = 5, h = 2$

5 $j = 7, k = 1$

6 $l = -1, m = 2$

7 $n = 3, p = -2$

8 $q = 5, r = -3$

9 $s = -2, t = -3$

10 $u = 1, v = -1$

✿ Practical examples of using simultaneous equations

The lengths of the sides of this rectangle are expressed algebraically.

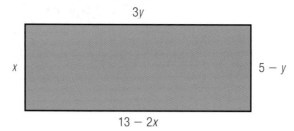

Because opposite sides of a rectangle are the same length, two equations can be formed:

$$3y = 13 - 2x \quad \text{and} \quad x = 5 - y$$

These form a pair of simultaneous equations in x and y. If we solve these equations, we can work out the lengths of the sides of the rectangle.

First rearrange the equations to form a pair:

$$2x + 3y = 13 \quad \text{equation 1}$$
$$x + y = 5 \quad \text{equation 2}$$

Multiply equation 2 by 2 and call this equation 3:

$$2x + 3y = 13 \quad \text{equation 1}$$
$$2x + 2y = 10 \quad \text{equation 3}$$

Subtract equation 3 from equation 1:

$$2x + 3y = 13$$
$$\underline{2x + 2y = 10}$$
$$y = 3$$

Substitute $y = 3$ in equation 1:

$$2x + 3y = 13$$
$$2x + 9 = 13$$
$$2x = 13 - 9$$
$$2x = 4$$
$$x = 2$$

Check by substituting $x = 2$, $y = 3$ in equation 2:

$$x + y = 5$$
$$2 + 3 = 5 \checkmark$$

In the original diagram, the lengths of the sides were:

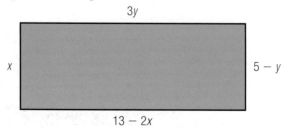

By substitution, the lengths of the sides are:

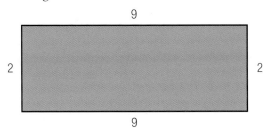

Worked example

Find the lengths of the sides
of this rectangle.

First, form two equations:

$$4x = y + 9 \qquad 7x = y + 18$$

Rearrange the equations to give:

$$4x - y = 9 \qquad \text{equation 1}$$
$$7x - y = 18 \qquad \text{equation 2}$$

Subtract equation 1 from equation 2:

$$7x - y = 18$$
$$\underline{4x - y = 9}$$
$$3x = 9$$

Therefore $x = 3$.
Substitute $x = 3$ in equation 1:

$$4x - y = 9$$
$$12 - y = 9$$
$$12 - 9 = y$$
$$y = 3$$

Check by substituting $x = 3$, $y = 3$ in equation 2:

$$7x - y = 18$$
$$21 - 3 = 18 \checkmark$$

The lengths of the sides are:

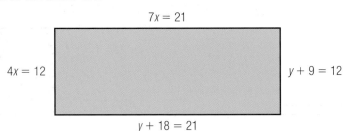

Problem solving using simultaneous equations

Worked example

The sum of two numbers is 27, and their difference is 9. By forming two equations and solving them, find the two numbers.

$$x + y = 27 \quad \text{equation 1}$$
$$x - y = 9 \quad \text{equation 2}$$

Adding the equations gives:

$$x + y = 27$$
$$\underline{x - y = 9}$$
$$2x = 36$$

Therefore $x = 18$.

Substitute $x = 18$ in equation 1:

$$x + y = 27$$
$$18 + y = 27$$
$$y = 27 - 18$$
$$y = 9$$

Check by substituting $x = 18$, $y = 9$ in equation 2:

$$x - y = 9$$
$$18 - 9 = 9 \checkmark$$

The two numbers are 18 and 9.

EXERCISE 9.3E

For each of the following problems, form two equations and solve them to find the two numbers.

1 The sum of two numbers is 10, and their difference is 2.

2 The sum of two numbers is 26, and their difference is 2.

3 The sum of two numbers is 50, and their difference is 18.

4 The sum of two numbers is 12, and their difference is 8.

5 The sum of two numbers is 60, and half of their difference is 10.

6–10 Make up five questions of this kind. Ask a friend to try to solve them.

Expanding two linear expressions

Worked example

Write an expression for the area of this rectangle.

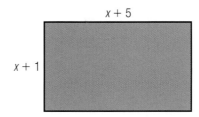

The rectangle can be split into four like this:

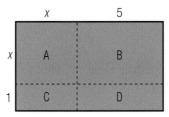

The area of A is $x \times x = x^2$.
The area of B is $5 \times x = 5x$.
The area of C is $1 \times x = x$.
The area of D is $1 \times 5 = 5$.

The total area is given by the expression

$$x^2 + 5x + x + 5 = x^2 + 6x + 5$$

The area of the rectangle can also be expressed using brackets like this:

$$(x + 1)(x + 5)$$

Therefore

$$(x + 1)(x + 5) = x^2 + 6x + 5$$

To expand brackets, you multiply all the terms in one set of brackets by the terms in the other set of brackets.

$$(x + 1)(x + 5) = x^2 + 5x + x + 5$$

$$= x^2 + 6x + 5$$

EXERCISE 9.4A

For each of the following shapes:
   a) write an expression for the area, using brackets
   b) expand your expression in part **a)** by multiplying out the brackets.

1

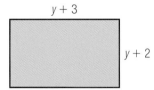

$y + 3$

$y + 2$

2

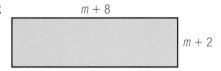

$m + 8$

$m + 2$

3

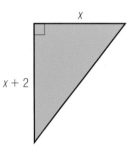

x

$x + 2$

4

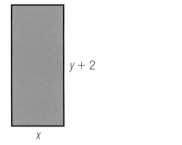

$y + 2$

x

5

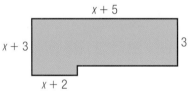

$x + 5$

$x + 3$

3

$x + 2$

6

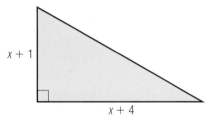

$x + 1$

$x + 4$

7

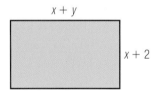

$x + y$

$x + 2$

8

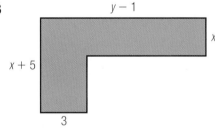

$y - 1$

x

$x + 5$

3

9

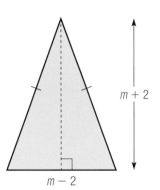

$m + 2$

$m - 2$

10

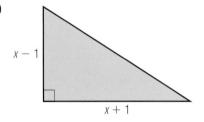

$x - 1$

$x + 1$

EXERCISE 9.4B

Expand each of the following and simplify your answer.

1 **a)** $(x-2)(x+3)$ **b)** $(x+8)(x-3)$

2 **a)** $(x+1)(x-3)$ **b)** $(x-7)(x+9)$

3 **a)** $(x-3)(x-3)$ **b)** $(x-7)(x-5)$

4 **a)** $(x+6)^2$ **b)** $(7-y)^2$

Inequalities

You are already familiar with the equals sign, used in equations to show that one thing is equal to another. There are a number of other signs which show that one thing *is not equal* to another. These are called **inequality** signs and they are used in **inequalities**.

The basic inequality signs are $<$ and $>$.

$x < y$ means x **is less than** y.
$x > y$ means x **is greater than** y.

So a sentence such as 'Everyone in a class of students is less than 13 years old' could be expressed as:

$a < 13$ where a is the age of a student, in years.

Two more signs $\leqslant$ and $\geqslant$ are formed by putting part of an equals sign under the inequality sign.

$x \leqslant y$ means x **is less than or equal to** y.
$x \geqslant y$ means x **is greater than or equal to** y.

So a sentence such as 'This nursery school takes children who are four years old or more' could be expressed as:

$a \geqslant 4$ where a is the age of a child, in years.

The following pairs of inequalities mean the same:

$x < y$ (x is less than y)   and $y > x$ (y is greater than x)
$x \leqslant y$ (x is less than or equal to y) and $y \geqslant x$ (y is greater than or equal to x)

So $5 < x$ is usually written as $x > 5$.

Another sign used is $\neq$, which means **is not equal to**. So

$x \neq 5$ means x is not equal to 5.

Worked examples

a) Write the inequality $a \leqslant 8$ in words.

   $a \leqslant 8$ means a is less than or equal to 8, i.e. a is at most 8.

b) Write the inequality $b \geqslant 5$ in words.

   $b \geqslant 5$ means b is greater than or equal to 5, i.e. b is at least 5.

EXERCISE 9.5A

Write these inequalities in words.

1 **a)** $a < 6$ **b)** $b > 5$ **c)** $c \neq 10$

2 **a)** $a \leq 7$ **b)** $b \geq 3$ **c)** $c \leq 10$

3 **a)** $4 < a$ **b)** $7 > b$ **c)** $c \neq 8$

4 **a)** $8 > a$ **b)** $5 < b$ **c)** $5 \neq c$

5 **a)** $6 \geq a$ **b)** $9 \leq b$ **c)** $3 \neq c$

EXERCISE 9.5B

Copy and complete the following statements, writing one of the signs =, > or < to make the statement true.

1 5×3 _____ $7 + 8$ 2 $6 + 4$ _____ 3×4

3 8×7 _____ 9×6 4 5^2 _____ 5×5

5 5×4 _____ 3×6 6 $1\,m$ _____ $75\,cm$

7 1 litre _____ $1000\,ml$ 8 $10\,cm$ _____ $1000\,mm$

9 5 tonnes _____ $3000\,kg$ 10 $1\,cm^2$ _____ $100\,mm^2$

Showing inequalities on a number line

The inequality $x \geq 5$ means that x is greater than or equal to 5. This can be shown on a number line like this:

Note that all values are included, not just whole numbers.

The inequality $x < 7$ means that x is less than 7. This is shown on the number line like this:

Notice that ○———➤ means the number *is not included*.

●———➤ means the number *is included*.

EXERCISE 9.5C

Show each of the following inequalities on a number line.

1 $a \geqslant 3$ **2** $b \leqslant 6$

3 $c > 4$ **4** $d < 5$

5 $4 \leqslant e$ **6** $7 \geqslant f$

7 $3 < g$ **8** $6 > h$

9 $i > 0.7$ **10** $j < 2.5$

Combined inequalities

It is possible to combine two inequalities. For example, $p > 7$ and $p < 10$ can be combined as $7 < p < 10$, which means that p is greater than 7 but less than 10. This can be shown on a number line like this:

$7 \leqslant q \leqslant 10$ means that q is greater than or equal to 7 but less than or equal to 10. This can be shown on a number line like this:

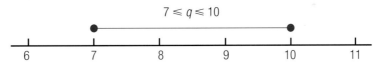

EXERCISE 9.5D

Represent each of the following inequalities on a number line.

1 $4 < a < 7$ **2** $5 \geqslant b \geqslant 2$

3 $8 \leqslant c \leqslant 11$ **4** $6 > d > 1$

5 $3 < e \leqslant 6$ **6** $5 \geqslant f > 3$

7 $-5 < g < -2$ **8** $-5 \geqslant h > -8$

9 $-2 \leqslant i < 2$ **10** $4 > j \geqslant 0$

EXERCISE 9.5E

Write the inequality shown by each of the following number lines, using the given letter for the unknown.

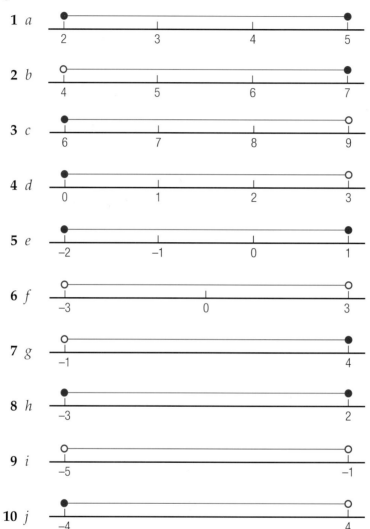

1 a

2 b

3 c

4 d

5 e

6 f

7 g

8 h

9 i

10 j

Vocabulary of inequalities

English words and phrases that express inequalitities, such as 'at least', 'at most', 'maximum', 'minimum', 'between', 'inclusive', 'including' and 'not more than', are used in ordinary conversation but they are not as exact in their meaning as a clear statement using inequality signs.

With the help of your teacher, decide how the words and phrases above can be shown using inequality signs. Can you think of any other words or phrases that express inequalities?

EXERCISE 9.5F

Re-write each of the following sentences using the correct inequality signs. Choose a suitable letter to represent the unknown in each case.

1 To go to a particular secondary school a student must be at least 11 years old and not more than 18 years old.

2 To register as a firefighter an adult must be at least 21 years old and not older than 40 years old.

3 To ride on a roller coaster a person must be at least 160 cm tall and not taller than 2 m.

4 The temperature in August in London was at least 14 °C at night and reached a maximum of 28 °C during the day.

5 In an orchard the trees had between 300 and 400 pears on each tree.

6 The tallest student in a class is 185 cm and the shortest is 155 cm.

7 The maximum number of players from each side on the pitch in a football league game is 11. The minimum number is 7.

8 A lift can carry between 1 and 8 people.

9 Apples are sorted for market and must be between 10 cm and 12 cm in diameter.

10 A box of matches contains more than 40 matches and up to 50 matches.

Solving inequalities

You have looked at the meaning of an inequality and how it can be represented on a number line.

More complex inequalities such as $x - 2 > 4$ need to be **solved** to give $x > 6$. To solve inequalities you can use a similar method to the one you use to solve equations: whatever you do to one side of the inequality, you must also do to the other side.

Worked examples

a) Solve the following inequality and represent the solution on a number line.
$$3x - 2 > x + 2$$

$3x - 2 > x + 2$
$2x - 2 > 2$ (subtract x from both sides)
$2x > 4$ (add 2 to both sides)
$x > 2$ (divide both sides by 2)

b) Solve the following inequality and represent the solution on a number line.
$$4x + 1 \geqslant 5x - 3$$

$4x + 1 \geqslant 5x - 3$
$1 \geqslant x - 3$ (subtract $4x$ from both sides)
$4 \geqslant x$ (add 3 to both sides)
Therefore $x \leqslant 4$.

EXERCISE 9.6A

Solve the following inequalities.

1   **a)** $x - 3 \leqslant 4$ **b)** $x + 2 > 1$

2   **a)** $2x + 4 \geqslant 0$ **b)** $3x + 1 < 4$

3   **a)** $3x - 2 \leqslant 2x$ **b)** $6x + 4 \geqslant 5x$

4   **a)** $5x + 6 > 3x + 8$ **b)** $7x - 3 < 4x + 3$

5   **a)** $3x - 4 < 5x + 2$ **b)** $5x + 1 \leqslant 9x - 5$

6   **a)** $x + 8 \geqslant 5x - 1$ **b)** $2x \leqslant 5x$

Solving combined inequalities

You have seen that some inequalities can be described with two inequality signs, for example $3 \leqslant x < 7$. You show this on a number line like this:

An inequality with two inequality signs can still be solved in the same way as before, if it is broken down into two separate inequalities. For example, to solve
$$6 \leqslant 2x - 2 < 15$$
first split it into two:
$$6 \leqslant 2x - 2 \quad \text{and} \quad 2x - 2 < 15$$
Solving each inequality separately gives:

$$6 \leqslant 2x - 2$$
$$8 \leqslant 2x \qquad \text{(add 2 to both sides)}$$
$$4 \leqslant x \qquad \text{(divide both sides by 2)}$$
$$x \geqslant 4$$

$$2x - 2 < 15$$
$$2x < 17 \qquad \text{(add 2 to both sides)}$$
$$x < 8\tfrac{1}{2} \qquad \text{(divide both sides by 2)}$$

These solutions can be represented on the following number line.

EXERCISE 9.6B

Solve the following inequalities. Represent each solution on a number line.

1 $3 < x + 2 \leqslant 6$

2 $5 \leqslant 3x - 1 \leqslant 11$

3 $8 < 2(x - 4) \leqslant 10$

4 $12 \leqslant 3(1 - x) < 21$

5 $1 \geqslant x \geqslant 2$

6 $6 \geqslant 2(x + 1) > 12$

7 $12 \geqslant 3(2x - 1) \geqslant 33$

8 $-2 + x < -x \leqslant 4x - 10$

(10) Pythagoras' theorem

◆ Know and use Pythagoras' theorem to solve two-dimensional problems involving right-angled triangles.

This clay tablet dates from about 1800 BCE and came from what is now Iraq. It is known as 'Plimpton 322', after the man who bought it in the 1920s and left it to Columbia University in the USA.

The cuneiform writing on it is an example of Babylonian mathematics. It has a table of numbers which some mathematicians think are sets of Pythagorean triples. These are whole numbers where the square of the third number is equal to the sum of the squares of the other two numbers, for example 3, 4 and 5 or 5, 12 and 13.

Practical task

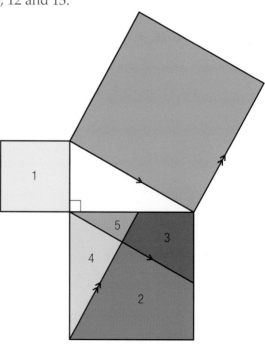

- In the centre of a piece of paper, draw a right-angled triangle.
- Off each of the sides of the triangle, construct a square, as shown in the diagram.
- Divide up one of the smaller squares as shown, making sure the dividing lines run parallel to the sides of the largest square.
- Cut out the shapes numbered 1, 2, 3, 4 and 5, and try to arrange them on top of the largest square so that they fit without any gaps.
- What conclusions can you make about the areas of the three squares?

This dissection to prove Pythagoras' theorem was constructed by Thabit ibn Quarra in Baghdad in 836 BCE.

Pythagoras' theorem states the relationship between the lengths of the three sides of a right-angled triangle:

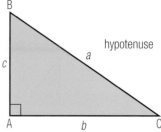

$$a^2 = b^2 + c^2$$

In words, the theorem states that the square of the length of the hypotenuse is equal to the sum of the squares of the other two sides.

Worked examples

a) Calculate the length of the side marked a in this diagram.

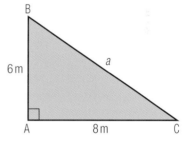

Using Pythagoras' theorem:
$$a^2 = b^2 + c^2$$
$$a^2 = 8^2 + 6^2$$
$$a^2 = 64 + 36 = 100$$
$$a = \sqrt{100} = 10$$
The length of side a is 10 m.

b) Calculate the length of the side marked b in this diagram.

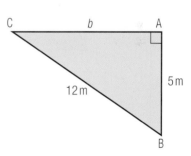

Pythagoras' theorem states that
$$a^2 = b^2 + c^2$$
Rearranging to make b^2 the subject gives:
$$b^2 = a^2 - c^2$$
$$b^2 = 12^2 - 5^2$$
$$b^2 = 144 - 25 = 119$$
$$b = \sqrt{119}$$
The length of side b is 10.9 m (to one decimal place).

EXERCISE 10.1A

Use Pythagoras' theorem to calculate the length of the hypotenuse in each of these right-angled triangles.

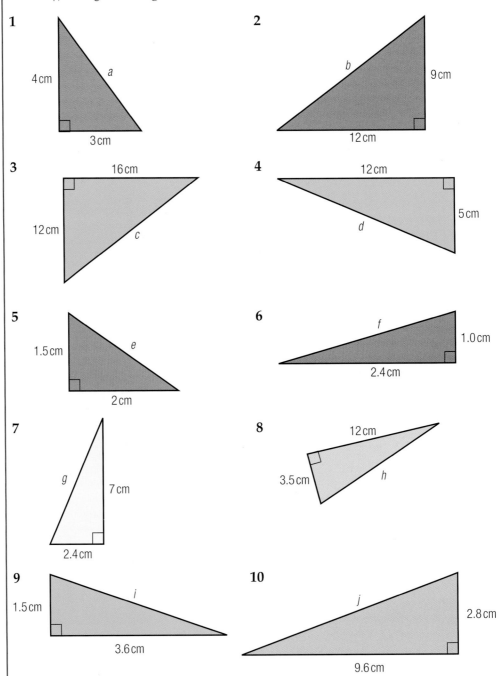

1   4 cm   a   3 cm

2   b   9 cm   12 cm

3   16 cm   12 cm   c

4   12 cm   5 cm   d

5   1.5 cm   e   2 cm

6   f   1.0 cm   2.4 cm

7   g   7 cm   2.4 cm

8   12 cm   3.5 cm   h

9   1.5 cm   i   3.6 cm

10   j   2.8 cm   9.6 cm

EXERCISE 10.1B

Use Pythagoras' theorem to calculate the length of the unknown side in each of these diagrams.

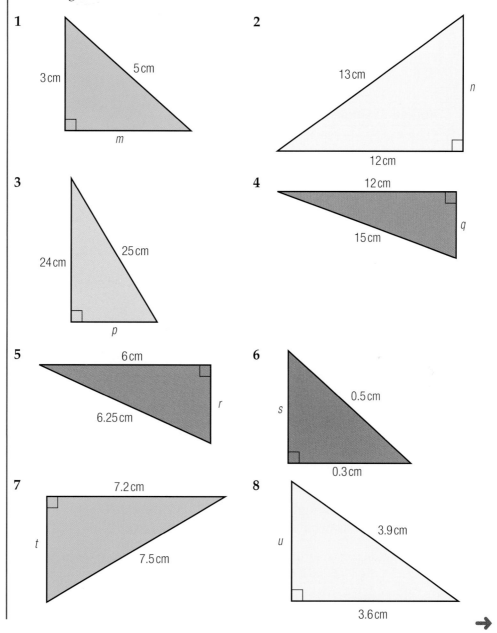

1

3 cm · 5 cm · *m*

2

13 cm · 12 cm · *n*

3

24 cm · 25 cm · *p*

4

12 cm · 15 cm · *q*

5

6 cm · 6.25 cm · *r*

6

0.5 cm · 0.3 cm · *s*

7

7.2 cm · 7.5 cm · *t*

8

3.9 cm · 3.6 cm · *u*

➡

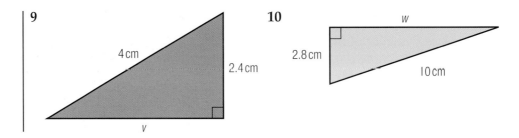

9   4 cm   2.4 cm   V

10   W   2.8 cm   10 cm

Worked example

An isosceles triangle has a base of 6 cm and a height of 8 cm.
Calculate the length of its other two sides.
Draw a diagram to show the information.

Use Pythagoras' theorem:

$$x^2 = 8^2 + 3^2$$
$$x^2 = 64 + 9$$
$$x^2 = 73$$
$$x = \sqrt{73}$$

The length of each of the other two sides is 8.5 cm
(to one decimal place).

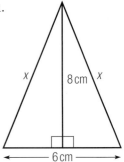

x   8 cm   x

6 cm

EXERCISE 10.1C

For each of these questions, draw a diagram to show the information and use
Pythagoras' theorem to solve the problem.

1   A rectangle is 8 cm by 6 cm. Calculate the length of one of its diagonals.

2   An isosceles triangle has a base of 10 cm and a height of 12 cm.
Calculate the length of its other two sides.

3   An isosceles triangle has a base of 14 cm and sides of 50 cm.
Calculate its height.

4   A ladder 7.5 m long rests against a wall. The bottom of the ladder is 2.1 m
from the wall. Calculate how far the ladder reaches up the wall.

5   An explorer marches 120 km north from his camp and then 35 km east.
What is the length of his shortest return journey?

6   A vertical mast is held in place by wires from the top of it to the ground.
The mast is 60 m tall and the wires are fixed in the ground 25 m from the
foot of the mast.
How long is each of the wires?

7   The screen of a laptop computer measures 24 cm by 10 cm.
    What is the length from corner to corner?

8   A ship sails 360 km due south from a port and then 105 km due west.
    What is the shortest distance from the ship to the port?

9   A rectangular playing field measures 180 m by 37.5 m.
    How long is its diagonal?

10 A swimming pool is 20 m wide and has a diagonal length of 52 m.
    How much shorter is it than a 50 m long pool?

Worked example

Find the lengths (in centimetres) of the sides marked p and q in this diagram.

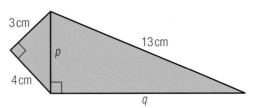

Using Pythagoras' theorem:
$$p^2 = 4^2 + 3^2$$
$$p^2 = 16 + 9$$
$$p^2 = 25$$
$$p = 5$$
Using Pythagoras' theorem again:
$$13^2 = p^2 + q^2$$
$$13^2 = 5^2 + q^2$$
$$13^2 - 5^2 = q^2$$
$$169 - 25 = q^2$$
$$144 = q^2$$
$$q = 12$$
Therefore $p = 5$ cm and $q = 12$ cm.

EXERCISE 10.1D

Find the lengths of the unknown sides in each of these diagrams.

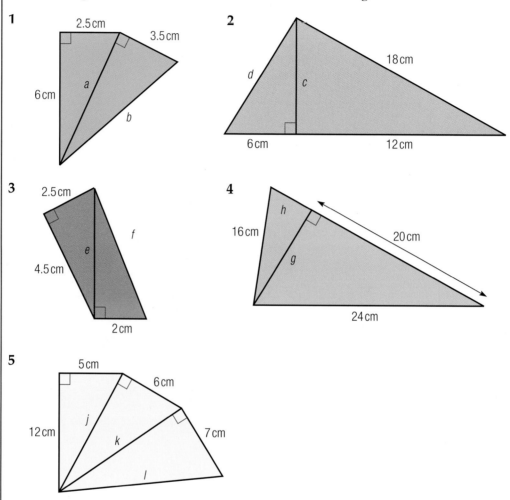

1

2.5 cm
3.5 cm
6 cm
a
b

2

18 cm
d
c
6 cm
12 cm

3

2.5 cm
f
e
4.5 cm
2 cm

4

h
16 cm
g
20 cm
24 cm

5

5 cm
6 cm
12 cm
j
k
7 cm
l

11 Compound measures and motion

◆ Solve problems involving average speed.
◆ Use compound measures to make comparisons in real-life contexts, e.g. travel graphs and value for money.

Measures of speed, distance and time

We can measure the speed of a car in kilometres per hour (km/h). This is a **compound measure** as it involves more than one type of measure (in this case, distance and time).

A speed of 50 kilometres per hour (km/h) is a way of saying that the car will travel 50 km in 1 hour travelling at a constant speed. Other units of speed are miles per hour (used in England and the USA, among other countries), centimetres per second (cm/s) and metres per second (m/s).

We can represent the relationship between distance, speed and time on a diagram like this:

The layout of the diagram helps you to remember the formulae linking the three measures.

To calculate average speed, the formula is:

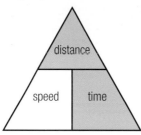

$$\text{speed} = \frac{\text{distance}}{\text{time}}$$

We can rearrange this to give the formula for the distance travelled:

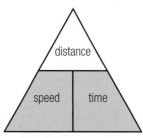

$$\text{distance} = \text{speed} \times \text{time}$$

We can also rearrange the formula again to give the time taken:

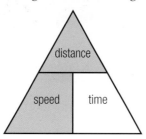

$$\text{time} = \frac{\text{distance}}{\text{speed}}$$

Worked examples

a) Calculate the average speed of a car which makes a journey of 200 km in $2\frac{1}{2}$ hours.

$$\text{Speed} = \frac{\text{distance}}{\text{time}}$$
$$= \frac{200}{2.5}$$
$$= 80$$

The car's average speed is 80 km/h.

b) How far does a car, travelling at an average speed of 120 km/h, cover in $3\frac{1}{4}$ hours?

Distance = speed × time
$$= 120 \times 3.25$$
$$= 390$$

The distance travelled by the car is 390 km.

c) How long does it take a train to make a journey of 720 km at a speed of 160 km/h?

$$\text{Time} = \frac{\text{distance}}{\text{speed}}$$
$$= \frac{720}{160}$$
$$= 4.5$$

The train's journey takes $4\frac{1}{2}$ hours.

Sometimes the journey time is given in hours and minutes and is not a simple fraction of an hour involving a half or quarters. You need to convert the time to a decimal before using it in speed calculations.

Worked examples

a) Convert 3.6 hours to hours and minutes.

3.6 hours is 3 hours plus 0.6 of an hour.
An hour has 60 minutes, so 0.6 of an hour is
$$0.6 \times 60 = 36$$
3.6 hours is equivalent to 3 hours and 36 minutes.

b) Convert 54 minutes to a decimal part of an hour.

54 minutes is $\frac{54}{60}$ of an hour.
$$\frac{54}{60} = \frac{9}{10} = 0.9$$
54 minutes is 0.9 hour.

EXERCISE 11.1A

Do not use a calculator for this exercise.

Find the average speed of an object that travels:

1 80 km in 2 hours	**2** 300 km in 4 hours
3 650 km in 5 hours	**4** 70 m in 5 seconds
5 400 m in 25 seconds	**6** 150 m in 6 seconds

➜

7   4 km in 30 minutes (give your answer in km/h)

8   12 km in 15 minutes (give your answer in km/h)

9   2 km in 1 minute (give your answer in km/h)

10   1.5 km in 30 seconds (give your answer in km/h)

EXERCISE 11.1B

Do not use a calculator for this exercise.

How far does an object travel in:

1   2 hours at 75 km/h

2 $4\frac{1}{2}$ hours at 120 km/h

3 $6\frac{1}{4}$ hours at 80 km/h

4   30 minutes at 60 km/h

5   15 minutes at 320 km/h

6   1 minute at 120 km/h

7   10 seconds at 12 m/s

8   45 seconds at 60 m/s

9   2 minutes at 10 m/s

10   30 minutes at 20 m/s?

EXERCISE 11.1C

Do not use a calculator for this exercise.

How long does an object take to travel:

1   20 km at 5 km/h

2   400 km at 80 km/h

3   15 km at 30 km/h (give your answer in minutes)

4   10 km at 40 km/h (give your answer in minutes)

5   50 km at 100 km/h (give your answer in minutes)

6   4 km at 40 km/h (give your answer in minutes)

7   20 m at 4 m/s

8   400 m at 80 m/s

9   10 m at 40 m/s

10   1 m at 40 m/s?

EXERCISE 11.1D

1 A car travels 90 km in 2 hours. What is its average speed?

2 A train takes 3 hours 30 minutes to travel a distance of 280 km.
   What is its average speed?

3 A boy cycles at an average speed of 22 km/h.
   How long does it take him to travel 55 km?

4 How far will a girl walk in 4 hours 15 minutes at an average speed of 6 km/h?

5 A plane makes a return journey across the Atlantic Ocean, a distance
   of 3800 km each way. From west to east the journey time is 6 hours
   12 minutes. Because of the jet stream the plane takes 7 hours 18 minutes
   to fly the same journey east to west.
   Find the average speed of the plane for each crossing.

6 A train travels for 2 hours 30 minutes at an average speed of 120 km/h and
   then for 5 hours 20 minutes at an average speed of 180 km/h.
   How far does it travel altogether?

Travel graphs

You already know from Student's Books 1 and 2 that travel graphs can be used to
display the movement of an object over time.

This distance–time graph shows the movement of a person leaving home and
going for a walk.

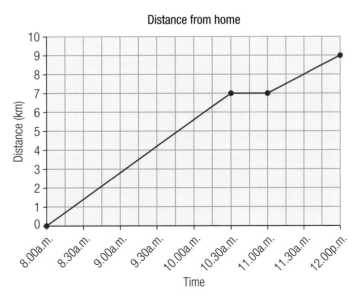

Distance from home

We can deduce a number of things from the shape of the graph. These include:

- The person set off at 8.00a.m.
- The person took a rest between 10.30a.m. and 11.00a.m.

> We can tell this because the line is horizontal between these times.

- Between 8.00a.m. and 10.30a.m. the person was travelling at an average speed of $\frac{7}{2.5} = 2.8\,\text{km/h}$.

However, not all travel graphs are distance–time graphs. It is also possible to show the motion of an object using a **speed–time graph**.

For example, this graph shows the speed of a cyclist over a 3-hour period.

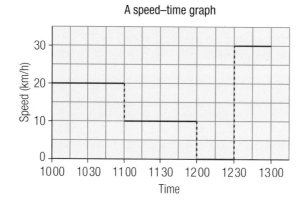

A speed–time graph

> The horizontal lines show that the cyclist is travelling at a constant speed. The dashed vertical lines simply show that one horizontal line is connected to the next.

Worked example

Use the graph above to answer these questions.
a) What is the cyclist's speed between 10 00 and 11 00?
b) Between which times is the cyclist stationary?
c) What is the cyclist's fastest speed and when does this occur?

a) The horizontal line between 10 00 and 11 00 shows that the cyclist is travelling at a constant speed of 20 km/h.
b) The cyclist is stationary when the speed is 0 km/h.
    This happens between 12 00 and 12 30.
c) The fastest speed is 30 km/h.
    This occurs between 12 30 and 13 00.

EXERCISE 11.2

1 This graph shows the speed of a car during a journey.

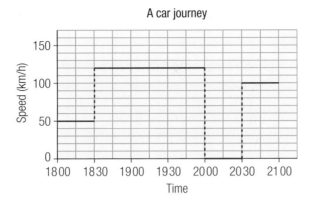

A car journey

a) What time did the car set off on its journey?

b) How fast did the car travel for the first 30 minutes?

c) For how long did the car travel at 120 km/h?

d) The driver stopped for a snack along the route.
At what time did this occur?

e) How far did the car travel during the first half-hour?

f) How far did the car travel on the whole journey?

2 Two walkers leave at different times of the day on the same route.
This graph shows their journeys.

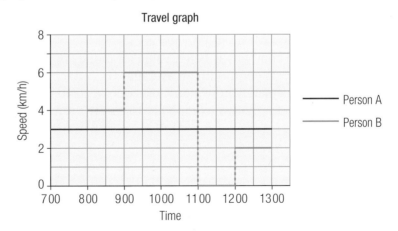

Travel graph

Person A
Person B

a) What time did person A set off?   **b)** At what speed did person A walk?

c) For how long did person A walk?   **d)** How far did person A walk?

e) What time did person B set off?

f) At what speed did person B walk between 9 00 and 11 00?

g) How far did person B walk between 11 00 and 12 00?

h) Who had walked further by 11 00? Show your method clearly.

Graphs in real-life contexts

Graphs can be used to represent many different real-life situations.

EXERCISE 11.3

1 Two mobile phone companies are advertising their tariffs for the cost of sending text messages.

         Company A: Unlimited texts for $10 per month
         Company B: 100 texts cost $1.50

This graph shows the cost of the two tariffs.

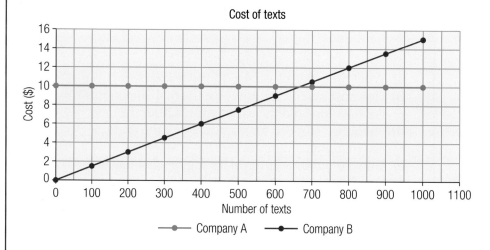

a) Which company is better value for money for a customer who sends 500 texts per month on average?

b) Which company is better value for money for a customer who sends 1000 texts per month on average?

c) Approximately how many texts does a customer need to send each month for the two companies to cost the same?

2 Two new cars are bought at the same time. Car X costs $45 000 and car Y costs $20 000. This graph shows their value over the next ten years.

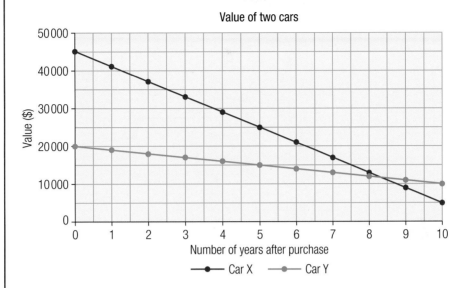

a) Which car is better value for money for a buyer who wants a car which does not depreciate (lose its value) quickly?

b) How can you tell which car depreciates more quickly from the shape of the graph?

c) What is the approximate difference in the two cars' value after five years? Show your method clearly.

d) Which car is worth more after ten years?

e) Approximately how many years after they are bought are the two cars worth the same?

➜

3 A gardener is using a watering can filled from a tank to water his garden. This graph shows the water level (in centimetres) in the tank over a one-hour period.

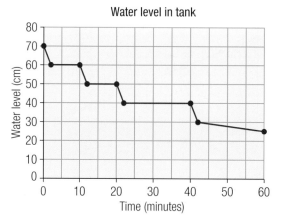

Water level in tank

a) What was the level of the water in the tank at the start?
b) Assuming that the gardener fills the watering can at the same rate each time, how many times does he fill the watering can?
c) The gardener finishes watering his garden and leaves after 50 minutes. Give one possible reason why the level in the water tank continues to drop.

4 A boy decides to have a bath. This graph shows the water level (in centimetres) in the bath over time.

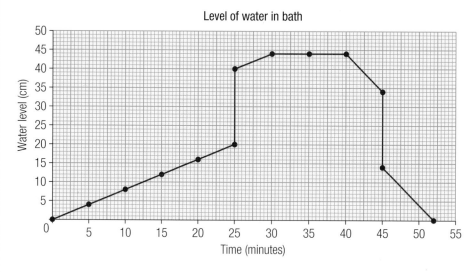

Level of water in bath

a) Give a possible explanation for the shape of the graph during the first 25 minutes.
b) When did the boy get into the bath?
   Justify your answer by referring to the graph.
c) How long did the boy stay in the bath?
d) Give a possible explanation for the shape of the graph after 45 minutes.

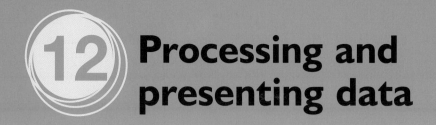

12 Processing and presenting data

♦ Calculate statistics and select those most appropriate to the problem.
♦ Select, draw and interpret diagrams and graphs, including:
   – frequency diagrams for discrete and continuous data
   – line graphs for time series
   – scatter graphs to develop understanding of correlation
   – back-to-back stem-and-leaf diagrams.

Selecting statistics

You are already familiar with using statistical calculations in order to give raw data some meaning and to help make some conclusions about the data. These include **averages** such as the mean, the median and the mode. You have also met the **range**, which gives an indication of the spread of the data.

A large number of different types of calculation is available, so it is important to be able to select the most appropriate method for the data collected. Picking an inappropriate method may lead to misleading information and incorrect conclusions.

Worked example

The heights (in centimetres) of ten Year 9 students are given below.
     159   162   165   166   167   168   169   170   185   185
Choose a statistical calculation which best describes the heights of these students.

The calculations possible include the mean, median, mode and range.

$$\text{Mean} = \frac{159 + 162 + 165 + 166 + 167 + 168 + 169 + 170 + 185 + 185}{10} = 169.6\,\text{cm}$$

The data is already in order of size. The median is the mean of the middle pair of values.
     159   162   165   166   (167   168)   169   170   185   185
     Median = 167.5 cm

The mode is the value which occurs most often.
     Mode = 185 cm
     Range = 185 − 159 = 26 cm

In this example, the mode does not give an accurate representation of the data as it is distorted by the two values of 185 cm.

The range on its own also serves little purpose, as it gives no indication of the actual heights.

In this case, either the mean or the median would appropriate and give an accurate representation of the students' heights.

EXERCISE 12.1

In each of the following questions choose the most appropriate calculation to use.

1   The masses (in grams) of 15 similar packets of biscuits are given below.
        199   200   200   200   200   200   200   200
        200   200   200   201   202   203   203
    a) What is the average mass of a packet of these biscuits?
    b) Justify your answer to part **a)**.

2   A pole vaulter recorded his highest jump (in metres) in each of his last nine competitions. The results are shown below.
        3.23   4.24   4.24   5.33   5.34   5.35   5.36   5.37   5.38
    a) How high can the pole vaulter jump on average?
    b) Justify your answer to part **a)**.

3   Two cucumber farmers each pick 12 cucumbers at random from their crop and measure their lengths to the nearest centimetre. The results are shown below.

    Farmer A
    25   28   26   31   27   27   30   31   32   32   31   29
    Farmer B
    25   28   16   26   15   34   27   26   28   17   42   18

    They can sell their cucumbers to a local supermarket if they are longer than 25 cm on average and are reasonably consistent in length.
    a) Which farmer is more likely to be able to sell his cucumbers to the supermarket?
    b) Justify your answer to part **a)**.

4   The times taken (in seconds) for ten runners to complete a 400 m race are given below.
        55   58   51   82   61   63   62   59   54   60
    a) What time best describes the average time of the ten athletes?
    b) Justify your answer to part **a)**.

Selecting, drawing and interpreting graphs

You are already familiar with many different types of graph for displaying data. These include frequency diagrams for both discrete and continuous data and line graphs for data involving time.

When presented with a set of data, it is important to be able to select which type of graph to use to display the data as clearly as possible. The decision will depend on the type and quantity of the data.

EXERCISE 12.2

1 The table below records the height of a sunflower as it grows.

Day	0	7	14	21	28	35	42	49	56	63	70	77	84
Height (cm)	0	18	36	68	100	131	170	206	230	247	251	254	255

a) What type of graph would be the most appropriate to display this data?
b) Plot the graph you chose in part a).
c) Use your graph to estimate the height of the sunflower after 33 days.
d) Use your graph to find when the sunflower is growing at its fastest. Justify your answer.

2 The wing lengths (in millimetres) of 50 flies of a particular species are recorded. The results are shown below.

```
36  38  38  40  41  41  41  42  43  43  44  44  44
44  44  44  44  45  45  45  45  46  46  46  46  46
47  47  47  47  47  47  48  48  48  48  49  49
49  50  50  50  50  50  50  52  52  53  54  57
```

a) What type of graph would be the most appropriate to display this data?
b) Plot the graph you chose in part a).
c) Describe the shape of the graph.

The wing lengths (in millimetres) of 50 flies of a different species are also recorded. The results are shown below.

```
36  36  36  36  36  37  38  38  38  39  39  39  40
40  40  40  40  40  41  41  41  41  41  42  42  42
42  42  42  43  43  43  43  44  44  44  44  45
45  45  46  46  47  47  48  49  51  52  54  57
```

d) Plot a similar graph to the one in part b).
e) Describe the shape of this graph.
   How does it differ from the graph for the first species of fly?

→

3 The population of the USA has been recorded through census data since 1830.

This table shows the population (in millions) at 10-year intervals.

Year	1830	1840	1850	1860	1870	1880	1890	1900	1910
Population (millions)	12.9	17.1	23.2	31.4	38.6	50.2	63.0	76.2	92.2
Year	1920	1930	1940	1950	1960	1970	1980	1990	2000
Population (millions)	106.0	123.2	132.1	151.3	179.3	203.3	226.5	248.7	281.4

a) What type of graph would be the most appropriate to display this data?

b) Plot the graph you chose in part a).

c) Use your graph to estimate the population of the USA in 1975.

d) Use the shape of your graph to describe the change in the population of the USA since 1830.

e) Use your graph to deduce when the population of the USA was growing at its fastest. Justify your answer.

4 The football World Cup is played every four years. The table lists the top ten goal-scoring countries in all the competitions so far.

Ranking	Country	Total number of goals
1	Brazil	201
2	Germany	190
3	Italy	122
4	Argentina	113
5	France	95
6	Hungary	87
7	Spain	80
8	England	74
8	Sweden	74
10	Uruguay	65

a) Is the total number of goals an example of discrete or continuous data?

b) What type of graph would be the most appropriate to display this data?

c) Plot the graph you chose in part b).

5 The tables below show the mean maximum daily temperature for each month of the year in Sydney in Australia and Moscow in Russia.

Sydney

Month	Jan	Feb	Mar	Apr	May	June	July	Aug	Sept	Oct	Nov	Dec
Mean maximum temperature (°C)	26	26	25	23	20	17	17	18	20	22	24	26

Moscow

Month	Jan	Feb	Mar	Apr	May	June	July	Aug	Sept	Oct	Nov	Dec
Mean maximum temperature (°C)	−6	−5	1	10	18	22	23	22	16	8	1	−4

a) Plot a graph that will enable you to compare the temperatures in the two cities against each other.

b) Describe any differences in the shapes of the two graphs.

Scatter graphs and correlation

Scatter graphs are particularly useful if we wish to see if there is a **correlation** (relationship) between two sets of data. The two sets of data are collected. Each pair of values then form the coordinates of a point, which is plotted on a graph.

There are several types of correlation, depending on the arrangement of the points plotted on the scatter graph.

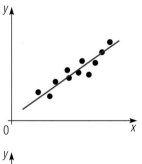

A **strong positive correlation** between the values of x and y. The points lie very close to the line of best fit.

As x increases, so does y.

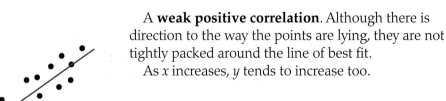

A **weak positive correlation**. Although there is direction to the way the points are lying, they are not tightly packed around the line of best fit.

As x increases, y tends to increase too.

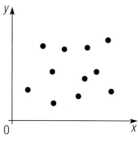

No correlation. As there is no pattern in the way the points are lying, there is no correlation between the variables x and y. As a result there can be no line of best fit.

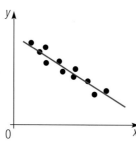

A **strong negative correlation**. The points lie close to the line of best fit.
As x increases, y decreases.

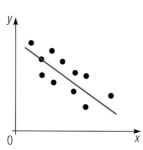

A **weak negative correlation**. There is direction to the way the points are lying but they are not tightly packed around the line of best fit.
As x increases, y tends to decrease.

Worked example

Different cars have different engine sizes. A student decides to see if a car's engine size affects its fuel economy, i.e. how many kilometres it can travel (on average) on 1 litre of fuel. She randomly selects 14 cars and records their engine size (in litres) and their average fuel economy (in kilometres per litre). The results are given in the table below.

Engine size (litres)	3.2	1.8	1.8	2.4	1.5	2.0	1.9	2.8	1.8	2.0	2.0	4.3	1.9	2.8
Fuel economy (km/l)	10.2	14.2	13.6	14.0	15.7	11.9	16.2	12.3	15.7	12.5	14.5	9.8	16.1	11.1

a) Plot a scatter graph to represent this data.
b) Comment on any relationship that you see.
c) If another car was found to have an engine size of 2.5 litres, approximately what fuel economy would you expect it to have?

a)

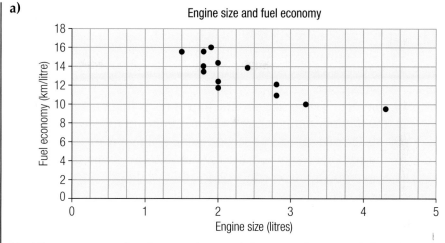

b) The points tend to lie in a diagonal direction from top left to bottom right. This suggests that as engine size increases then, in general, fuel economy decreases. Therefore there is a **negative correlation** between engine size and fuel economy.

c) We need to assume that this car follows the trend set by the other 14 cars. To work out an approximate value for the fuel economy, we draw a **line of best fit**.

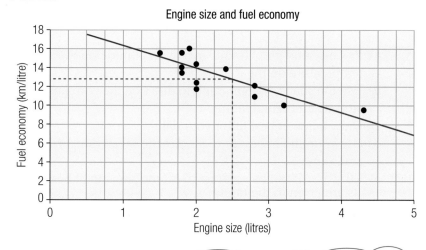

The line of best fit is a solid straight line which best passes through the points. Notice that it does not need to pass through the origin.

Then we draw a vertical line up from 2.5 litres on the horizontal axis until it reaches the line of best fit and read off the value for the fuel economy from the vertical axis.

The fuel economy of a car with an engine size of 2.5 litres is likely to be about 13 kilometres per litre.

EXERCISE 12.3

1   What type of correlation might you expect, if any, if the following data was collected and plotted on a scatter graph? Give reasons for your answers.
   a) a student's score in one maths exam and their score in another maths exam
   b) a student's shoe size and the time it takes them to walk to school
   c) the outdoor temperature and the number of ice-creams sold by a shop
   d) the age of a car and its second-hand selling price
   e) the size of a restaurant and the number of customers it can seat
   f) the temperature on a mountain and the altitude at which the reading was taken
   g) a person's weight and their waist size
   h) a car's top speed and its engine size

2   The temperature of the Earth's atmosphere is measured at different altitudes.
   The table shows the mean temperature (in °C) at increasing altitudes (in kilometres).

Altitude (km)	0	1	2	3	4	5	6	7	8	9	10	11
Mean temperature (°C)	15	9	2	−5	−11	−17	−24	−31	−37	−43	−50	−56

   a) Plot a scatter graph of the data with altitude on the x-axis and mean temperature on the y-axis.
   b) Use the shape of your graph to describe the correlation (if any) between altitude and temperature.
   c) Draw a line of best fit for your data.
   d) Use your line of best fit to predict the mean temperature at an altitude of 6.5 km.
   e) Why may it not be accurate to extend the line of best fit to predict the mean temperature at altitudes greater than the ones given?

3 This scatter graph shows people's life expectancy (in years) plotted against the percentage of the population who are literate, for most countries in the world.

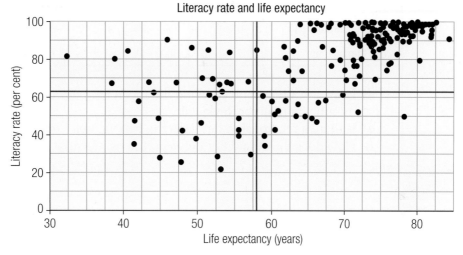

Literacy rate and life expectancy

a) A horizontal and a vertical line have been drawn over the graph, splitting it into four sections. Describe the life expectancy and literacy levels in those countries found in the bottom left section.

b) Describe the life expectancy and literacy levels in those countries found in the bottom right section.

c) Use the graph to describe the relationship (if any) between life expectancy and literacy levels.

4 The mean temperature (in °C) and the mean rainfall (in millimetres) in Rio de Janeiro in Brazil are recorded over a 12-month period. The data is shown in the table.

Month	Jan	Feb	Mar	Apr	May	June	July	Aug	Sept	Oct	Nov	Dec
Mean temperature (°C)	26.2	26.5	26.0	24.5	23.0	21.5	21.3	21.8	21.8	22.8	24.2	25.2
Mean rainfall (mm)	114	105	103	137	86	80	56	51	87	88	96	169

a) What are the highest and the lowest mean monthly temperatures?

b) Using an appropriate scale on each axis, draw a scatter graph to show the relationship between mean temperature and mean monthly rainfall.

c) Describe the relationship (if any) between the two variables.

→

The mean temperature (in °C) and the mean rainfall (in millimetres) are also recorded in Reykjavik in Iceland. The data is shown in the table.

Month	Jan	Feb	Mar	Apr	May	June	July	Aug	Sept	Oct	Nov	Dec
Mean temperature (°C)	−0.5	0.4	0.5	2.9	6.3	9	10.6	10.3	7.4	4.4	1.1	−0.2
Mean rainfall (mm)	76	72	82	58	44	50	52	62	67	86	73	79

d) Draw a scatter graph showing the mean temperature and the mean monthly rainfall for Reykjavik.

e) Is there a relationship between the two variables in Reykjavik?

f) How does the data differ between the two locations?

Stem-and-leaf diagrams

You already know from Student's Book 2 that stem-and-leaf diagrams are a special type of bar chart in which the 'bars' are made from the data itself. This has the advantage that the original data can still be seen in the diagram.

Worked example

This data records the ages of people on a bus to the seaside.

2	4	25	31	3	23	24	26	37	42
60	76	33	24	25	18	20	77	5	13
18	13	15	49	70	48	27	25	24	29

Display the data on a stem-and-leaf diagram.

```
0 | 2 3 4 5
1 | 3 3 5 8 8
2 | 0 3 4 4 4 5 5 5 6 7 9
3 | 1 3 7
4 | 2 8 9
5 |
6 | 0
7 | 0 6 7
```

Key

|2| 5 means 25 years

The diagram must have a key to explain what the stem means. If the data were 1.8, 2.7, 3.2, etc., the key would state that ' |2| 7 means 2.7'.

Stem-and-leaf diagrams can also be used to compare two different sets of data by arranging them 'back to back'.

Worked example

Another bus picks up 30 people from a care home to take them to a local supermarket. Their ages are:

72	74	65	81	83	73	64	66	77	72
60	76	83	84	85	68	80	77	75	73
88	73	75	79	70	88	67	65	74	69

Display this data on a back-to-back stem-and-leaf diagram with the data for the seaside trip from the example on the previous page.

Supermarket trip		Seaside trip
	0	2 3 4 5
	1	3 3 5 8 8
	2	0 3 4 4 4 5 5 5 6 7 9
	3	1 3 7
	4	2 8 9
	5	
9 8 7 6 5 5 4 0	6	0
9 7 7 6 5 5 4 4 3 3 3 2 2 0	7	0 6 7
8 8 5 4 3 3 1 0	8	

Key
9 |6| means 69 years
|2| 5 means 25 years

By arranging the stem-and-leaf diagrams back to back, it is easy to compare the age distributions of the two sets of data.

EXERCISE 12.4

1 20 students sit two maths tests, A and B. Each test is marked out of 50. The results are shown below.

Test A

8	10	12	16	20	21	21	23	24	26
29	34	34	35	36	36	38	38	41	42

Test B

18	26	27	27	29	34	34	35	35	36
38	38	39	41	41	43	45	48	48	49

a) Display the data on a back-to-back stem-and-leaf diagram.

b) From the diagram, which test appears to have been the harder of the two? Justify your answer.

2 A basketball team plays 25 matches during one season. They keep a record of the number of points they score in each game and the number of points scored against them. The results are shown below.

Points for					**Points against**				
64	72	84	46	53	51	72	40	66	69
69	62	71	71	79	43	58	81	78	60
80	47	53	69	69	60	42	57	69	74
56	82	84	78	78	40	41	72	66	54
72	68	66	54	64	72	66	51	53	67

a) Draw a back-to-back stem-and-leaf diagram showing the numbers of points for and against the team during the season.

b) By looking at the shape of the diagram, is the team likely to have won more games than they lost, or the other way round?

3 15 people take part in a fitness assessment. Their pulse rates are taken before and after exercise. The results are recorded in this back-to-back stem-and-leaf diagram.

```
    4  3  1 │ 5 │
       9  6 │ 5 │ 8
 4  3  3  0 │ 6 │ 1  3
    8  8  7 │ 6 │ 8  8  9
          1 │ 7 │ 0  2  3  4
       9  9 │ 7 │ 7
            │ 8 │ 1  3
            │ 8 │ 9
            │ 9 │ 3
```

Key
4 |5| means 54 beats per minute
|6| 8 means 68 beats per minute

a) Which side of the diagram is likely to show the readings taken after exercise? Justify your answer.

b) Calculate the mean, median, mode and range for the pulse rates before and after exercise.

(13) Calculations and mental strategies 2

◆ Multiply by decimals, understanding where to position the decimal point by considering equivalent calculations.

Multiplying by decimals

You already know how to multiply whole numbers without using a calculator.
For example, the multiplication 437×263 can be done like this:

$$437 \times 263 = 400 \times 263 + 30 \times 263 + 7 \times 263$$

$$100 \times 263 = 26\,300$$
so $\quad 200 \times 263 = 52\,600$
and $\quad 400 \times 263 = 105\,200$

> *First make an estimate.*
> $400 \times 250 = 100\,000$

$$10 \times 263 = 2630$$
so $\quad 30 \times 263 = 7890$

$$2 \times 263 = 526$$
and $\quad 5 \times 263 = 1315$
so $\quad 7 \times 263 = 1841$

So $\quad 437 \times 263 = 105\,200 + 7890 + 1841$
$$= 114\,931$$

Another way is to use long multiplication:

```
        4  3  7
×       2  6  3
  ─────────────
  8  7  4  0  0    (multiplying 437 by 200)
  2  6  2  2  0    (multiplying 437 by 60)
     1  3  1  1    (multiplying 437 by 3)
  ─────────────
1 1  4  9  3  1
```

You can use this result to deduce the answers to other multiplications involving decimals.

Worked examples

a) Work out 4.37×263.

$$4.37 \times 263 = (437 \div 100) \times 263$$
$$= (437 \times 263) \div 100$$
$$= 114\,931 \div 100$$
$$= 1149.31$$

First make an estimate.
$4 \times 250 = 1000$

b) Work out 4.37×2.63.

$$4.37 \times 2.63 = (437 \div 100) \times (263 \div 100)$$
$$= (437 \times 263) \div 10\,000$$
$$= 114\,931 \div 10\,000$$
$$= 11.4931$$

First make an estimate.
$4 \times 2.5 = 10$

EXERCISE 13.1A

For each of the following:
   (i) estimate the answer to the calculation
   (ii) work out the exact answer using an appropriate method.

1 **a)** 39×51 **b)** 3.9×5.1

2 **a)** 78×19 **b)** 7.8×1.9

3 **a)** 72×58 **b)** 720×5.8

4 **a)** 98×45 **b)** 0.98×4.5

5 **a)** 76×33 **b)** 7600×0.33

6 **a)** 839×11 **b)** 83.9×1.1

7 **a)** 7798×19 **b)** 77.98×1.9

8 **a)** 172×58 **b)** 1720×5.8

9 **a)** 9458×5 **b)** 0.9458×0.5

10 **a)** 1276×93 **b)** $127\,600 \times 0.93$

EXERCISE 13.1B

1 Use the fact that $651 \times 25 = 16\,275$ to work out:
   a) 6.51×25 **b)** 6.51×2.5

2 Use the fact that $1385 \times 67 = 92\,795$ to work out:
   a) 1385×6.7 **b)** 13.85×6.7

3   Use the fact that $541 \times 331 = 179\,071$ to work out:
    a) 541×0.331 **b)** 5.41×33.1

4   Use the fact that $793 \times 540 = 428\,220$ to work out:
    a) 7.93×54 **b)** 7.93×0.54

5   Use the fact that $867 \times 512 = 443\,904$ to work out:
    a) 8.67×5.12 **b)** 867×0.0512

6   Use the fact that $939 \times 610 = 572\,790$ to work out:
    a) 93.9×0.61 **b)** 0.939×61

7   Use the fact that $44 \times 1237 = 54\,428$ to work out:
    a) 44×12.37 **b)** 0.44×1.237

8   Use the fact that $22 \times 9878 = 217\,316$ to work out:
    a) 2.2×9.878 **b)** 2.2×0.9878

9   Use the fact that $103 \times 901 = 92\,803$ to work out:
    a) 1.03×0.901 **b)** $1.03 \times 90\,100$

10 Use the fact that $1273 \times 12 = 15\,276$ to work out:
    a) 12.73×1.2 **b)** 1.273×1200

Worked example

a)   Work out 1868×312.
b)   Use your answer to part **a)** to work out 1.868×3.12.

a) $1868 \times 312 = 1868 \times 300 + 1868 \times 10 + 1868 \times 2$
         $1868 \times 100 = 186\,800$
    so $1868 \times 300 = 560\,400$
         $1868 \times 10 = 18\,680$
         $1868 \times 2 = 3736$
    So $1868 \times 312 = 560\,400 + 18\,680 + 3736$
                         $= 582\,816$

First make an estimate. $2000 \times 300 = 600\,000$

b) $1.868 \times 3.12 = (1868 \div 1000) \times (312 \div 100)$
                       $= (1868 \times 312) \div 100\,000$
                       $= 582\,816 \div 100\,000$
                       $= 5.828\,16$

First make an estimate. $2 \times 3 = 6$

EXERCISE 13.1C

1   Use the fact that $1651 \times 25 = 41275$ to work out:
     a) 16.51×0.25 **b)** 0.1651×25

2   Use the fact that $7385 \times 46 = 339710$ to work out:
     a) 73.85×4.6 **b)** 73.85×0.46

3   Use the fact that $9541 \times 37 = 353017$ to work out:
     a) 95.41×0.37 **b)** 95.41×0.037

4   Use the fact that $49793 \times 4 = 199172$ to work out:
     a) 497.93×0.4 **b)** 497.93×0.04

5   Use the fact that $12847 \times 5 = 64235$ to work out:
     a) 128.47×0.5 **b)** 128.47×0.005

6   Use the fact that $59 \times 677 = 39943$ to work out:
     a) 5.9×0.677 **b)** 590×0.0677

7   Use the fact that $74 \times 74 = 5476$ to work out:
     a) 7.4×0.74 **b)** 0.74×0.74

8   Use the fact that $2312 \times 8 = 18496$ to work out:
     a) 23.12×0.8 **b)** 2.312×800

9   Use the fact that $103 \times 99 = 10197$ to work out:
     a) 1.03×0.99 **b)** 103×0.099

10   Use the fact that $27350 \times 2 = 54700$ to work out:
     a) 2.735×0.2 **b)** 2.735×20000

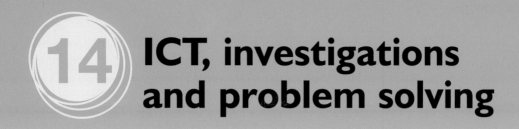

14 ICT, investigations and problem solving

1 Pythagoras and semicircles

You already know about Pythagoras' rule. It states a relationship between the lengths of the three sides of a right-angled triangle.

In this diagram:

$$a^2 = b^2 + c^2$$

The letter a represents the length of the hypotenuse and b and c represent the lengths of the other two sides. So a^2, b^2 and c^2 are the areas of the squares drawn on each of the sides.

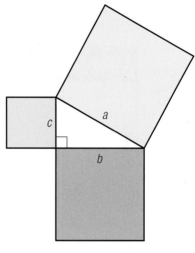

Pythagoras' rule states that the area of the square on the hypotenuse is equal to the sum of the areas of the squares on the other two sides.

But what if a semicircle is drawn on each of the sides? Is the area of the semicircle on the hypotenuse equal to the sum of the areas of the semicircles on the other two sides?

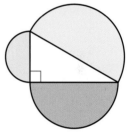

a) **(i)** Draw a right-angled triangle with side lengths 3 cm, 4 cm and 5 cm.
   (ii) Construct a semicircle on each side using a pair of compasses.
   (iii) Calculate the area of each semicircle.
   (iv) Does Pythagoras' rule still hold?
b) Draw two more right-angled triangles and repeat part **a)**. Does Pythagoras' rule hold for each of these triangles?
c) In this diagram, the lengths of the sides of the triangle are a, b and c as shown.
   (i) What is the radius of the semicircle drawn on the hypotenuse?
   (ii) What is the area of the semicircle, in terms of a?
   (iii) What are the areas of the other two semicircles, in terms of b and c respectively?

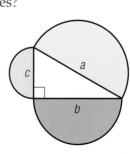

d) (i) Assuming that Pythagoras' rule always holds true for semicircles, write an equation linking the areas of the three semicircles.
 (ii) Simplify your equation from part **(i)**.
 (iii) What conclusion can you make?
e) You can use a geometry package, such as Cabri Géomètre II, to demonstrate this.

The picture below shows a right-angled triangle, with a circle drawn on each side. The centre of each circle lies on the midpoint of a side. The diameter of the circle is equal to the length of the side on which it is constructed.

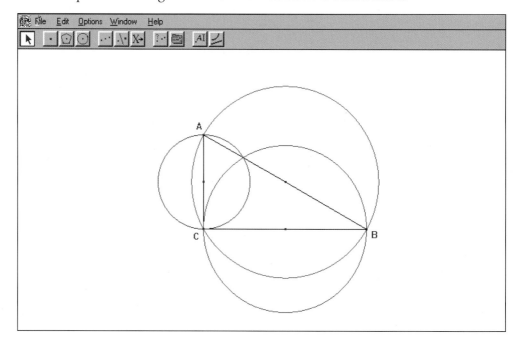

 (i) Use the program to work out the area of each of the circles.
 (ii) Use these to work out the areas of semicircles drawn on each of the sides.
 (iii) Produce a display of your findings using print-outs from the screen.

2 Pulse rates

You will need a stop watch for this activity.

For this activity you will need to do some exercise and record how your pulse rate changes over a period of time.

- Work in pairs and try to find each other's pulse.
- Record how many times your partner's heart beats in one minute *before* exercise. This is known as the resting pulse rate.
- Draw a table in which to record your results. A suggested one is shown below.

Name: _____	Resting pulse rate = _____ beats per minute	
Time after exercise (minutes)	Pulse rate (30 seconds)	Pulse rate (1 minute)
1		
2		
3		
4		
5		
⋮		
15		

From now on, one of you will be doing the exercise, and the other will be taking the pulse and recording the results.

- Exercise for 5 minutes (ask your teacher for suitable exercises).
- Once you have finished the exercise, your partner will record your pulse rate over a period of 15 minutes. At one-minute intervals, count the pulse rate for 30 seconds and then double it to give the pulse rate in beats per minute.
- Once your table of results is complete, swap roles and repeat the activity so that your partner's results can also be collected.
- Plot a line graph to show the change in the pulse rate over time.

   a) Draw a smooth line which best fits the data.
   b) How does your pulse rate after 15 minutes compare with your resting pulse rate?
   c) Compare your graph with those of other students in the class. What similarities or differences are there in the shapes of the graphs?
   d) Do 'sporty' students have different-shaped graphs to those of other students?

Review 2A

1 Write each of the following numbers to two significant figures.
   a) 5947   **b)** 54 904
   c) 5.552   **d)** 28.8

2 Round each of the following numbers to two decimal places.
   a) 5.4503   **b)** 15.3789
   c) 8.005 03   **d)** 4.2049

3 Solve the following linear equations.
   a) $x + 10 = 22$ **b)** $3y - 4 = 23$
   c) $3q = 11q + 24$ **d)** $6(3n - 1) = 4(n + 4)$

4 Solve each of these pairs of simultaneous equations by elimination.
   a) $6x + 3y = 12$ **b)** $12x - 5y = 22$
       $4x + 3y = 8$ $12x + 5y = 2$

5 Expand each of the following and simplify your answer.
   a) $(x - 5)(x + 4)$ **b)** $(x + 1)(x - 4)$

6 Use Pythagoras' theorem to calculate the length of the unknown side in
   each of the following right-angled triangles. Give your answers to one
   decimal place.
   a)
   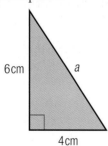
   6cm   a
   4cm

   b)
   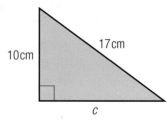
   10cm   17cm
   c

7 Find the average speed of an object that travels:
   a) 450 km in 9 hours
   b) 30 km in 10 minutes (give your answer in km/h).

8 The graph on the next page shows the speed of a car during a journey.
   a) What time did the car set off on its journey?
   b) How fast was the car travelling at 10 00?
   c) For how long did the car travel at 50 km/h?

d) How far did the car travel between 1100 and 1200?

e) How far did the car travel on the whole journey?

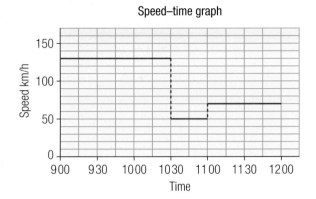

Speed–time graph

9 Two banana producers each pick ten bananas at random from their plantations and weigh them to the nearest gram. The results are shown below.

Producer A

155   156   158   151   160   163   156   157   152   151

Producer B

128   123   154   180   156   173   133   167   189   156

They can sell their bananas to a supermarket if they are heavier than 140 g on average and are reasonably consistent in weight.

a) Which producer is more likely to be able to sell his bananas to the supermarket?

b) Justify your answer to part **a)**, showing appropriate use of calculations.

10 What type of correlation is shown on each of the scatter graphs below?

a) 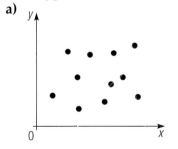   **b)**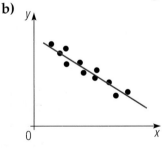

11 What type of correlation might you expect, if any, if the following data was collected and plotted on a scatter graph? Give reasons for your answers.

a) a student's score in a biology exam and their score in a chemistry exam

b) the number of people on a bus and the number of unoccupied seats

c) the number of pages in a book and the price of the book

12 For each of the following:

(i) estimate the answer to the calculation

(ii) work out the exact answer using an appropriate method.

a) 78×41 **b)** 109×88 **c)** 4921×18

Review 2B

1 Work out the following.
   a) $2^3 + 3^2$

   b) $4(5^2 + 4^2)$

   c) $\dfrac{(15^2 - 5^2)}{5}$

⭐ **2** By forming and solving a pair of simultaneous equations, find the lengths of the sides of this rectangle.

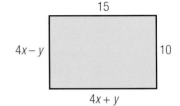

3 For each of the following problems, form two equations and solve them to find the two numbers.
   a) The sum of two numbers is 13, and their difference is 3.
   b) One number plus double another number is 11. The difference between the numbers is −1.
   c) Double one number take away another number is −3. The difference between the numbers is 1.

4 Represent each of the following inequalities on a number line.
   a) $7 \leqslant a < 10$ **b)** $-2 \leqslant b < 3$

5 Solve the following inequalities.
   a) $x + 3 \leqslant 9$ **b)** $2x + 7 > 1$

6 **a)** A rectangle is 15 cm by 2 cm. Calculate the length of one of its diagonals.
   b) An equilateral triangle has side lengths of 10 cm. Calculate its height.

7 Find the lengths of the unknown sides in this diagram.
Give your answers to one decimal place.

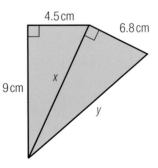

8 How far does an object travel in:
   a) 8 hours at 45 km/h
   b) 5 minutes at 156 km/h?

9 Two new cars are bought at the same time. Car X costs $15 000 and car Y costs $10 000. This graph shows their value over the next six years.

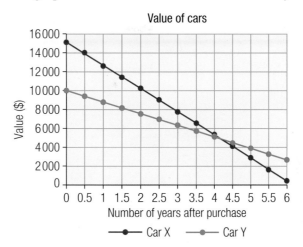

a) Which car depreciates more quickly?
b) How can you tell which car depreciates more quickly from the shape of the graph?
c) Approximately how many years after they are bought are the two cars worth the same?

10 The numbers of sweets in 15 similar packets are given below.

66 68 69 68 67 70 70 66 80 71 68 70 66 71 80

a) The manufacturer wishes to advertise the average number of sweets in a packet. What number should he state?
b) Justify your answer to part **a)**.

11 16 students sit two English exams. Each exam is marked out of 40.
The results are shown below.

Test 1
11 13 18 24 24 26 27 32 34 36 36 39 39 39 40 40
Test 2
4 5 5 8 11 12 13 13 17 24 25 25 25 28 31 34

a) Display the data on a back-to-back stem-and-leaf diagram.
b) From the diagram, which test appears to have been the harder of the two? Justify your answer.

12 For each of the following:
(i) estimate the answer to the calculation
(ii) work out the exact answer using an appropriate method.

a) 452×31
b) 2021×47
c) 1.9×5.04

SECTION ③

Twee motieven, Systeem V D, variant 2   Baarn XI-'61

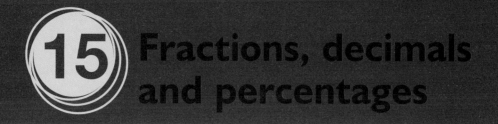

15 Fractions, decimals and percentages

◆ Consolidate writing a fraction in its simplest form by cancelling common factors.
◆ Add, subtract, multiply and divide fractions, interpreting division as a multiplicative inverse, and cancelling common factors before multiplying or dividing.
◆ Solve problems involving percentage changes, choosing the correct numbers to take as 100% or as a whole, including simple problems involving personal or household finance, e.g. simple interest, discount, profit, loss and tax.

Fractions

Writing a fraction in its simplest form

To simplify a fraction, divide both the numerator and denominator by a common factor (a whole number that divides into both of them exactly).

This is often called 'cancelling'.

    To write the fraction in its **simplest form**, divide the numerator and denominator by their **highest common factor** (the biggest number that divides into both of them exactly).

Worked examples

a) Write $\frac{24}{84}$ as a fraction in its simplest form.

The highest common factor of 24 and 84 is 12, i.e. 12 is the largest number that divides into both 24 and 84 exactly.
$$24 \div 12 = 2$$
$$84 \div 12 = 7$$
Therefore $\frac{24}{84}$ simplifies to $\frac{2}{7}$.

b) Write $\frac{75}{225}$ as a fraction in its simplest form.

The highest common factor of 75 and 225 is 75.
$$75 \div 75 = 1$$
$$225 \div 75 = 3$$
Therefore $\frac{75}{225}$ simplifies to $\frac{1}{3}$.

The simplification can be done in steps if the highest common factor is not known.
$$75 \div 25 = 3 \quad and \quad 225 \div 25 = 9$$
So $\frac{75}{225}$ simplifies to $\frac{3}{9}$.
But $\frac{3}{9}$ simplifies further, giving $\frac{1}{3}$.

EXERCISE 15.1A

Write each of the following fractions in its simplest form.

1 **a)** $\frac{16}{36}$ **b)** $\frac{36}{54}$ **c)** $\frac{27}{45}$

  d) $\frac{144}{156}$ **e)** $\frac{75}{125}$ **f)** $\frac{78}{130}$

2 **a)** $\frac{4}{10}$ **b)** $\frac{12}{27}$ **c)** $\frac{28}{48}$

  d) $\frac{8}{56}$ **e)** $\frac{26}{65}$ **f)** $\frac{36}{45}$

3 **a)** $\frac{25}{75}$ **b)** $\frac{39}{130}$ **c)** $\frac{39}{65}$

  d) $\frac{99}{165}$ **e)** $\frac{58}{145}$ **f)** $\frac{128}{384}$

Addition and subtraction of fractions

You already know that adding or subtracting fractions with the same denominator is relatively straightforward. For example,

$$\frac{5}{17} + \frac{11}{17} = \frac{16}{17}$$

Simply add the numerators together and keep the denominator as it is. Adding or subtracting fractions with different denominators requires an extra step. For example,

$$\frac{3}{8} + \frac{4}{9}$$

Both fractions need to be converted into equivalent fractions with a common denominator. The **lowest common multiple** of both denominators is 72, i.e. 72 is the smallest number that both 8 and 9 divide into. Therefore we need to find equivalent fractions to those given, with 72 as a denominator.

$$\frac{3}{8} = \frac{27}{72} \quad \text{and} \quad \frac{4}{9} = \frac{32}{72}$$

Therefore $\frac{3}{8} + \frac{4}{9}$ is the same as $\frac{27}{72} + \frac{32}{72}$.

$$\frac{27}{72} + \frac{32}{72} = \frac{59}{72}$$

The same method applies when subtracting: it is also necessary to work with fractions with a common denominator.

EXERCISE 15.1B

1 Do the following calculations. Simplify your answers where possible.

  a) $\frac{3}{9} + \frac{4}{9}$ **b)** $\frac{5}{11} + \frac{4}{11}$ **c)** $\frac{4}{7} - \frac{2}{7}$

  d) $\frac{7}{13} + \frac{3}{13} - \frac{5}{13}$ **e)** $\frac{16}{23} + \frac{17}{23} - \frac{19}{23}$

2   Do the following calculations.

a) $\frac{5}{9} - \frac{2}{9} + \frac{4}{9}$ b) $\frac{5}{7} - \frac{4}{7} + \frac{6}{7}$ c) $\frac{8}{13} - \frac{5}{13} - \frac{1}{13}$

d) $\frac{26}{29} - \frac{19}{29} + \frac{5}{29}$ e) $\frac{33}{50} - \frac{21}{50} + \frac{7}{50}$

3   Do the following calculations. Show your working clearly and simplify your answers where possible.

a) $\frac{1}{5} - \frac{1}{6}$ b) $\frac{1}{2} - \frac{1}{5}$ c) $\frac{1}{4} - \frac{1}{7}$

d) $\frac{1}{2} + \frac{1}{4} - \frac{1}{8}$ e) $\frac{13}{18} - \frac{2}{9} + \frac{1}{6}$

4   Do the following calculations. Simplify your answers where possible.

a) $\frac{4}{7} + \frac{4}{21}$ b) $\frac{8}{9} - \frac{5}{18}$ c) $\frac{14}{15} + \frac{7}{45}$

d) $\frac{19}{24} + \frac{7}{72}$ e) $\frac{1}{3} + \frac{4}{5} - \frac{3}{4}$

5   Do the following calculations. Simplify your answers where possible.

a) $\frac{2}{3} + \frac{4}{7}$ b) $\frac{3}{7} - \frac{2}{9}$ c) $\frac{5}{8} - \frac{3}{7}$

d) $\frac{2}{3} - \frac{8}{9} + \frac{1}{2}$ e) $\frac{4}{5} + \frac{3}{10} - \frac{1}{6}$

Multiplication of fractions

Multiplying fractions is relatively straightforward. For example,

$$\frac{1}{3} \times \frac{3}{5}$$

This can be read as '$\frac{1}{3}$ of $\frac{3}{5}$' and is visually represented as follows:

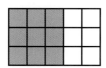

Once again the lowest common multiple of the denominators has been identified, i.e. 15. $\frac{3}{5}$ of the rectangle has been shaded. This is equivalent to $\frac{9}{15}$.

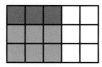

Now $\frac{1}{3}$ of the $\frac{3}{5}$ has been shaded. This is $\frac{3}{15}$ of the original rectangle.

Therefore is $\frac{1}{3}$ of $\frac{3}{5}$ equal to $\frac{3}{15}$.

Doing this is equivalent to simply multiplying the numerators together and multiplying the denominators together to give the answer. For example,

$$\frac{1}{3} \times \frac{3}{5} = \frac{3}{15} = \frac{1}{5}$$

To keep calculations simple, it is helpful to look for common factors first. If there are common factors in fractions which are being multiplied, then these can be cancelled *before* doing the multiplication.

In the multiplication $\frac{1}{3} \times \frac{3}{5}$, for example, 3 is a common factor of the numerator and denominator and can be cancelled:

$$\frac{1}{\cancel{3}} \times \frac{\cancel{3}}{5} = \frac{1}{1} \times \frac{1}{5} = \frac{1}{5}$$

Worked example

By cancelling any common factors first, work out $\frac{4}{9} \times \frac{3}{16} \times \frac{4}{7}$.

Cancel the common factors in stages.

$$\frac{4}{9} \times \frac{3}{16} \times \frac{4}{7} = \frac{4}{3\cancel{9}} \times \frac{\cancel{3}}{16} \times \frac{4}{7}$$

3 is a common factor of 3 and 9.

$$= \frac{\cancel{4}}{3} \times \frac{1}{4\cancel{16}} \times \frac{4}{7}$$

4 is a common factor of 4 and 16.

$$= \frac{1}{3} \times \frac{1}{\cancel{4}} \times \frac{\cancel{4}}{7}$$

4 is a common factor again.

$$= \frac{1}{3} \times \frac{1}{1} \times \frac{1}{7}$$

This multiplication is easy.

$$= \frac{1}{21}$$

Without any cancelling, the multiplication is $\frac{4}{9} \times \frac{3}{16} \times \frac{4}{7} = \frac{48}{1008}$.

This then can be simplified to $\frac{1}{21}$ (not a straightforward process).

Division of fractions

To understand division involving fractions, it can be helpful to look at the problem visually. For example, $\frac{2}{3} \div \frac{1}{4}$ can be read as 'How many quarters go into $\frac{2}{3}$?'

$\frac{1}{4}$ is equivalent to $\frac{3}{12}$.

$\frac{2}{3}$ is equivalent to $\frac{8}{12}$.

 or

Therefore we are trying to see how many lots of $\frac{3}{12}$ go into $\frac{8}{12}$.

We can see from this diagram that there are $2\frac{2}{3}$.

Another way of carrying out a division involving fractions is to transform it into a multiplication. For example, dividing by $\frac{1}{4}$ is equivalent to multiplying by $\frac{4}{1}$. So

$$\frac{2}{3} \div \frac{1}{4} \quad \text{is equivalent to} \quad \frac{2}{3} \times \frac{4}{1} = \frac{8}{3} = 2\frac{2}{3}$$

A division can be changed to a multiplication by using the **multiplicative inverse**.

> *Dividing by 7 is equivalent to multiplying by $\frac{1}{7}$.*
>
> *Dividing by $\frac{3}{2}$ is equivalent to multiplying by $\frac{2}{3}$.*

Worked examples

a) Work out $\frac{5}{16} \div \frac{5}{9} \div \frac{7}{8} \times \frac{7}{9}$.

First re-write the divisions as equivalent multiplications.

$$\frac{5}{16} \div \frac{5}{9} \div \frac{7}{8} \times \frac{7}{9} = \frac{5}{16} \times \frac{9}{5} \times \frac{8}{7} \times \frac{7}{9}$$

5 and 7 are common factors, so cancel.

$$= \frac{\cancel{5}}{16} \times \frac{9}{\cancel{5}} \times \frac{8}{\cancel{7}} \times \frac{\cancel{7}}{9}$$

It is possible to cancel more common factors.

$$= \frac{1}{{}_2 16} \times \frac{\cancel{9}}{1} \times \frac{\cancel{8}}{1} \times \frac{1}{\cancel{9}}$$

$$= \frac{1}{2}$$

Without any cancelling, the multiplication is
$\frac{5}{16} \times \frac{9}{5} \times \frac{8}{7} \times \frac{7}{9} = \frac{2520}{5040}$.
This then can be simplified to $\frac{1}{2}$.

b) Work out $2\frac{1}{2} \times 3\frac{3}{4} \div 3\frac{1}{8}$.

$$2\frac{1}{2} \times 3\frac{3}{4} : 3\frac{1}{8} = \frac{5}{2} \times \frac{15}{4} \div \frac{25}{8}$$

> First write the mixed numbers as improper fractions.

$$= \frac{5}{2} \times \frac{15}{4} \times \frac{8}{25}$$

> Re-write the division as an equivalent multiplication.

$$= \frac{5}{2} \times \frac{^{3}\cancel{15}}{\cancel{4}} \times \frac{^{2}\cancel{8}}{_{5}\cancel{25}}$$

> 5 and 4 are common factors, so cancel.

$$= \frac{\cancel{5}}{\cancel{2}} \times \frac{3}{1} \times \frac{\cancel{2}}{\cancel{5}}$$

> It is possible to cancel more common factors.

$$= 3$$

EXERCISE 15.1C

In this exercise, simplify your calculations by cancelling any common factors first.

1 Do the following calculations. Give your answers in their simplest form.

   a) $\frac{5}{6} \times \frac{3}{8}$ **b)** $\frac{3}{5} \times \frac{5}{12}$

   c) $\frac{7}{10} \times \frac{5}{7}$ **d)** $\frac{1}{3} \times 1\frac{1}{4} \times \frac{1}{5}$

2 Do the following calculations. Show your working clearly and give your answers in their simplest form.

   a) $\frac{4}{9} \div \frac{2}{3}$ **b)** $\frac{9}{14} \div \frac{3}{7} \times \frac{1}{2}$

   c) $\frac{9}{16} \div \frac{3}{4} \times \frac{2}{3}$ **d)** $\frac{1}{2} \div \frac{1}{8} \times \frac{1}{4}$

3 Do the following calculations. Give your answers in their simplest form.

   a) $\frac{5}{8} \times \frac{3}{10}$ **b)** $\frac{3}{7} \times \frac{14}{15}$

   c) $\frac{11}{20} \times \frac{15}{22}$ **d)** $\frac{2}{3} \times \frac{5}{6} \times \frac{3}{5}$

4 Do the following calculations. Show your working clearly and give your answers in their simplest form.

   a) $\frac{15}{19} \div \frac{10}{19} \times \frac{2}{3}$ **b)** $\frac{11}{14} \div \frac{33}{21}$

   c) $\frac{9}{16} \div \frac{9}{8} \times 1\frac{3}{4} \div \frac{7}{8}$ **d)** $\frac{1}{2} \div \frac{1}{3} \times \frac{1}{4} \div \frac{3}{8}$

Finance – discount, profit and loss, interest and tax

Banks in Europe, America, Japan and many other places in the world will pay you money if you place your savings with them. They will also lend you money but will charge you to do so. The amount of money that you save or borrow is called the **principal**. The amount paid or charged by the bank is called **interest**.

The interest paid on money saved depends upon the amount of the principal, the amount of time you are prepared to leave it in the bank and the rate that the bank pays in percentage terms.

The formula for calculating **simple interest** is

$$I = \frac{ptr}{100}$$

where *I* **is the interest paid by the bank**
p **is the principal**
t **is the time in years**
r **is the rate per year (percentage).**

Worked examples

a) Find the simple interest earned on a deposit of $400 saved for three years at a rate of 5% per year.

$$I = \frac{ptr}{100}$$

$$I = \frac{400 \times 3 \times 5}{100} = 60$$

So the simple interest paid is $60.

b) How long will it take a principal of $200 to earn simple interest of $80 at 8% per year?

$$I = \frac{ptr}{100}$$

$$80 = \frac{200 \times t \times 8}{100}$$

$$80 = 16t$$

$$80 \div 16 = t$$

$$5 = t$$

Therefore it will take five years.

EXERCISE 15.2A

All the rates of interest in this exercise are annual rates of simple interest.

1 Calculate the interest paid in each of the following cases.
   a) principal $500   time 2 years   rate 3%
   b) principal $800   time 4 years   rate 5%
   c) principal $750   time 3 years   rate 4%
   d) principal $400   time 6 years   rate 2.5%
   e) principal $6000   time 2 years   rate 3.75%

2 Calculate how many years it will take to earn the given amount of interest in each of the following cases.
   a) principal $200   rate 5%   interest $30
   b) principal $500   rate 2%   interest $40
   c) principal $750   rate 4%   interest $150
   d) principal $2500   rate 3%   interest $450
   e) principal $4000   rate 2.5%   interest $350

Worked examples

a) What percentage rate per year is paid for a principal of $400 to earn simple interest of $60 in three years?

$$I = \frac{ptr}{100}$$

$$60 = \frac{400 \times 3 \times r}{100}$$

$$60 = 12r$$

$$5 = r$$

Therefore the rate is 5% per year.

b) What principal will earn simple interest of $360 in three years at an annual rate of 8%?

$$I = \frac{ptr}{100}$$

$$360 = \frac{p \times 3 \times 8}{100}$$

$$36\,000 = 24p$$

$$1500 = p$$

The principal is $1500.

EXERCISE 15.2B

All the rates of interest in this exercise are annual rates of simple interest.

1   What rate of interest per year will earn the given amount of interest in each of the following cases?
    a) principal $400   time 4 years   interest $80
    b) principal $200   time 3 years   interest $36
    c) principal $850   time 5 years   interest $340
    d) principal $1200   time 6 years   interest $540
    e) principal $4000   time 3 years   interest $540

2   What principal will earn the given amount of interest in each of the following cases?
    a) interest $112   time 4 years   rate 7%
    b) interest $224   time 7 years   rate 4%
    c) interest $210   time 6 years   rate 7.5%
    d) interest $340   time 5 years   rate 8%

Profit, loss and tax

Things made in a factory are made at a **cost price**. They are then sold at a **selling price**. When the selling price is greater than the cost price, a **profit** is made. A **loss** is made when the selling price is less than the cost price.

A **tax** is a payment made to the government. In most countries people pay tax on income and a tax is added to the prices of goods and materials.

Worked example

a)   A man buys a box of 100 apples in a market for $44.
      He sells all the apples for 50 cents each.
      What is his profit or loss?
b)   The same man buys a box of 100 oranges for $35 and sells them for 40 cents each, but 20 of the oranges are bad and he throws them away. What is his profit or loss?

a)   Cost price = $44
      Selling price = 100×50 cents = $50
      Profit = selling price − cost price
           = $50 − $44 = $6
      His profit is $6.
b)   Cost price = $35
      Selling price = 80×40 cents = $32
      He has paid more than he received, so he has made a loss.
      His loss is cost price − selling price.
      $35 − $32 = $3
      His loss is $3.

EXERCISE 15.2C

Calculate the profit or loss in each of the following cases.

1   cost price $70   selling price $50

2   cost price $35   selling price $29

3   cost price $45 for 12   selling price $4 each

4   cost price $70 for 100   selling price 65 cents each

5   cost price $35 000 for 8   selling price $4200 each

Percentage profit and loss

Profit and loss can be shown as a percentage using the formula below.

$$\text{Percentage profit or loss} = \frac{\text{profit or loss}}{\text{cost price}} \times 100$$

Worked example

A woman buys a car for $8000 and sells it the following year for $6000. What is her percentage loss?

Loss = $8000 − $6000 = $2000

$$\text{Percentage loss} = \frac{\text{loss}}{\text{cost price}} \times 100$$

$$= \frac{2000}{8000} \times 100$$

$$= 25\%$$

Her percentage loss was 25%.

EXERCISE 15.2D

A company produces kitchen equipment for the home.
a) Work out the percentage profit on each of the following items.
b) Tax at 15% is added to the selling price of each item.
How much tax is added in each case?

1	toaster	cost price $20	selling price $34
2	coffee maker	cost price $30	selling price $45
3	food processor	cost price $40	selling price $70
4	fridge	cost price $60	selling price $75
5	freezer	cost price $48	selling price $72
6	cooker	cost price $340	selling price $544
7	microwave	cost price $44	selling price $55
8	washing machine	cost price $240	selling price $420
9	dryer	cost price $160	selling price $280
10	dishwasher	cost price $200	selling price $340

EXERCISE 15.2E

Cars which are bought new and sold after 3 years are all worth less than they cost. This loss is called **depreciation**. Find the loss or depreciation on each of the following makes of cars as a percentage of its cost price.

1	Ford	cost price $8000	selling price $3000
2	Vauxhall	cost price $10 000	selling price $4000
3	Fiat	cost price $5000	selling price $2500
4	Renault	cost price $12 000	selling price $8400
5	Toyota	cost price $10 800	selling price $7200
6	Nissan	cost price $13 440	selling price $9600
7	Mazda	cost price $18 000	selling price $10 800
8	Lexus	cost price $24 000	selling price $15 600
9	Audi	cost price $32 000	selling price $18 560
10	Mercedes	cost price $40 000	selling price $25 000

16 Sequences

◆ Generate terms of a sequence using term-to-term and position-to-term rules.
◆ Derive an expression to describe the *n*th term of an arithmetic sequence.

Leonardo Pisano Bigollo was born in Italy in about 1170 CE and died in about 1250 CE. He has been described as 'the most talented Western mathematician of the Middle Ages' and is better known by the name Fibonacci.

Fibonacci is famous for his 'Book of Calculation', the *Liber Abaci*, which brought the Arabic number system to Europe in the 13th century, and which uses this sequence of numbers as an example.

    0   1   1   2   3   5   8   13   . . .

In the sequence, each number is the sum of the two numbers before it. Fibonacci did not discover the sequence but it is now named after him. It is found in nature and in many other situations, for example architecture and the movement of stocks and shares.

Sequences

A **sequence** is an ordered set of numbers. Each number in the sequence is called a **term**. The terms of a sequence form a regular pattern and are produced by following a **rule**.

Below are three examples of different types of sequence.

● 6   8   10   12   14   16   . . .
  In this sequence the rule is 'Add 2 to each term to give the next term.'
  This is an **arithmetic** sequence.

  Arithmetic sequences are ones where there is a **common difference** between consecutive terms. This can be positive, for example in the sequence 3, 7, 11, 15, . . . (where the common difference is +4) or negative, for example in the sequence 28, 20, 12, 4, . . . (where the common difference is −8).

- **4   8   16   32   64**   ...
  In this sequence the rule is 'Double the number to give the next term.'
  This is a **geometric** sequence.
    Geometric sequences are ones where there is a **common ratio** between consecutive terms. This can be by multiplying, for example in the sequence 2, 8, 32, 128, . . . (where the common ratio is ×4) or by dividing, for example in the sequence 432, 144, 48, 16, . . . (where the common ratio is ÷3 or ×$\frac{1}{3}$).
- **9   16   25   36   49   64**   ...
  In this sequence the difference between consecutive terms increases by 2 each time. It is also the sequence of square numbers.

Term-to-term rules

A rule which describes how to get from one term to the next is called a **term-to-term** rule.

Worked examples

a)   Here is an arithmetic sequence of numbers.

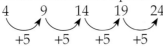

$$4 \quad 9 \quad 14 \quad 19 \quad 24$$
$$+5 \quad +5 \quad +5 \quad +5$$

The term-to-term rule for this sequence is +5. What is the tenth term?

To calculate the tenth term in the sequence, the pattern can be continued using the term-to-term rule:

   4   9   14   19   24   29   34   39   44   **49**

b)   Here is a geometric sequence of numbers.

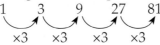

$$1 \quad 3 \quad 9 \quad 27 \quad 81$$
$$×3 \quad ×3 \quad ×3 \quad ×3$$

The term-to-term rule for this sequence is ×3. What is the eighth term?

To calculate the eighth term in the sequence, the pattern can be continued using the term-to-term rule:

   1   3   9   27   81   243   729   **2187**

EXERCISE 16.1A

For each of the sequences in questions 1–10:
   a) write if it is arithmetic (A), geometric (G) or neither (N)
   b) describe the term-to-term rule
   c) calculate the next two terms.

1   5   10   20   40   80

2   4   5   7   10   14

3   2   4   6   8   10

→

4   5   7   9   11   13

5   2   4   8   16   32

6   4   7   10   13   16

7   2   6   10   14   18

8   144   121   100   81   64

9   1   8   15   22   29

10   14   21   28   35   42

EXERCISE 16.1B

For each of the sequences in questions 1–10:
   a) write if it is arithmetic (A), geometric (G) or neither (N)
   b) describe the term-to-term rule
   c) calculate the next two terms.

1   9   18   27   36   45

2   1.5   2   2.5   3   3.5

3   1   1   2   3   5

4   0.5   0.75   1   1.25   1.5

5   24   12   6   3   1.5

6   7   5   3   1   −1

7   64   32   16   8   4

8   144   132   120   108   96

9   1   10   100   1000   10000

10   1   8   27   64   125

Position-to-term rules – the nth term

This table gives the first terms of a sequence and their positions in the sequence.

Position	1	2	3
Term	1	4	7

We can write
$t_1 = 1$, $t_2 = 4$, $t_3 = 7$ and so on.

The terms are the numbers of the sequence.

The term-to-term rule is +3 and we can continue the table to give the values of higher terms.

Position	1	2	3	4	5	6
Term	1	4	7	10	13	16

We can write, for example, $t_6 = 16$.

We can use the letter d for the difference between consecutive terms. So for this sequence, $d = +3$ and we can write the terms like this:

$$t_1 = 1$$
$$t_2 = 4 = t_1 + d$$
$$t_3 = 7 = t_2 + d = t_1 + d + d = t_1 + 2d$$
$$t_4 = 10 = t_3 + d = t_1 + d + d + d = t_1 + 3d$$
$$t_5 = 13 = t_4 + d = t_1 + d + d + d + d = t_1 + 4d$$

In general, the value of the nth term of an arithmetic sequence is

$t_n = t_1 + (n - 1)d$ where t_1 is the value of the first term and d is the difference between consecutive terms.

This expression connects a term's position in the sequence with its value. It is called the **position-to-term** rule or the **nth term**.

Worked examples

a) For the sequence 1, 4, 7, 10, 13, ...
   (i) find the 11th term in the sequence
   (ii) derive a simplified formula for the nth term of the sequence.

   (i) Using the general formula:
   $$t_n = t_1 + (n - 1)d$$
   $$t_{11} = t_1 + (11 - 1) \times 3$$
   $$t_{11} = 1 + (10 \times 3)$$
   $$t_{11} = 31$$

   $t_1 = 1, d = 3$ and $n = 11$

   The 11th term is 31.

   (ii)
   $$t_n = t_1 + (n - 1)d$$
   $$t_n = 1 + (n - 1)3$$
   $$t_n = 1 + 3n - 3$$
   $$t_n = 3n - 2$$

b) For the sequence 42, 39, 36, 33, 30, ...
   (i) find the 31st term in the sequence
   (ii) derive a simplified formula for the nth term of the sequence.

   (i) Using the general formula:
   $$t_n = t_1 + (n - 1)\, d$$
   $$t_{31} = 42 + (31 - 1) \times (-3)$$
   $$t_{31} = 42 + (30 \times -3)$$
   $$t_{31} = 42 - 90$$
   $$t_{31} = -48$$

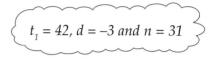

   $t_1 = 42,\ d = -3\ and\ n = 31$

   The 31st term is –48.
   (ii) $t_n = t_1 + (n - 1)d$
   $$t_n = 42 + (n - 1) \times (-3)$$
   $$t_n = 42 - 3n + 3$$
   $$t_n = 45 - 3n$$

EXERCISE 16.2A

For each of the sequences in questions 1–10:
   a) derive a simplified formula for the nth term of the sequence
   b) use the position-to-term rule to find the value of the term shown in brackets.

1 2   4   6   8   10   ... (t_{21}) **2** 5   10   15   20   ... (t_{11})

3 5   7   9   11   13   ... (t_{12}) **4** 27   24   21   18   15   ... (t_{14})

5 91   81   71   61   ... (t_{10}) **6** –6   –3   0   3   6   ... (t_{16})

7 24   30   36   42   48   ... (t_{21}) **8** –4   1   6   11   16   ... (t_{12})

9 –83   –78   –73   –68   ... (t_{31}) **10** 2   13   24   35   46   ... (t_{17})

EXERCISE 16.2B

For each of the sequences in questions 1–10:
   a) use the position-to-term rule to find the value of the nth term
   b) find the value of the 20th term in the sequence.

1 5   7   9   11   13   ...   **2** 12   14   16   18   20   ...

3 4   9   14   19   24   ...   **4** 27   24   21   18   15   ...

5 63   53   43   33   23   ...   **6** 102   202   302   402   502   ...

7 87   76   65   54   43   32   ...   **8** 0   15   30   45   60   ...

9 –15   –10   –5   0   5   10   ...   **10** –96   –84   –72   –60   –48   ...

17 Position and movement

◆ Tessellate triangles and quadrilaterals and relate to angle sums and half-turn rotations; know which regular polygons tessellate, and explain why others will not.

◆ Use the coordinate grid to solve problems involving translations, rotations, reflections and enlargements.

◆ Transform two-dimensional shapes by combinations of rotations, reflections and translations; describe the transformation that maps an object on to its image.

◆ Enlarge two-dimensional shapes, given a centre and positive integer scale factor; identify the scale factor of an enlargement as the ratio of the lengths of any two corresponding line segments.

◆ Recognise that translations, rotations and reflections preserve length and angle, and map objects on to congruent images, and that enlargements preserve angle but not length.

◆ Know what is needed to give a precise description of a reflection, rotation, translation or enlargement.

Tessellations

The Alhambra is a walled city and fortress in Granada, Spain. It is one of Spain's major tourist attractions and is a UNESCO World Heritage Site.

It was built in the 14th century by the Moorish rulers during the last Islamic sultanate on the Iberian Peninsula. It is an outstanding example of Islamic art and architecture, and has a wonderful collection of Islamic tiles lining many of the walls.

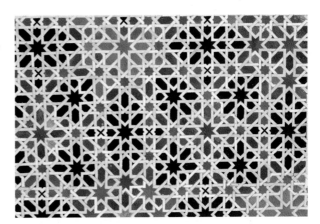

From a mathematical point of view, the tiles are exceptional as they show intricate **tessellating patterns**. A tessellating pattern is one where all the shapes form a repeating pattern and fit together without any gaps. The picture on the previous page shows an example.

The 20th century Dutch artist, M. C. Escher, visited the Alhambra and was inspired by the patterns he saw there. He went on to draw many pictures based on the different types of symmetry, including tessellations. An example of one of his works is shown on page 142.

Triangles

Here are some examples of patterns made by tessellating triangles.

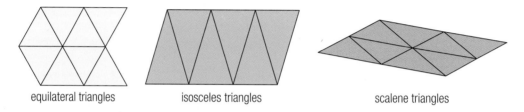

| equilateral triangles | isosceles triangles | scalene triangles |

These diagrams show that it is possible to tessellate these triangles with themselves.

However, does this work for *any* triangle? Does *any* triangle tessellate with itself? In Exercise 17.1A you will find out.

EXERCISE 17.1A

You will need squared or isometric dot paper for this exercise.

1   On squared paper (or isometric dot paper) draw ten identical triangles. Cut them out carefully and try to arrange them so that they tessellate.

2   Repeat question 1 for a different triangle. Do these triangles tessellate?

3   Compare your results with those of other students in your class. Have all the different types of triangle tessellated? Were there any which did not tessellate?

4   This diagram shows six equilateral triangles tessellating.
    a) What is the size of each of the angles a, b, c, d, e and f?
    b) Calculate the value of $a + b + c + d + e + f$.

5 This diagram shows an isosceles triangle *ABC*.
The angle at *A* is 40°.
a) What is the size of angle *B*?
b) What is the size of angle *C*?
c) The diagram below shows triangle *ABC* and
two identical triangles arranged together.

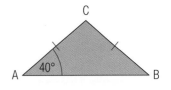

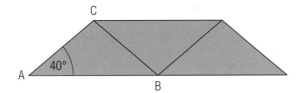

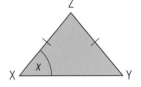

*The middle triangle
is a rotation of the
other two by 180°.*

   (i) Copy the diagram and label all of the angles with their size.
   (ii) What is the sum of the three angles at *B*?
   (iii) Will this pattern continue to tessellate in all directions?
   Explain your answer.

6 This diagram shows an isosceles triangle *XYZ*.
The size of the angle at *X* is *x*.
a) What is the size of angle *Y* in terms of *x*?
b) What is the size of angle *Z* in terms of *x*?
c) The diagram below shows triangle *XYZ* and
two identical triangles arranged together.

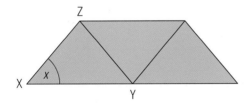

   (i) Copy the diagram and label all of the angles with their size in terms
   of *x*.
   (ii) What is the sum of the three angles at *Y*?
   (iii) Will this pattern continue to tessellate in all directions?
   Explain your answer.

7 This diagram shows a scalene triangle *PQR*.
The size of angle *P* is *a*.
The size of angle *Q* is *b*.

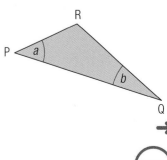

a) What is the size of angle R in terms of a and b?

b) The diagram below shows triangle XYZ and two identical triangles arranged together.

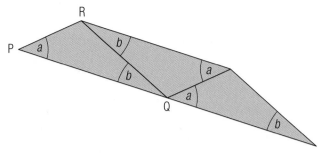

(i)   What is the size of the unmarked angle at Q in terms of a and b?

(ii) Write an equation in terms of a and b for the sum of the three angles at Q.

(iii) Will this pattern of scalene triangles continue to tessellate in all directions? Explain your answer.

You will have seen from Exercise 17.1A that it is possible to tessellate any type of triangle with itself, simply by rotating alternate triangles by 180° and placing them together. Three identical triangles can always be arranged to form an angle of 180°. Therefore six triangles can always be arranged around a point to complete 360°.

> *Remember, two shapes are congruent if they are exactly the same shape and size.*

The triangles which make up each tessellation are **congruent**.

Quadrilaterals

The diagrams below show some tessellations of different quadrilaterals.

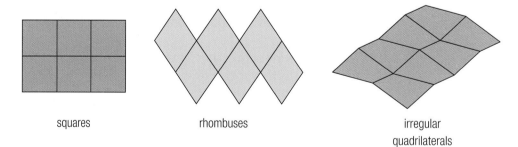

squares   rhombuses   irregular
                                                        quadrilaterals

Does *any* quadrilateral tessellate with itself?

EXERCISE 17.1B

You will need squared or isometric dot paper for this exercise.

1 On squared paper (or isometric dot paper) draw ten identical irregular quadrilaterals. Cut them out carefully and try to arrange them so that they tessellate.

> *In an irregular quadrilateral, all the angles and side lengths are different.*

2 Repeat question 1 for a different irregular quadrilateral. Can these be tessellated?

3 Compare your results with those of other students in your class. Have all the different irregular quadrilaterals tessellated? Were there any which did not tessellate?

4 This irregular quadrilateral has angles of sizes *a*, *b*, *c* and *d*.
   a) Write an equation for the sum of the four angles.
   b) An identical quadrilateral is rotated by 180° and placed next to the original one like this: Copy the diagram and label each of the unmarked angles with its size, *a*, *b*, *c* or *d*.
   c) The diagram below shows two more identical quadrilaterals placed next to the existing ones. Add these two quadrilaterals to your diagram and label the remaining unmarked angles that meet at the centre.
   d) Write an equation for the sum of the four angles that meet at the centre.

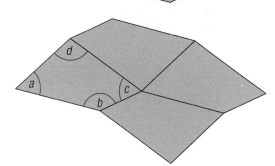

You will have seen from Exercise 17.1B that any quadrilateral can be made to tessellate. This is because, by rotations of 180°, the four corners of the quadrilateral meet around a point. This is not surprising, because any quadrilateral can be split into two triangles and Exercise 17.1A showed that any triangle can be made to tessellate with itself.

As with the tessellations of triangles, the quadrilaterals which make up each tessellation are congruent.

Other polygons

So far we have seen that all triangles and all quadrilaterals tessellate by themselves. However, this is not the case for *all* polygons.

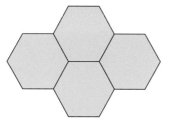

Regular hexagons tessellate.

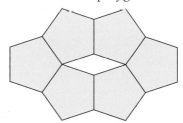

Regular pentagons do no tessellate.

How can we decide whether a polygon will tessellate with itself or not?

EXERCISE 17.1C

1 Look at this regular hexagon.
   a) From your work in Chapter 3, write down the size of each interior angle.
   b) Three regular hexagons can be arranged around a point. By considering the size of the internal angles, explain why this is possible.

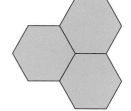

2 a) Calculate the size of an interior angle of a regular pentagon.
   b) Three regular pentagons are arranged around a point as shown. By considering the size of the internal angles, explain why regular pentagons do not tessellate.

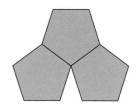

3 a) Regular pentagons can be arranged as shown. What is the name of the shape in the centre?
   b) Calculate the size of each of the interior angles of the centre shape.

4 A regular octagon is shown.
   a) Calculate the size of each internal angle.
   b) Will regular octagons tessellate with themselves? Justify your answer.
   c) Will regular octagons tessellate with another regular shape? If so, which shape? Justify your answer.

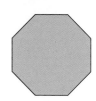

5 This tessellation is made of different shapes.
   a) Write down the names of the different shapes that make up this pattern.
   b) Write down the size of the internal angles of each of the shapes you named in part **a)**.
   c) By considering the sizes of the internal angles, explain why the shapes tessellate.

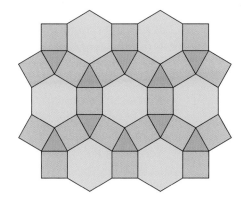

6 This tessellation is made of different shapes.
   a) Write down the names of the different shapes that make up this pattern.
   b) Write down the size of the internal angles of each of the shapes you named in part **a)**.
   c) By considering the sizes of the internal angles, explain why the shapes tessellate.

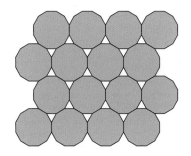

7 A regular hexagon, a square and a third regular polygon tessellate.
   a) Work out what shape the third polygon is. Write down its name.
   b) Justify your answer to part **a)**.

Transformations

Enlargement

You are already familiar with some types of transformation from Student's Books 1 and 2. These include reflection, rotation and translation. In these transformations the image produced is congruent to the original object. Both the angles and the lengths of the sides remain the same after the transformation.

Another type of transformation is **enlargement**. If an object is enlarged, the image is mathematically similar to the object, but of a different size. The angles remain the same after the transformation but the lengths of the sides change. The image can be larger or smaller than the original object. In this chapter, we will only look at enlargements where the image is larger than the original object.

When describing an enlargement, two pieces of information need to be given. These are the position of the **centre of enlargement** and the **scale factor of enlargement**.

This diagram shows a triangle *ABC* enlarged to form triangle *A'B'C'*. The centre of enlargement is *O* and the scale factor of enlargement is 2.

Lines can be drawn from the centre of enlargement through each of the vertices *A*, *B* and *C*. When extended, these lines also pass through the corresponding vertices *A'*, *B'* and *C'*.

As the scale of enlargement is 2, each length in the triangle *A'B'C'* is double the length of the corresponding side in triangle *ABC*. That is,

$$\frac{A'B'}{AB} = \frac{A'C'}{AC} = \frac{B'C'}{BC} = 2$$

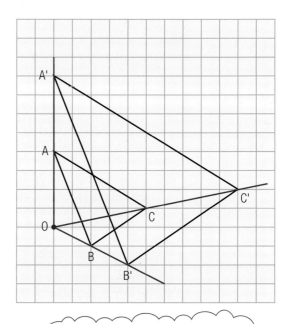

Notice that the angles remain the same. The angle at A is the same size as the angle at A'.

Worked example

Enlarge the triangle *XYZ* by a scale factor of 2 and from the centre of enlargement *O*. Label the image *X'Y'Z'*.

To draw the enlargement, use the following steps.

- Draw lines from the centre of enlargement *O* through each of the vertices *X*, *Y* and *Z*.
- As the scale factor of enlargement is 2, draw the lines such that *OX'* is twice the length of *OX*, *OY'* is twice the length of *OY* and *OZ'* is twice the length of *OZ*.
- Join the ends of the lines *OX'*, *OY'* and *OZ'* to form the enlarged shape *X'Y'Z'*.

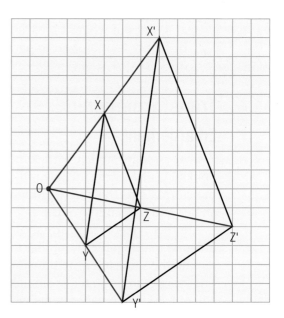

When the enlargement is done on a grid, it is sometimes easier to count squares. For example, OX is 3 across and 4 up, so OX' is 6 across and 8 up.

EXERCISE 17.2A

You will need squared paper for this exercise.

Copy each of the diagrams below on to squared paper. Enlarge each of the objects by the given scale factor and from the centre of enlargement O.

1

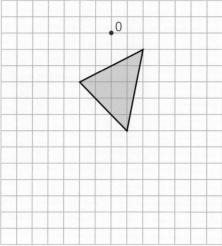

Scale factor of enlargement 2

2

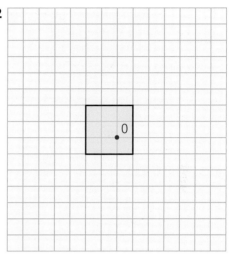

Scale factor of enlargement 3

3

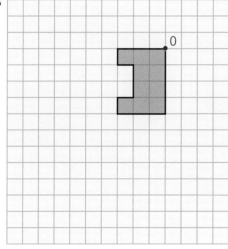

Scale factor of enlargement 2

4

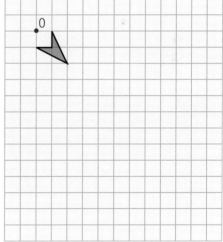

Scale factor of enlargement 4

EXERCISE 17.2B

In each of the following diagrams, the larger shape is an enlargement of the smaller one from the centre of enlargement O. Work out the scale factor of enlargement in each case.

1

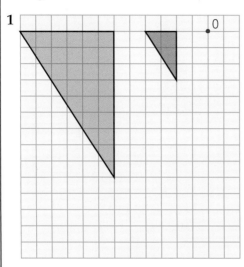

2

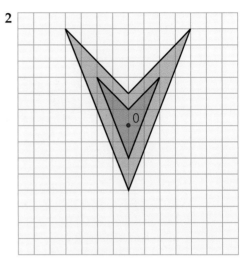

3

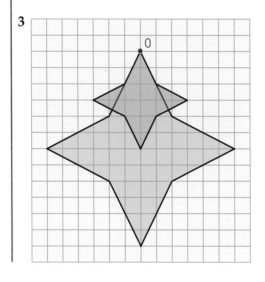

4

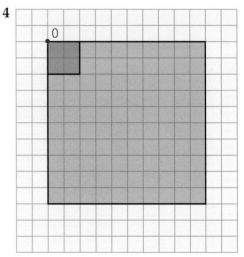

Combining transformations

You already know from Student's Book 2 that it is possible to *combine* transformations, so that an object undergoes more than one transformation to map it on to an image.

The types of transformation and the order in which they are carried out affect where the image appears.

Worked example

The trapezium X undergoes two transformations:

- a translation of $\begin{pmatrix} 5 \\ -2 \end{pmatrix}$
- a reflection in the line $y = -x$.

Draw the images, labelling the image after the first transformation Y and the image after the second transformation Z.

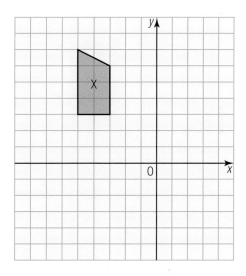

To draw the transformations, use the following steps.

- The translation has been described as a **vector**. The top number gives the horizontal movement and the bottom number gives the vertical movement. So image Y is located by translating each vertex of X by 5 units to the right and −2 units up (i.e. 2 units down).
- The reflection has been described by the equation of the mirror line on the coordinate grid. The straight line $y = -x$ is a downward sloping straight line through the origin. Draw this on the coordinate grid and reflect Y in it to locate the image Z.

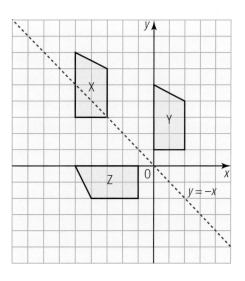

EXERCISE 17.2C

You will need squared paper for this exercise.

In each of the following questions, the object X undergoes two transformations. The first transformation maps X on to an image Y, the second maps Y on to an image Z.

Copy each diagram on to squared paper and draw each of the images Y and Z, labelling them clearly.

1

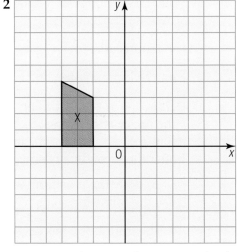

Reflection in the line $y = 3$

Translation of $\begin{pmatrix} -6 \\ -3 \end{pmatrix}$

2

Rotation of 180° with centre at $(0, 2)$
Reflection in the line $y = x + 2$

3

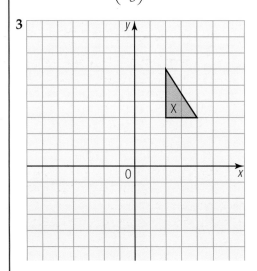

Enlargement with scale factor 2 and centre of enlargement at $(2, 7)$
Rotation of 90° clockwise about O

4

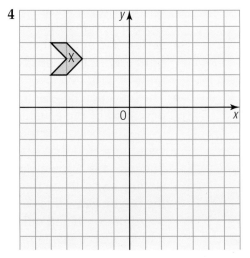

Reflection in the line $y = 0$
Enlargement with scale factor 3 and centre of enlargement at $(-7, -5)$

EXERCISE 17.2D

In each of the following questions, the object X undergoes two transformations.
The first transformation maps X on to the image Y, the second maps Y on to the image Z.
Fully describe the two transformations in each case.

> For a reflection, give the equation of the mirror line.
> For a rotation, give the angle, the direction and the coordinates of the centre of rotation.
> For an enlargement, give the scale factor and the coordinates of the centre of enlargement.
> For a translation, give the vector.

1

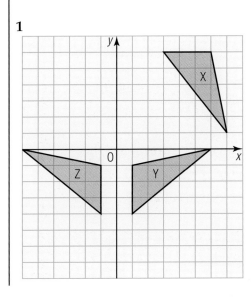

2

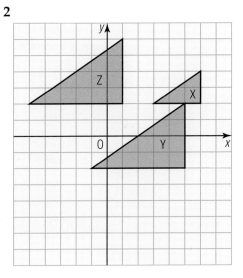

18 Area and volume

◆ Convert between metric units of area (e.g. mm^2 and cm^2, cm^2 and m^2) and volume (e.g. mm^3 and cm^3, cm^3 and m^3); know and use the relationship $1\,cm^3 = 1\,ml$.

◆ Know that land area is measured in hectares (ha), and that 1 hectare = $10\,000\,m^2$; convert between hectares and square metres.

Metric units of area

You already know from Student's Book 2 how to convert between metric units of area. These drawings will remind you.

This is a 1 cm × 1 cm square.

1 cm

1 cm

Area = 1 cm × 1 cm = $1\,cm^2$

But 1 cm = 10 mm, so the square can also be drawn like this:

10 mm

10 mm

Area = 10 mm × 10 mm = $100\,mm^2$

The two squares have the same area, so $1\,cm^2 = 100\,mm^2$.

To convert:
> **from cm to mm, multiply by 10**
> **from cm² to mm², multiply by 100**
> **from mm to cm, divide by 10**
> **from mm² to cm², divide by 100.**

Similarly, a square of side 1 m has the same area as a square of side 100 cm, so
$$1\,m^2 = 100\,cm \times 100\,cm = 10\,000\,cm^2$$

To convert:
> **from m to cm, multiply by 100**
> **from m² to cm², multiply by 10 000**
> **from cm to m, divide by 100**
> **from cm² to m², divide by 10 000.**

172

EXERCISE 18.1

Find the area of each of the rectangles in questions 1–4.

Give your answers:
   a) in mm²   **b)** in cm².

> *The formula for calculating the area of a rectangle is Area = length × width*

1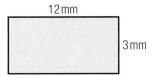
12 mm

3 mm

2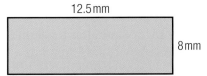
12.5 mm

8 mm

3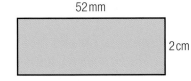
52 mm

2 cm

4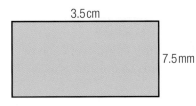
3.5 cm

7.5 mm

Find the area of each of the rectangles in questions 5–8.
Give your answers:
   a) in cm²   **b)** in m².

5 length = 50 cm   width = 25 cm

6 length = 6 m   width = 3 m

7 length = 750 cm   width = 4 m

8 length = 1.2 m   width = 40 cm

Metric units of volume and capacity

Since 1 cm = 10 mm, the two cubes below have the same dimensions.

1 cm
1 cm
1 cm

Volume = 1 cm × 1 cm × 1 cm = 1 cm³

10 mm
10 mm
10 mm

Volume = 10 mm × 10 mm × 10 mm = 1000 mm³

To convert:
   from cm³ to mm³, multiply by 1000
   from mm³ to cm³, divide by 1000.

Similarly, a cube of side 1 m has the same volume as a cube of side 100 cm, so
$$1 \, m^3 = 100 \, cm \times 100 \, cm \times 100 \, cm = 1\,000\,000 \, cm^3$$

To convert:
> **from m³ to cm³, multiply by 1 000 000**
> **from cm³ to m³, divide by 1 000 000.**

Litres and millilitres are units of liquid measure and capacity.
   1 m*l* of liquid has a volume of 1 cm³ and 1 litre is 1000 m*l*.
   A cube of side 10 cm has a volume of 10 cm × 10 cm × 10 cm = 1000 cm³, which is the same as 1000 m*l* or 1 litre.

EXERCISE 18.2

Find the volume of each of the cuboids in questions 1–3.

Give your answers:
   a) in mm³   **b)** in cm³.

> *The formula for calculating the volume of a cuboid is*
> *Volume = length × width × height*

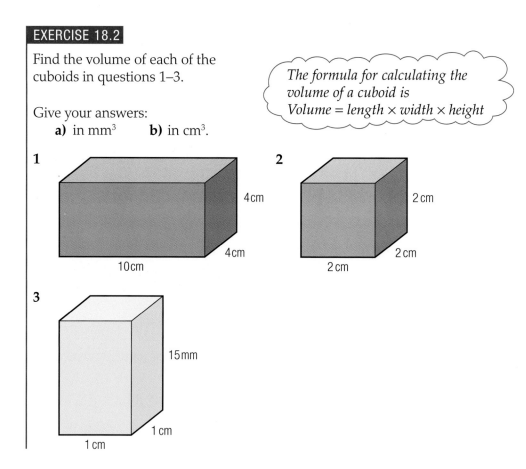

1   10 cm, 4 cm, 4 cm

2   2 cm, 2 cm, 2 cm

3   15 mm, 1 cm, 1 cm

Find the volume of each of the cuboids in questions 4–6.
Give your answers:
   a) in cm³   **b)** in m³.

4

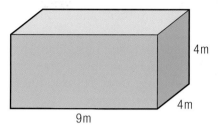

5

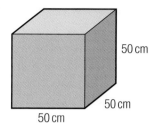

6

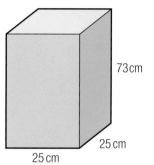

7 A net is a two-dimensional shape which can be folded to create a three-dimensional object. For example, this is the net of a cuboid.

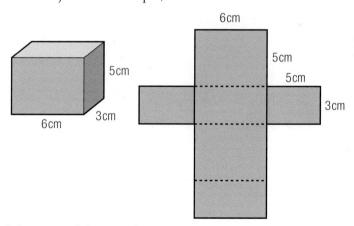

  a) Find the area of the net above:
     (i) in cm²   **(ii)** in mm².
  b) If the net is folded into the cuboid, find the volume of the cuboid:
     (i) in cm³   **(ii)** in mm³.
  c) What quantity of liquid will the cuboid in part **b)** hold:
     (i) in m*l*   **(ii)** in litres?

8 The dimensions of the cuboid in question 7 are all doubled.
  a) Find the volume of the new cuboid in cm³.
  b) What is the capacity of the new cuboid in litres?

Land area

When early people moved about in search of food for themselves and their animals, land area was not really important. But as towns and cities grew up and farms were needed to feed the people in them, the area of a farmer's land became important.

Different units of area came naturally from the units of length and width in use at the time. In England, the length turned over by a horse-drawn plough (the length of a furrow, or furrowlong or **furlong**, about 200 m) multiplied by a width called a **chain** (about 20 m) gives a unit called an **acre**.

In the metric system, the unit used to measure land area is the **hectare**, which is the area of a square of side 100 m. It is not difficult to convert between hectares and square metres.

Area = 100 m × 100 m = 10 000 m² = 1 hectare

100m

100m

The area of a large football pitch is about 1 hectare.

100 hectares = 100 × 10 000 m² = 1 000 000 m² = 1 square kilometre

Worked examples

a) The football pitch played on by Real Madrid in Spain measures 120 m by 80 m (including the area of grass around the pitch).
What is the area in hectares?

$$\text{Area of rectangle} = \text{length} \times \text{width}$$
$$\text{Area} = 120\,\text{m} \times 80\,\text{m}$$
$$= 9600\,\text{m}^2$$
$$9600\,\text{m}^2 = 9600 \div 10\,000$$
$$= 0.96\,\text{hectare}$$

b) A golf course covers an area of 16.35 hectares.
What is the area in square metres?

1 hectare = $10\,000\,m^2$
The area is $16.35 \times 10\,000 = 163\,500\,m^2$.

EXERCISE 18.3

1 Convert each of these areas to hectares.
   a) $42\,500\,m^2$ **b)** $780\,500\,m^2$ **c)** $\frac{1}{2}$ million m^2

2 Convert each of these areas to square metres.
   a) 3.142 hectares   **b)** 0.787 hectare   **c)** 0.084 hectare

3 A New York city block measures 300 m by 300 m.
What is its area in hectares?

4 A castle and its grounds occupy 7.2 hectares.
What is the area in square metres?

5 A paddock for four horses has an area of 0.75 hectare for each horse.
What is the area of the paddock in square metres?

6 A builder buys a plot of land on which to build houses.
The plot is in the shape of a right-angled triangle with sides of 300 m, 400 m and 500 m.
   a) What is the area of the plot in hectares?
   b) 75% of the land will be occupied by houses.
   What area will be occupied by houses (in hectares)?
   c) 15 houses are built. What is the mean area of land for each house?
   Give your answer in square metres.

7 A woman buys a plot of land of area 0.36 hectare.
She pays $8.50 per square metre for the land. What is the total cost?

8 In Argentina, a cow on a ranch is expected to need an average of $4200\,m^2$ of grassland for food.
What size does a ranch need to be to feed 4500 cows?
Give your answer in hectares.

9 A small island measures 5.2 km by 1.8 km.
What is its area in hectares?

10 A sheep farm in Australia is in the shape of a rectangle 18 km long by 23.5 km wide.
What is its area in hectares?

19 Interpreting and discussing results

◆ Interpret tables, graphs and diagrams and make inferences to support or cast doubt on initial conjectures; have a basic understanding of correlation.
◆ Compare two or more distributions; make inferences, using the shape of the distributions and appropriate statistics.
◆ Relate results and conclusions to the original question.

You are already familiar with many ways of recording and displaying data, including tables, frequency charts, pie charts, line graphs and stem-and-leaf diagrams. It is also important to be able to interpret results that have been presented in these ways.

In Exercise 19.1 you will concentrate on interpreting data through looking at some graphs and questioning their meaning.

EXERCISE 19.1

1   A group of students believed that the time students took to get to school depended largely on how far away they lived. They collected data to test this theory, recording how far each student lived from school (in kilometres) and the time it took them to get to school (in minutes).

This is a graph of their results.

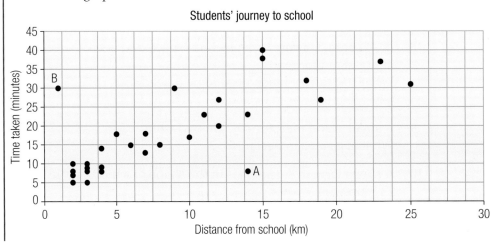

a) What type of graph has been plotted?

b) Does the graph support the students' theory that the further away a student lives from school, the longer it takes to travel? Justify your answer.

c) Explain why some students who live further away may get to school more quickly than other students who live nearer.

d) The data points for two students, A and B, have been highlighted on the graph.

    (i) What does the position of point A tell you about student A's distance from school and travel time?

    (ii) Give a possible reason for the position of point A.

    (iii) What does the position of point B tell you about student B's distance from school and travel time?

    (iv) Give a possible reason for the position of point B.

2 A newspaper report states that

    'On average, women live longer than men.'

The United Nations keeps an up-to-date database of statistical information on its member countries. Some of the data, giving the life expectancies of men and women is shown in this table.

Country	Life expectancy at birth (years, 1990–99)		Country	Life expectancy at birth (years, 1990–99)	
	Female	Male		Female	Male
Australia	81	76	Iraq	64	61
Barbados	79	74	Israel	80	76
Brazil	71	63	Japan	83	77
Chad	49	46	Kenya	53	51
China	72	68	Mexico	76	70
Colombia	74	67	Nepal	57	58
Congo	51	46	Portugal	79	72
Cuba	78	74	Russian Federation	73	61
Egypt	68	65			
France	82	74	Saudi Arabia	73	70
Germany	80	74	UK	80	75
India	63	62	USA	80	73

→

One of the newspaper's readers wants to check the statement in the newspaper. They use the United Nations data to plot this scatter graph.

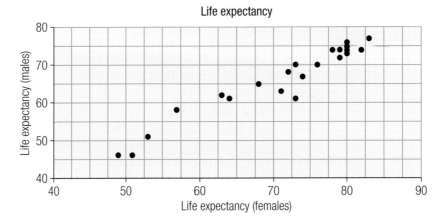

a) Is there a correlation between the life expectancies of males and females? Justify your answer.

b) Do the data and the graph support the statement made by the newspaper? Justify your answer.

3 In a science experiment, a spring is attached to a clamp stand as shown. Different weights are hung from the end of the spring.

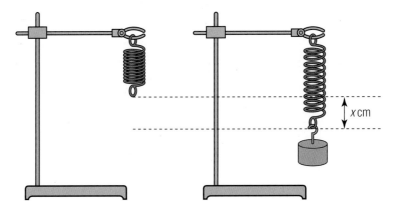

The students record the mass, m (in grams) and the amount by which the spring stretches, x (in centimetres) each time. Their data is shown in this table.

Mass (g)	50	100	150	200	250	300	350	400	450	500
Extension (cm)	2.5	5.2	7.2	10.4	12.7	15.1	17.7	19.6	22.0	24.4

a) Plot a graph of extension against mass.

b) Describe the correlation (if any) between the extension and the mass.

c) Draw a line of best fit for the data.

d) Use your graph to predict the extension of the spring if a mass of 375 g is hung from it.

e) A student extends the line of best fit to predict what the extension will be if 4 kg is hung from the spring. Explain why this prediction is not likely to be accurate.

4   The graph below shows the distribution of the weights of birds of two different species, P and Q. The mean weight of a bird from species P is M_1; the mean weight of a bird from species Q is M_2.

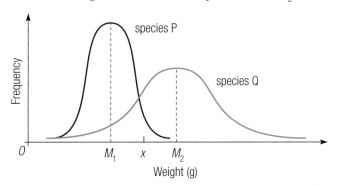

a) Which species has the larger mean weight?

b) Which species has weights which are within a smaller range? Justify your answer.

c) Another bird is caught and its weight is measured. Its weight is x g (shown on the graph). Is this bird more likely to be from species P or species Q? Justify your answer.

5   The manufacturers of two different brands of batteries, X and Y, collect data about how long their batteries last under 'average' usage. This graph shows their data.

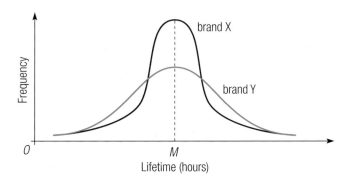

Both brands of battery have the same mean lifetime, M, as shown. Which brand is more consistent? Justify your answer.

6 This graph shows the distributions of the ages of the members of two clubs, A and B. One is an athletics club; the other is a golf club.

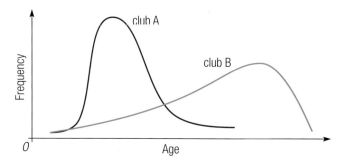

Which club is more likely to be the golf club? Justify your answer.

7 The heights of competitors at a sporting event are shown in the table.
One observer states that the data shows that the heights of the competitors are evenly distributed. Comment on the accuracy of this statement.

Height (cm)	Frequency
$160 \leqslant h < 165$	6
$165 \leqslant h < 170$	6
$170 \leqslant h < 172$	6
$172 \leqslant h < 173$	6
$173 \leqslant h < 175$	6
$175 \leqslant h < 185$	6

8 Students from two classes took the same test.
This back-to-back stem-and-leaf diagram shows their results.

a) Compare the distribution of results from the two classes, commenting on any similarities and/or differences.

b) One class of students is set by ability and the other is a mixed ability class. From the results, deduce which class is likely to be set by ability. Justify your answer.

Class X		Class Y
8 8 6 6	1	1
7 4 3 2	2	6 7 9
8 6 6 4 4	3	4 5 5 5 5 6 6 7 8 9 9 9 9
9 9 7 7	4	6 8 8
8 5 5 5	5	2

Key
|1| 1 means 11 marks.

20 Calculations and mental strategies 3

◆ Extend mental methods of calculation, working with decimals, fractions, percentages and factors, with jottings where appropriate.

Factors

When finding the factors of a number it is helpful to write them in order of size. For example, the factors of 50 are

$$1 \quad 2 \quad 5 \quad 10 \quad 25 \quad 50$$

Unless the number is a square number, the factors occur in pairs. Each pair multiplies together to give the number being considered. That is,

Check your list of factors to make sure each one has a 'partner'. That way, you are less likely to miss out the higher factors.

$$1 \times 50 = 50 \quad 2 \times 25 = 50 \quad 5 \times 10 = 50$$

If the number being considered is a square number, the middle factor forms a 'pair' with itself. For example, the factors of 64 are

$$1 \quad 2 \quad 4 \quad 8 \quad 16 \quad 32 \quad 64$$

The highest common factor (HCF) of 50 and 64 is 2, as this is the highest number that appears in both lists.

EXERCISE 20.1

Find the highest common factor of the following pairs of numbers.

1	30, 35	**2**	15, 18	**3**	24, 36
4	27, 45	**5**	49, 63	**6**	39, 52
7	34, 51	**8**	121, 66	**9**	38, 57
10	77, 132	**11**	16, 24	**12**	63, 84

Fractions

Writing a fraction in its simplest form

In Chapter 15 you saw that you can use factors to simplify fractions. To write a fraction in its simplest form, divide the numerator and denominator by their highest common factor.

Worked example

Write $\frac{50}{75}$ as a fraction in its simplest form.

The highest common factor of 50 and 75 is 25.

$$50 \div 25 = 2$$
$$75 \div 25 = 3$$

Therefore $\frac{50}{75}$ simplifies to $\frac{2}{3}$.

EXERCISE 20.2A

Write each of the following fractions in its simplest form. You may make jottings if necessary.

1 $\frac{15}{24}$ 2 $\frac{9}{18}$ 3 $\frac{27}{36}$ 4 $\frac{75}{100}$

5 $\frac{9}{45}$ 6 $\frac{66}{77}$ 7 $\frac{19}{57}$ 8 $\frac{17}{51}$

9 $\frac{64}{72}$ 10 $\frac{33}{88}$ 11 $\frac{51}{68}$ 12 $\frac{57}{76}$

Converting a decimal to a fraction

You can also use factors to convert a decimal to a fraction or mixed number.

Worked example

Convert 2.375 to a mixed number in its simplest form.

2.375 is equivalent to 2 units and the fraction $\frac{375}{1000}$.

The highest common factor of 375 and 1000 is 125.

$$375 \div 125 = 3$$
$$1000 \div 125 = 8$$

Remember that you can simplify in steps if you cannot spot the highest common factor. For example, you could cancel by 5 three times, like this:

$$\frac{{}^{75}\cancel{375}}{{}_{200}\cancel{1000}} = \frac{{}^{15}\cancel{75}}{{}_{40}\cancel{200}} = \frac{{}^{3}\cancel{15}}{{}_{8}\cancel{40}} = \frac{3}{8}$$

So $\frac{375}{1000}$ simplifies to $\frac{3}{8}$.

Therefore 2.375 is equivalent to the mixed number $2\frac{3}{8}$.

EXERCISE 20.2B

Convert each of these decimals to a fraction or mixed number in its simplest form. You may make jottings if necessary.

> *Start by writing each decimal as a fraction with denominator 10, 100 or 1000.*

1	0.8	**2**	1.9	**3**	2.3
4	0.25	**5**	0.75	**6**	4.25
7	0.35	**8**	0.65	**9**	7.95
10	0.125	**11**	0.875	**12**	1.625

Finding a fraction of a quantity

You can use factors to help you find a fraction of a quantity.

Worked example

Work out $\frac{5}{8}$ of 72.

$72 = 8 \times 9$ so $\frac{1}{8}$ of 72 is 9.

$\frac{5}{8}$ of 72 is 5 times as much as $\frac{1}{8}$.

Therefore $\frac{5}{8}$ of 72 is $9 \times 5 = 45$.

EXERCISE 20.2C

Work out these calculations without using a calculator.
You may make jottings if necessary.
Give each answer in its simplest form.

1 a) $\frac{1}{5}$ of 62	**b)** $\frac{2}{5}$ of 62	**c)** $\frac{2}{5}$ of 0.62
2 a) $\frac{1}{8}$ of 33	**b)** $\frac{3}{8}$ of 33	**c)** $\frac{7}{8}$ of 3.3
3 a) $\frac{1}{10}$ of 340	**b)** $\frac{1}{2}$ of 340	**c)** $\frac{6}{10}$ of 340
4 a) $\frac{1}{9}$ of 369	**b)** $\frac{8}{9}$ of 369	**c)** $\frac{8}{9}$ of 0.369

Addition and subtraction of fractions

EXERCISE 20.2D

Work out these calculations without using a calculator.
You may make jottings if necessary.
Give your answers in their simplest form.

1   $\frac{2}{3} + \frac{1}{3} - 1$ 2 $\frac{5}{9} + \frac{4}{9} + \frac{1}{9} - \frac{7}{9}$

3   $\frac{2}{7} + \frac{3}{7} + \frac{2}{7}$ 4 $\frac{5}{11} + \frac{4}{11} - \frac{3}{11}$

5   $\frac{1}{9} + \frac{1}{3}$ 6 $\frac{1}{4} + \frac{3}{8}$

7   $\frac{9}{11} - \frac{3}{11}$ 8 $1 - \frac{4}{5} - \frac{1}{5}$

9   $1 - \frac{8}{9} + \frac{4}{9}$ 10 $1 - \frac{6}{13} - \frac{1}{13}$

11   $\frac{1}{3} - \frac{1}{9}$ 12 $\frac{3}{4} - \frac{3}{8}$

13   $2\frac{2}{3} + 1\frac{1}{3}$ 14 $1\frac{1}{4} + 2\frac{3}{4}$

15   $5\frac{1}{3} + \frac{1}{9}$ 16 $6\frac{1}{2} - 2\frac{3}{4}$

17   $7\frac{3}{10} - 3\frac{7}{10}$ 18 $5\frac{1}{2} - 4\frac{3}{4}$

19   $1 - \frac{3}{16}$ 20 $4 - 3\frac{9}{20}$

Multiplication of fractions

You can use factors to simplify multiplications involving fractions.

Worked example

Work out $25 \times \frac{2}{5}$.

25 can be written as a fraction as $\frac{25}{1}$.

Therefore $25 \times \frac{2}{5} = \frac{{}^{5}\cancel{25}}{1} \times \frac{2}{\cancel{5}}$

$$= \frac{5}{1} \times \frac{2}{1}$$

$$= 10$$

EXERCISE 20.2E

Work out these calculations without using a calculator.
You may make jottings if necessary.
Give your answers in their simplest form.

Simplify each calculation beforehand if possible.

1 $6 \times \frac{2}{3}$ 2 $8 \times \frac{3}{4}$ 3 $15 \times \frac{3}{5}$

4 $9 \times \frac{2}{3}$ 5 $18 \times \frac{5}{6}$ 6 $24 \times \frac{7}{12}$

7 $6 \times \frac{3}{5}$ 8 $7 \times \frac{3}{8}$ 9 $2 \times \frac{4}{7}$

10 $8 \times \frac{3}{5}$ 11 $6 \times \frac{3}{11}$ 12 $9 \times \frac{7}{10}$

Dividing by a fraction

You already know from Chapter 15 that dividing by a fraction is equivalent to multiplying by its reciprocal. Again, you can use factors to simplify the calculations.

Worked example

Work out $24 \div \frac{6}{7}$.

$24 \div \frac{6}{7} = \frac{\overset{4}{\cancel{24}}}{1} \times \frac{7}{\cancel{6}}$

$= 4 \times \frac{7}{1}$

$= 28$

*The **reciprocal** of a number is 1 divided by that number. (For a fraction, this has the effect of swapping the numerator and denominator.)*

EXERCISE 20.2F

Work out these calculations without using a calculator.
You may make jottings if necessary.
Give your answers in their simplest form.

Simplify each calculation beforehand if possible.

1 $3 \div \frac{3}{5}$ 2 $5 \div \frac{5}{3}$ 3 $8 \div \frac{8}{7}$

4 $10 \div \frac{10}{11}$ 5 $9 \div \frac{3}{4}$ 6 $18 \div \frac{6}{7}$

7 $8 \div \frac{4}{5}$ 8 $16 \div \frac{4}{5}$ 9 $24 \div \frac{6}{7}$

10 $36 \div \frac{9}{10}$ 11 $42 \div \frac{7}{8}$ 12 $64 \div \frac{8}{9}$

Percentages

You should already be familiar with the percentage equivalents of simple fractions and decimals as outlined in the table.

Fraction	Decimal	Percentage
$\frac{1}{2}$	0.5	50%
$\frac{1}{4}$	0.25	25%
$\frac{3}{4}$	0.75	75%
$\frac{1}{8}$	0.125	12.5%
$\frac{3}{8}$	0.375	37.5%
$\frac{5}{8}$	0.625	62.5%
$\frac{7}{8}$	0.875	87.5%
$\frac{1}{10}$	0.1	10%
$\frac{2}{10}$ or $\frac{1}{5}$	0.2	20%
$\frac{3}{10}$	0.3	30%
$\frac{4}{10}$ or $\frac{2}{5}$	0.4	40%
$\frac{6}{10}$ or $\frac{3}{5}$	0.6	60%
$\frac{7}{10}$	0.7	70%
$\frac{8}{10}$ or $\frac{4}{5}$	0.8	80%
$\frac{9}{10}$	0.9	90%

EXERCISE 20.3A

Work with a partner to test each other on the equivalents in the table above. Take turns to give one value, for example 0.4. Your partner must give its equivalents.

EXERCISE 20.3B

1 Write each of these percentages as a fraction in its simplest form.
   a) 13%   **b)** 28%   **c)** 90%   **d)** 25%   **e)** 140%

2 Write each of these fractions as a percentage.
   a) $\frac{14}{100}$ **b)** $\frac{29}{1000}$ **c)** $\frac{3}{10}$ **d)** $\frac{47}{50}$ **e)** $3\frac{3}{4}$

3 Convert each of these percentages to a decimal.
   a) 69%   **b)** 350%   **c)** 123%   **d)** 275%   **e)** 111%

4 Convert each of these decimals to a percentage.
   a) 0.03   **b)** 0.44   **c)** 0.675   **d)** 3.8   **e)** 4.08

Finding a percentage of a quantity

It is sometimes easier to convert the percentage to a fraction or to start by working out 10%. You can use the conversion table on page 188.

Worked example

Work out 15% of $200.

$15\% = \frac{15}{100} = \frac{3}{20}$

Therefore 15% of 200 is

$$\frac{3}{20} \times {}^{10}200 = \frac{3}{1} \times 10 = 30$$

So 15% of $200 is $30.

> Another way is to start from 10%.
> 10% of 200 is 200 ÷ 10 = 20
> 5% of 200 is 10% ÷ 2 = 20 ÷ 2 = 10
> 15% of 200 is 10% + 5% = 20 + 10 = 30
> So 15% of $200 is $30.

EXERCISE 20.3C

Work out these calculations without using a calculator. You may make jottings if necessary.
Give your answers in their simplest form.

  1 20% of 60 minutes   **2** 25% of $360   **3** 40% of 350 days

  4 12.5% of $240   **5** 37.5% of 80 people **6** 80% of 37.5 hours

  7 50% of 96 marks   **8** 96% of 50 marks   **9** 24% of 50 adults

10 60% of 125 children **11** 6% of 125   **12** 125% of 6

13 10% of 240   **14** 90% of 240   **15** 90% of 480

16 480% of 45   **17** 250% of 80   **18** 125% of 200

19 250% of 60   **20** 175% of 160

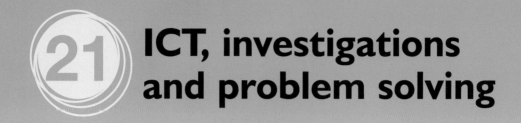

1 Totally tessellated

Starting from one shape that tessellates, it is possible to create a different shape that tessellates. For example, an irregular tessellating shape can be made from a square like this.

(i) A shape is cut out from one side.

(iii) A different shape is cut from one of the other sides and translated to the opposite side.

(ii) This shape is translated to the opposite side of the square.

(iv) The resulting shape tessellates with other identical shapes.

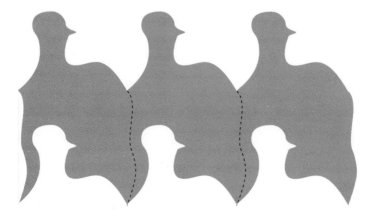

A simple drawing package can be used to create effective tessellating patterns on a computer. An example is shown below.

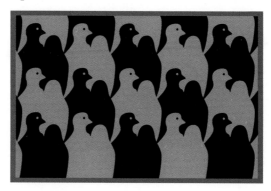

a) Create your own tessellating pattern.
b) Investigate M. C. Escher's tessellating drawings. Many of his patterns were created by rotating an original shape rather than translating it. Try to work out how he created some of his tessellating patterns. One of his patterns is shown on page 142.

2 Second-hand cars

In Chapter 15 you looked at how to work out percentage loss or depreciation when selling second-hand cars. An example is shown here.

Brand New $15\,000   Two Years Old $6000

$$\text{Percentage depreciation} = \frac{\text{change in price}}{\text{original price}} \times 100$$

$$= \frac{6000}{15000} \times 100$$

$$= 40\%$$

a) Look in newspapers or car magazines to find the selling price of a number of second-hand cars.
b) Using the internet or other methods, look up these second-hand cars and find their price when new.

→

c) Set up a spreadsheet to automatically calculate the total percentage depreciation and the 'average' yearly percentage depreciation for each of the cars. It may look similar to this one.

Enter data in these columns   Enter formulae in these columns

d) Using the findings from your spreadsheet, write a brief report suggesting the sort of car someone should buy if they do not want it to depreciate much.

1 Do the following calculations. Simplify your answers where possible.

a) $\frac{3}{13} + \frac{5}{13}$ b) $\frac{4}{31} + \frac{17}{31} - \frac{15}{31}$

c) $\frac{1}{3} + \frac{1}{6} - \frac{5}{18}$ d) $\frac{5}{24} - \frac{1}{12} + \frac{5}{18}$

e) $\frac{1}{7} \times \frac{3}{5}$ f) $\frac{1}{3} \times 1\frac{1}{7} \times \frac{1}{4}$

g) $\frac{7}{9} \div \frac{1}{2}$ h) $\frac{3}{7} \div \frac{3}{21} \times \frac{1}{2}$

2 Calculate the simple interest paid in each of the following cases.
(The rates of interest are annual rates.)
a) principal $2500   time 6 years   rate 2%
b) principal $500   time 3 years   rate 12%

3 For each of the following sequences:
   (i) describe the term-to-term rule
   (ii) calculate the next two terms.

a) 8   14   20   26
b) 0.6   0.2   −0.2   −0.6

4 For each of the following sequences, use the position-to-term rule to find the value of the term shown in brackets.
a) 15   18   21   24   ... (t_{10})
b) 45   41   37   33   ... (t_{50})

5 On squared paper draw a tessellating pattern of irregular quadrilaterals.

6 a) Write down the size of an interior angle of a regular octagon.
   b) By using your answer to part a), explain why regular octagons do not tessellate.
   c) Two regular octagons are arranged next to each other as shown.
   By using your answer to part a), explain why two octagons will tessellate with a square.

7 Copy each of the diagrams below on to squared paper. Enlarge each of the objects by the given scale factor and from the centre of enlargement *O*.

a)　　　　　　　　　　　　　　　　　**b)**

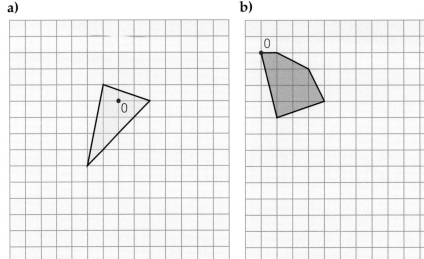

　　Scale factor of enlargement 2　　　　　Scale factor of enlargement 3

8 Convert each of these measures to the units shown in brackets.
　a) 2000 mm² 　　(cm²)
　b) 5 m² 　　　　(cm²)
　c) 250 cm² 　　(m²)

9 This is the net of a cube of side 1.5 cm.

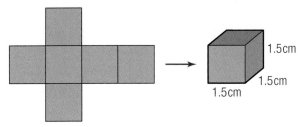

1.5cm
1.5cm
1.5cm

　a) Find the area of the net above:
　　(i) in cm² 　　　　**(ii)** in mm².
　b) If the net is folded into the cube, find the volume of the cube:
　　(i) in cm³ 　　　　**(ii)** in mm³.
　c) What is the capacity of the cube in part **b)** in millilitres?

10 A group of students think that a someone's weight (in kilograms) will give a
    good indication of that person's height (in centimetres). They collect data to
    test this theory.
    This is a graph of their results.

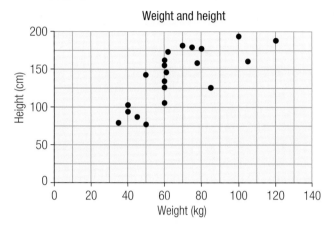

a) What type of graph has been plotted?
b) Does the graph support the students' theory that there is a correlation
   between someone's weight and their height? Justify your answer.
c) Another person, not included in the original data, has a weight of
   160 kg. Will extending the axes and using a line of best fit help in
   estimating this person's height? Explain your answer.

11 *Without using a calculator,* work out:
    a) 70% of 120   b) 145% of 80

12 Write each of these fractions as a percentage.
    a) $\frac{3}{20}$ b) $\frac{15}{1000}$

1   Do the following calculations. Simplify your answers where possible.

    a) $\frac{14}{35} - \frac{6}{35}$ **b)** $\frac{7}{40} - \frac{13}{40} + \frac{9}{40}$

    c) $\frac{5}{36} - \frac{7}{18} + \frac{1}{4}$ **d)** $\frac{1}{5} \times 2\frac{1}{3} \times \frac{3}{10}$

    e) $\frac{5}{14} \div \frac{6}{7} \times \frac{3}{4}$ **f)** $\frac{7}{15} \div \frac{3}{5} \div \frac{1}{2}$

2   Calculate how many years it will take to earn the given amount of simple interest in each of the following cases. (The rates of interest are annual rates.)
    a) principal $1250   rate 6%   interest $300
    b) principal $6000   rate 1.5%   interest $720

3   Calculate the percentage profit or loss in each of the following cases.
    a) cost price $35   selling price $50
    b) cost price $140   selling price $90

4   For each of the following sequences:
        (i) describe the term-to-term rule
        (ii) calculate the next two terms.

    a) 6.1   5.5   4.9   4.3
    b) −38   −29   −20   −11

5   For each of the following sequences:
        (i) derive a simplified formula for the nth term of the sequence
        (ii) use the position-to-term rule to find the value of the term shown in brackets.

    a) −11   −4   3   10   ... (t_{25})
    b) 56   55.5   55   54.5   ... (t_{120})

6   On isometric dot paper draw a tessellating pattern of scalene triangles.

7   **a)** Calculate the size of an interior angle of a regular hexagon.
    b) By considering the sizes of their interior angles, explain whether two squares, an equilateral triangle and a regular hexagon can tessellate.

8 The object X undergoes two transformations. The first transformation maps X on to an image Y, the second maps Y on to an image Z.
Copy the diagram on to squared paper and draw each of the images Y and Z, labelling them clearly.

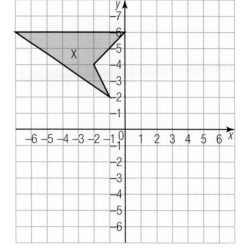

- An enlargement with scale factor 2 and centre of enlargement $(-7, 6)$
- A translation of $\begin{pmatrix} 0 \\ -4 \end{pmatrix}$

9 This is the net of a cuboid.

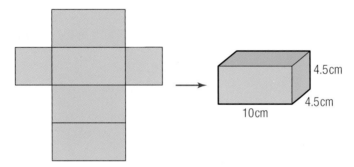

a) Find the area of the net above:
   (i) in cm² **(ii)** in mm².
b) If the net is folded into the cuboid, find the volume of the cuboid:
   (i) in cm³ **(ii)** in mm³.
c) What is the capacity of the cuboid in part **b)** in litres?

10 A field is a rectangle measuring 500 m by 250 m.
What is the area in hectares?

11 *Without using a calculator,* work out:
   a) $4 \div \frac{3}{8}$ **b)** $45 \div \frac{9}{4}$
   c) 12.5% of 60   **d)** 7.5% of 200

12 This graph shows the distribution of the weights of mammals of two different species, P and Q. The mean weight of a mammal from species P is M_1; the mean weight of a mammal from species Q is M_2.

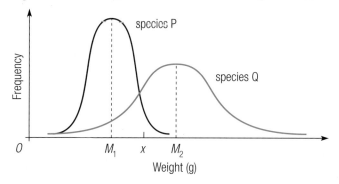

a) Which species has the larger mean weight?

b) Which species has weights which are within a smaller range? Justify your answer.

c) Another mammal is caught and its weight is recorded. Its weight is x kg (shown on the graph). Is this mammal more likely to be from species P or species Q? Justify your answer.

SECTION (4)

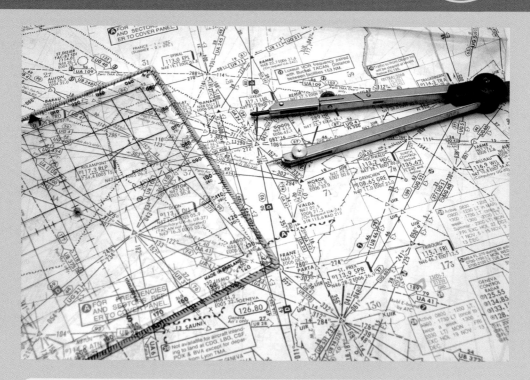

22 Ratio and proportion

◆ Recognise when fractions or percentages are needed to compare different quantities.
◆ Compare two ratios; interpret and use ratio in a range of contexts.
◆ Recognise when two quantities are directly proportional; solve problems involving proportionality, e.g. converting between different currencies.

Ratio

You already know from Student's Books 1 and 2 that a **ratio** shows the relative sizes of two numbers. It can be expressed in different ways.

Worked example

Zachary has a collection of toy cars.
He has 12 red cars, 9 silver cars and 4 blue cars.

a) What is the ratio of silver cars to red cars?

As a ratio: $\quad\text{silver}:\text{red} = 9:12 \qquad = 3:4$

As a fraction: $\quad\dfrac{\text{silver}}{\text{red}} = \dfrac{9}{12} \qquad = \dfrac{3}{4}$

As a percentage: $\quad\dfrac{\text{silver}}{\text{red}} \times 100 = \dfrac{9}{12} \times 100 = 75\%$

b) What is the ratio of red cars to the total number of cars?

The total number of cars is $12 + 9 + 4 = 25$.

As a ratio: $\quad\text{red}:\text{total} = 12:25$

As a fraction: $\quad\dfrac{\text{red}}{\text{total}} = \dfrac{12}{25}$

As a percentage: $\quad\dfrac{\text{red}}{\text{total}} \times 100 = \dfrac{12}{25} \times 100 = 48\%$

c) What is the ratio of red cars to blue cars?

As a ratio: $\quad\text{red}:\text{blue} = 12:4 \qquad = 3:1$

As a fraction: $\quad\dfrac{\text{red}}{\text{blue}} = \dfrac{12}{4} \qquad = \dfrac{3}{1}$

As a percentage: $\quad\dfrac{\text{red}}{\text{blue}} \times 100 = \dfrac{12}{4} \times 100 = 300\%$

d) What is the ratio of blue cars to red cars?

As a ratio: $\text{blue}:\text{red} = 4:12 \quad = 1:3$

As a fraction: $\dfrac{\text{blue}}{\text{red}} = \dfrac{4}{12} \quad = \dfrac{1}{3}$

As a percentage: $\dfrac{\text{blue}}{\text{red}} \times 100 = \dfrac{4}{12} \times 100 = 33\frac{1}{3}\%$

> *Parts **c)** and **d)** show that the order of the items in a ratio is important. For example, 3:5 is not the same as 5:3.*

Problems involving ratios can be answered in different ways.

Worked example

Ahmed works in a bank and earns \$2000 a month.
Ayse is a teacher and earns \$1500 a month.
What is the ratio of Ayse's salary to Ahmed's salary?

As a ratio: $1500:2000 = 3:4$

As a fraction: $\dfrac{1500}{2000} = \dfrac{3}{4}$

As a percentage: $\dfrac{1500}{2000} \times 100 = 75\%$

> *A ratio has no units.*

> *A percentage is the ratio as a fraction of 100.*

So Ayse earns $\frac{3}{4}$ of Ahmed's salary.

Another way of expressing this is that she earns 75% of his salary.

To compare two different ratios, it is often helpful to write each ratio as a percentage.

Worked examples

a) In a five-set tennis match, tennis player A hits 120 first serves.
84 of these first serves go in.
What is the success rate of player A's first serves?

As a ratio: $84:120 = 7:10$

As a fraction: $\dfrac{84}{120} = \dfrac{7}{10}$

As a percentage: $\dfrac{84}{120} \times 100 = 70\%$

b) In the same tennis match, player B hits 125 first serves and 90 go in.
What is the success rate of player B's first serves?

> *It is easy to see that player B has a higher success rate by looking at the percentages. It is not so obvious with the ratios or fractions.*

As a ratio: $90:125 = 18:25$

As a fraction: $\dfrac{90}{125} = \dfrac{18}{25}$

As a percentage: $\dfrac{90}{125} \times 100 = 72\%$

To divide a quantity in a given ratio, fractions are useful.

Worked example

A piece of wood is 150 cm long. It is cut into two pieces in the ratio 2 : 3.
How long is each piece?

2 : 3 gives 5 parts altogether.
One piece of wood is made of 2 parts, which is $\frac{2}{5}$ of the total.

$$\frac{2}{5} \times 150\,\text{cm} = 60\,\text{cm}$$

The other piece is made of 3 parts, which is $\frac{3}{5}$ of the total.

$$\frac{3}{5} \times 150\,\text{cm} = 90\,\text{cm}$$

Probabilities are also usually written and compared using fractions.

Worked example

The ratio of the numbers of red, white, blue and green balls in a bag is 3 : 4 : 5 : 8.
A ball is picked from the bag at random.
What is the probability that it is a red ball?

$$\text{Probability} = \frac{\text{number of successful outcomes}}{\text{number of possible outcomes}}$$

$$= \frac{\text{number of red balls}}{\text{total number of balls}}$$

$$= \frac{3}{3+4+5+8}$$

$$= \frac{3}{20}$$

EXERCISE 22.1A

1   In basketball, player A scores 142 times out of 200 attempts from the free
throw line. Player B scores 81 times out of 150 attempts and player C scores
76 times out of 120 attempts.
   a) What is each player's success rate:
      (i) as a ratio   (ii) as a percentage?
   b) Which player has the best success rate?

2   In football, player A scores 36 goals out of 96 penalty shots at goal. Player B
scores 24 goals out of 75 shots.
   a) What is each player's success rate:
      (i) as a ratio   (ii) as a percentage?
   b) Which player has the better success rate?

3 In rugby, player A scores 95 times from 160 penalty kicks. Player B scores 142 times from 210 kicks and player C scores 124 times from 180 kicks.
  a) What is each player's success rate:
   (i) as a ratio   **(ii)** as a percentage?
  b) Put these players in order of their success rates from lowest to highest.

4 $4000 is divided between three children in the ratio 2:3:5.
  How much does each child receive?

5 Peter is 150 cm tall. His friend Mehmet is 175 cm tall.
  What is the ratio of their heights in its simplest form?

6 A bag contains 90 balls. The ratio of the colours red to white to blue is 1:2:3.
  a) Calculate the probability of choosing:
   (i) a red ball
   (ii) not a red ball
   (iii) a white or a red ball.
  b) How many balls of each colour are there?

7 Asli has a number of coins in a box. There are thirty-four 25 cent coins, eighty-five 10 cent coins, seventy-two 5 cent coins and nine 1 cent coins.
  As a percentage, write down the ratio of:
  a) 25 cent coins to the total
  b) 10 cent coins to 25 cent coins
  c) 1 cent coins to 5 cent coins
  d) the total number of coins to 1 cent coins.

8 What is the ratio of:
  a) the number of days in July to the number of days in a non-leap year
  b) the number of days in a non-leap year to the number of days in August, September and October added together?

9 In golf, player A plays 320 good rounds out of a total of 400 rounds.
  Player B plays 300 good rounds out of a total of 350 rounds.
  What is each player's success rate:
  a) as a ratio   **b)** as a percentage?

10 Do the percentages in question 9 tell you which player is the better golfer? Justify your answer.

To compare ratios they can be written as fractions (or as percentages). If the fractions are equivalent, the ratios are equal.

Worked example

Are the ratios $5:10$ and $14:28$ equivalent?

The ratios can be re-written as the fractions $\frac{5}{10}$ and $\frac{14}{28}$.

$$\frac{5}{10} = \frac{1}{2} \quad \text{and} \quad \frac{14}{28} = \frac{1}{2}$$

Therefore the ratios are equivalent.

If fractions have different denominators it is not always easy to see whether they are equivalent. One way is by 'cross multiplying'.

Using the fractions $\frac{5}{10}$ and $\frac{14}{28}$, the method works like this:

$$\frac{5}{10} \times \frac{14}{28} \quad 5 \times 28 = 140 \quad \text{and} \quad 10 \times 14 = 140$$

If the two fractions are equivalent, the two multiplications have the same answer.

In effect, you are finding the numerators of equivalent fractions with a common denominator of $10 \times 28 = 280$. In this case, both numerators are 140 so the fractions are equivalent.

So one way of finding out whether two ratios are equivalent is to write each of them as a fraction and cross multiply.

Worked example

Are the ratios $5:30$ and $17:120$ equivalent?

Cross multiplying:

$$\frac{5}{30} \times \frac{17}{120} \quad 5 \times 120 = 600 \quad \text{and} \quad 30 \times 17 = 510$$

Therefore the ratios are not equivalent.

EXERCISE 22.1B

Use cross multiplication to find out which of the following pairs of ratios are equivalent.

1   $15:25$ and $3:5$

2   $6:10$ and $36:50$

3   $8:9$ and $24:30$

4   $7:12$ and $42:72$

5   $4:3$ and $3:4$

6   $7:10$ and $33:50$

7   $8:12$ and $72:108$

8   $1:3$ and $6:2$

9   $15:18$ and $70:90$

10   $23:46$ and $69:138$

Direct proportion

If two ratios are equivalent they are **in proportion**.

Worked example

A picture frame measures 12 cm by 20 cm. A second frame measures 36 cm by 60 cm. Are the picture frames in proportion?

The ratios of the dimensions of the two frames are 12:20 and 36:60.

The ratios can be re-written as the fractions $\frac{12}{20}$ and $\frac{36}{60}$.

Alternatively, cross multiplying:
$12 \times 60 = 720$ and $20 \times 36 = 720$

$$\frac{12}{20} = \frac{3}{10} \quad \text{and} \quad \frac{36}{60} = \frac{3}{10}$$

Therefore the ratios are equivalent and the picture frames are in the same proportion.

Proportion and rate

A **rate** is a proportion that involves two different units. For example, the time it takes to walk a given distance is a proportion involving time and distance, and the number of litres of petrol used to travel a given distance is a proportion involving volume and distance. They are examples of rates.

Worked example

Maria runs 6 km in 1 hour 30 minutes.
How long will it take her to run 10 km at the same rate?

Let x be the time Maria takes to run 10 km.
        Distance : Time
              6 : 1.5
             10 : x

1 hour 30 minutes = 1.5 hours

The ratios have to be in proportion because she runs at the same rate. So

$$\frac{6}{1.5} = \frac{10}{x}$$

$$6x = 10 \times 1.5$$

$$x = \frac{10 \times 1.5}{6} = \frac{15}{6} = 2.5$$

It will take her 2 hours 30 minutes.

EXERCISE 22.2A

Use proportion to work out these problems.
In each question assume that the rate stays the same.

1   A car uses 20 litres of petrol to travel 160 km.
    How much petrol does the car use to travel 400 km?

2   A 3 kg bag of potatoes costs $1.50. What does a 7 kg bag cost?

3   In January, £1 (pound sterling) was worth $1.60.
    a) How many pounds was $1200 worth?
    b) How many dollars was £1200 worth?

4   At the same time, £1 was worth €1.20 (euros).
    a) How many euros was £250 worth?
    b) How many pounds was €240 worth?

5   Using the information in questions 3 and 4, work out:
    a) how many dollars you would get for €2500
    b) how many euros you would get for $2500.

6   In June, $500 bought €350.
    a) What was the exchange rate for 1 dollar?
    b) What was the exchange rate for 1 euro?

7   In June, £800 bought €920.
    a) What was the exchange rate for £1?
    b) What was the exchange rate for €1?

8   In June, 50 000 Japanese yen bought €435.
    a) What was the exchange rate for €1?
    b) What was the exchange rate for 1 yen?

Proportions can also be used to solve problems involving percentages.
In this case

$$a:b = \frac{a}{b} = \frac{a}{b} \times 100\%$$

Worked examples

a)   25% of the 320 students in a year group take Spanish.
    How many students is this?

Let x be the number of students taking Spanish.
$$\frac{x}{320} = \frac{25}{100}$$
$$x = \frac{25 \times 320}{100} = 80$$

So 80 students take Spanish.

b) 240 out of 320 students in a year take science.
What percentage is this?

Let x be the percentage of the students taking science.
$$\frac{240}{320} = \frac{x}{100}$$
$$x = \frac{240 \times 100}{320} = 75$$
So 75% of the students take science.

c) 20% of the students in a school take geography.
The number of students taking geography is 65.
How many students are there in the school?

Let x be the number of students in the school.
$$\frac{65}{x} = \frac{20}{100}$$
$$65 \times 100 = 20x$$
$$x = \frac{65 \times 100}{20} = 325$$

So there are 325 students in the school.

EXERCISE 22.2B

1 What percentage of 64 is 16?

2 What percentage of 40 is 32?

3 What is 40% of 360?

4 At a school in Japan, 180 students take the bus to school.
This is 20% of all the students.
How many students are there in the school?

5 A football team won 75% of its matches. It played 44 matches in total.
How many matches did it win?

6 Maria earns $1625 a month. Of this, she pays $650 in rent on a flat.
What percentage of her earnings does Maria spend on rent?

7 40% of the students in a class got an A in a test.
If 18 students got an A, how many students are in the class?

8 35% of the workers in an office bring in lunch from home.
If there are 60 workers in the office, how many do not bring in lunch
from home?

9 I spend 25% of my income on food.
If I spend $138 a month on food, what is my monthly salary?

10 A doctor earns $2400 a month and saves 30% of this.
How much does she spend?

(23) Functions and graphs

◆ Find the inverse of a linear function.
◆ Construct tables of values and plot the graphs of linear functions, where y is given implicitly in terms of x, rearranging the equation into the form $y = mx + c$; know the significance of m and find the gradient of a straight-line graph.
◆ Find the approximate solutions of a simple pair of simultaneous linear equations by finding the point of intersection of their graphs.
◆ Use systematic trial and improvement methods to find approximate solutions of equations such as $x^2 + 2x = 20$.
◆ Construct functions arising from real-life problems; draw and interpret their graphs.
◆ Use algebraic methods to solve problems involving direct proportion, relating solutions to graphs of the equations.

Linear functions

You already know from Student's Books 1 and 2 that a line is made up of an infinite number of points. The position of each point on the line can be described using x and y coordinates.

The coordinates of every point on a straight line all have a common relationship. That is, there is a rule which links the x and the y values.

For example, the table below gives the x and y coordinates of some of the points along this straight line.

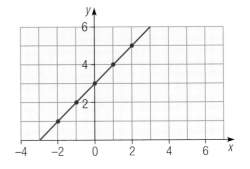

x	−2	−1	0	1	2
y	1	2	3	4	5

We can see that the y coordinates are always 3 more than the x coordinates. In algebra this can be written as $y = x + 3$. This is known as the **equation of the straight line** and simply describes the relationship between the x and y coordinates of all the points on the line.

Drawing straight-line graphs

To be able to draw a straight line, knowing the position of one point on the line is not enough. This diagram shows that, if only one point is given, then any number of lines can be drawn passing through it.

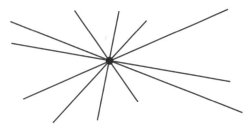

However, if the positions of two points are given, then only one line can pass through them both:

Therefore, to be able to draw a straight line from an equation, the positions of two points need to be calculated and plotted.

Worked example

Draw the line $y = 2x - 1$ on a coordinate grid.

To find the positions of two of the points on the line, choose two values for x.
Substitute each of these into the equation and calculate the y value.
When $x = 0$, $y = -1$, giving the coordinates $(0, -1)$.
When $x = 3$, $y = 5$, giving the coordinates $(3, 5)$.
Plotting these two points and drawing the line between them gives the following graph.

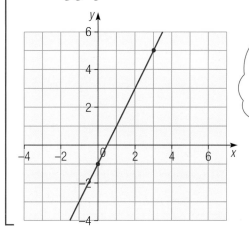

It is good practice to check a third point.
When $x = 1$, $y = 1$.
As the point $(1, 1)$ lies on the line, the graph is correct.

In the example on the previous page, the equation $y = 2x - 1$ gives the value of y **explicitly** in terms of x. That is, the relationship between x and y is stated directly.

Often, however, the relationship between x and y is given **implicitly**. The equation still describes a relationship between x and y, but it is not stated directly; it is implied. For example, the equation $y = 2x - 1$ could have been written as $y - 2x + 1 = 0$.

To draw a graph from an equation that is written implicitly, it is usually easier to rearrange it into explicit form first.

Worked example

Draw the line $2y + x - 4 = 0$ on a coordinate grid.

First re-write the equation in explicit form.

$$2y + x - 4 = 0$$
$$2y + x = 4 \qquad \text{(add 4 to both sides)}$$
$$2y = -x + 4 \qquad \text{(subtract } x \text{ from both sides)}$$
$$y = -\frac{1}{2}x + 2 \qquad \text{(divide both sides by 2)}$$

In explicit form the equation is $y = -\frac{1}{2}x + 2$.

Now find the positions of two of the points on the line. Choose two values for x, substitute each of these into the equation and calculate the y value, as before.
When $x = 0$, $y = 2$, giving the coordinates $(0, 2)$.
When $x = 4$, $y = 0$, giving the coordinates $(4, 0)$.
Plotting these two points and drawing the line between them gives the following graph.

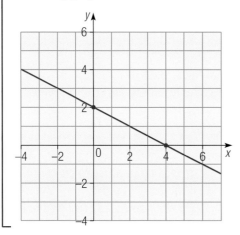

*Check: When $x = 2$, $y = 1$
As (2, 1) lies on the line,
the line is correct.*

EXERCISE 23.1

You will need squared paper for this exercise.

For each of the following equations:
  a) re-write the equation in explicit form
  b) produce a table of values giving the coordinates of at least three points on the line
  c) draw the straight line on a coordinate grid.

1	$y - x = 2$	**2**	$y - 2x + 3 = 0$
3	$2y = x + 2$	**4**	$y - 3 = 0$
5	$y - x = -1$	**6**	$x + 2 = 0$
7	$2y - x = 6$	**8**	$y + x - 3 = 0$
9	$2x + y = 2$	**10**	$y + x = -1$

The general equation of a straight line

Gradient

The **gradient** of a line is a measure of how steep the line is. The gradient of a straight line is **constant**, that is, it does not change.

The gradient of a straight line can be calculated from the coordinates of any two points on the line.

$$\text{Gradient} = \frac{\text{vertical distance between the two points}}{\text{horizontal distance between the two points}}$$

Worked examples

a) The equation of this line is $y = \frac{1}{2}x + 3$. Calculate its gradient.

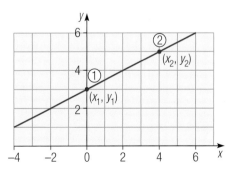

Taking two points on the line as shown,

$$\text{Gradient} = \frac{\text{vertical distance between the two points}}{\text{horizontal distance between the two points}}$$

So the gradient is the difference between the y coordinates, divided by the difference between the x coordinates.

$$\text{Gradient} = \frac{y_2 - y_1}{x_2 - x_1} = \frac{5 - 3}{4 - 0} = \frac{2}{4} = \frac{1}{2}$$

b) Calculate the gradient of the line passing through the points $(5, 2)$ and $(0, 7)$.

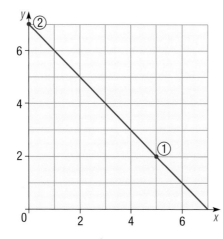

$$\text{Gradient} = \frac{y_2 - y_1}{x_2 - x_1} = \frac{7 - 2}{0 - 5} = \frac{5}{-5} = -1$$

A line with gradient 1 has the same steepness as a line with gradient −1, but the two lines slope in opposite directions. To check whether the sign of the gradient is correct, use the following guidelines:

A line sloping this way $\diagup$ has a positive gradient.

A line sloping this way $\diagdown$ has a negative gradient.

EXERCISE 23.2A

You will need squared paper for this exercise.

For each of questions 1–10:
   a) plot the two points on a coordinate grid
   b) calculate the gradient of the line passing through the two points.

1 $(5, 4)$ and $(2, 1)$ **2** $(4, 6)$ and $(1, 0)$

3 $(0, 1)$ and $(6, 4)$ **4** $(2, 4)$ and $(−1, −2)$

5 $(6, 0)$ and $(0, 3)$ **6** $(−1, −1)$ and $(1, 7)$

7 $(0, 5)$ and $(6, 3)$ **8** $(4, 0)$ and $(2, 6)$

9 $(7, 2)$ and $(0, 2)$ **10** $(2, 0)$ and $(2, 7)$

11 Comment on your answers to questions 9 and 10 above.

Intercept

Apart from straight lines that run parallel to the y axis, all straight lines cross the y axis at some point. This point is known as the **y intercept**.

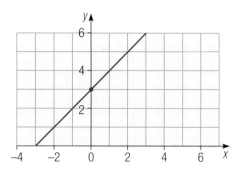

In this graph, the line crosses the y axis at $(0,3)$, so the y intercept is 3.

EXERCISE 23.2B

For each of the graphs in questions 1–5:
    a) work out the equation of the straight line
    b) calculate the gradient of the straight line
    c) give the value of the y intercept.

It may help to make a table of values first.

1

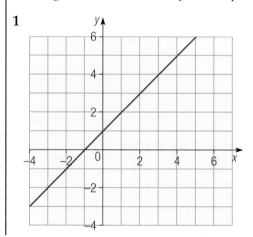

2

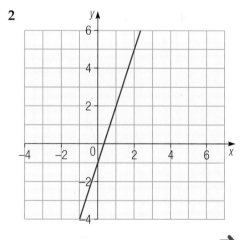

3

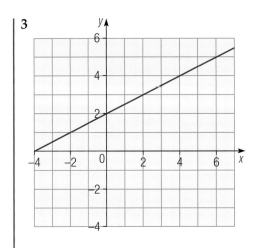

4

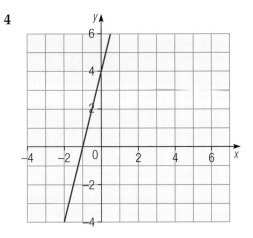

5

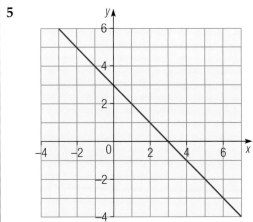

6 For each of the graphs in questions 1–5, describe what you notice about the connection between the equation of a line, its gradient and its y intercept.

You may have noticed in Exercise 23.2B that the values for the gradient and the y intercept form part of the equation of the straight line.

Every straight line takes the form

$y = mx + c$ where:
m = gradient
$c = y$ intercept

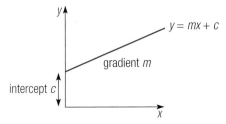

Therefore the equation $y = 3x - 5$ means that the straight line has a gradient of 3 and a y intercept of -5.

> *The equation $y = 3x$ is still of the form*
> *$y = mx + c$. In this case $c = 0$, that is, the line passes through the origin.*
> *Similarly, the equation $y = 2$ is still of the form $y = mx + c$. In this case*
> *$m = 0$, that is, the gradient is 0 and the line is therefore horizontal.*

If an equation is written implicitly, it is advisable to rearrange it into the explicit form $y = mx + c$ before deducing its gradient and y intercept.

Worked example

Find the gradient and y intercept of the straight line with equation $3y - 6x = 1$.

Rearrange the equation into the form $y = mx + c$.

$$3y - 6x = 1$$
$$3y = 6x + 1 \qquad \text{(add } 6x \text{ to both sides)}$$
$$y = 2x + \tfrac{1}{3} \qquad \text{(divide both sides by 3)}$$

Therefore the gradient is 2 and the y intercept is $\tfrac{1}{3}$.

EXERCISE 23.2C

For the straight line represented by each of these equations, find the value of the gradient and the y intercept.

1 **a)** $y = 2x + 1$ **b)** $y = 3x - 1$
    c) $y = \frac{1}{2}x - 3$ **d)** $y = x$
    e) $y = x - \frac{1}{2}$ **f)** $y = -3x + 4$
    g) $y = -x + 4$ **h)** $y = -x$

2 **a)** $y - 2x = 4$ **b)** $y - x = -2$
    c) $y - 3x = 0$ **d)** $y + 2x = 4$
    e) $y + 3x = -1$ **f)** $y - 1 - x = 0$
    g) $y - 5x + 4 = 0$ **h)** $y + 2x - 1 = 3$

3 **a)** $2y = 2x + 4$ **b)** $2y = 4x - 2$
    c) $3y = 9x + 3$ **d)** $5y = 5x$
    e) $\frac{1}{2}y = 2x - 4$ **f)** $\frac{1}{3}y = x - 1$
    g) $\frac{1}{4}y = 1$ **h)** $2y - x + 6 = 0$

Inverse functions

You already know from Student's Books 1 and 2 that a **function** describes the relationship between two variables. It describes how the value of an output variable depends on the value of the input variable.

In the equation $y = 2x - 1$, the variable y is dependent on the value of the variable x. We can also write this relationship as a function. The input variable is x. Using function notation:

$$f(x) = 2x - 1$$

> $y = 2x - 1$ and $f(x) = 2x - 1$ are different ways of writing the same thing.

The **inverse** of a function is its reverse, that is, it is a function that 'undoes' the effect of the original function. For example, the inverse of the function 'add 6' is 'subtract 6'.

If you enter an output value from the original function into the inverse function, you get back to the input value.

In function notation, the inverse of a function $f(x)$ is written as $f^{-1}(x)$.

Worked examples

a) Find the inverse of the function $f(x) = x + 3$.

Write the function as an equation in terms of y:
$$y = x + 3$$
Swap x and y:
$$x = y + 3$$
Rearrange to make y the subject:
$$y = x - 3$$
Therefore the inverse function is $f^{-1}(x) = x - 3$.

The output value from the original function is the input value for the inverse function.

b) Find the inverse of the function $f(x) = 2x + 6$.

Write the function as an equation in terms of y:
$$y = 2x + 6$$
Swap x and y:
$$x = 2y + 6$$
Rearrange to make y the subject:
$$x - 6 = 2y$$
$$y = \frac{x - 6}{2}$$
Therefore the inverse function is $f^{-1}(x) = \frac{x - 6}{2}$.

EXERCISE 23.3

Find the inverse of each of the following functions.

1   **a)** $f(x) = x + 7$ **b)** $f(x) = x - 4$
    c) $f(x) = x - 8$ **d)** $f(x) = x$
    e) $f(x) = 3x$ **f)** $f(x) = \frac{x}{4}$

2   **a)** $f(x) = 5x$ **b)** $f(x) = 3x + 5$
    c) $f(x) = 3x - 2$ **d)** $f(x) = \frac{x + 3}{3}$
    e) $f(x) = \frac{2x + 3}{4}$ **f)** $f(x) = \frac{4x - 6}{3}$

3   **a)** $f(x) = \frac{1}{2}x - 2$ **b)** $f(x) = \frac{1}{4}x + 5$
    c) $f(x) = 4(3x + 2)$ **d)** $f(x) = 6(2x - 3)$

Approximate solutions to equations

Simultaneous linear equations

In Chapter 9 you saw how to solve a pair of simultaneous linear equations algebraically, by eliminating one of the variables. You can also solve a pair of simultaneous linear equations by drawing a graph. This method gives an approximate solution, as it depends on the accuracy of the drawing.

Worked example

Solve these simultaneous equations by drawing a graph.

$$y = \tfrac{1}{2}x - 2$$
$$y = -2x + 2$$

● First draw the straight line $y = \tfrac{1}{2}x - 2$ on a coordinate grid.

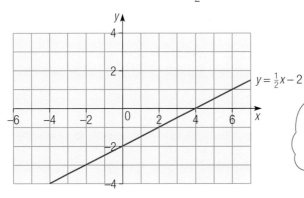

> The x and y values of all the points along this line satisfy the equation $y = \tfrac{1}{2}x - 2$.

● Now draw the line $y = -2x + 2$ on the same axes.

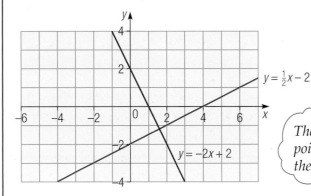

> The x and y values of all the points along the blue line satisfy the equation $y = -2x + 2$.

● At the point where the two graphs intersect, *both* equations are satisfied.
From the graph we can see that the coordinates of this point are approximately $(1.6, -1.2)$.

> If an exact solution is needed, it can be found by solving the two equations algebraically.

● The x and y values of this point are the solution of the two equations.
So the approximate solution of the pair of simultaneous equations is
$$x = 1.6, \ y = -1.2$$

EXERCISE 23.4A

You will need squared paper for this exercise.

For each of these pairs of equations:
   a) draw the two straight lines on the same coordinate grid
   b) use the coordinates of the point of intersection to find an approximate solution to the simultaneous equations.

1 $y = x + 3$ $y = -2x + 1$

2 $y = \frac{1}{3}x - 1$ $y = -x + 1$

3 $y = 2x - 3$ $y = \frac{1}{2}x + 1$

4 $y + 2x - 3 = 0$ $2y = x - 6$

5 $3y + x = 3$ $y + 3x + 3 = 0$

Solving equations by trial and improvement

You have seen that it is possible to find an approximate solution to an equation using graphical methods. It is also possible to find approximate solutions using other methods. One of these is the method of **trial and improvement**.
   This involves a process of getting closer and closer to the solution.

Worked examples

a)   One solution to the equation $x^2 + 2x = 20$ is between $x = 0$ and $x = 5$. Use the method of trial and improvement to find this solution. Give your answer to one decimal place.

Choose a starting value for x and substitute it into the left-hand side of the equation.

Try $x = 4$: $4^2 + 2(4) = 24$ *24 is bigger than 20, so a smaller value of x is needed.*

Try $x = 3$: $3^2 + 2(3) = 15$ *15 is smaller than 20, so a value of x between 3 and 4 is needed.*

Try $x = 3.5$: $(3.5)^2 + 2(3.5) = 19.25$ *The value of x must be between 3.5 and 4.*

Try $x = 3.6$: $(3.6)^2 + 2(3.6) = 20.16$ *The value of x must be between 3.5 and 3.6.*

We need a solution correct to one decimal place. It is either $x = 3.5$ or $x = 3.6$. Of these, $x = 3.6$ gives a result closer to 20 than $x = 3.5$ does. Therefore the solution to the equation $x^2 + 2x = 20$ is $x = 3.6$ (to one decimal place).

b) Use the method of trial and improvement to find the solutions to the equation $x^2 - 3x - 5 = 0$. Give your answers to the nearest whole number.

> *The question implies that there is more than one solution to the equation. As the highest power of x is x^2, there can be two solutions.*

Choose a starting value for x and substitute it into the left-hand side of the equation.

Try $x = 5$: $5^2 - 3(5) - 5 = 5$

> *5 is bigger than 0, so x must be smaller than 5.*

Try $x = 4$: $4^2 - 3(4) - 5 = -1$

> *−1 is less than 0, so x must be between 4 and 5.*

We need a solution correct to the nearest whole number. It is either $x = 4$ or $x = 5$. Of these, $x = 4$ gives a result closer to 0 than $x = 5$ does. So one solution is $x = 4$.

To find the second solution, repeat the process with another starting value for x.

Try $x = -3$: $(-3)^2 - 3(-3) - 5 = 13$

> *13 is bigger than 0, so x must have a smaller **magnitude** than −3.*

Try $x = -2$: $(-2)^2 - 3(-2) - 5 = 5$

> *5 is bigger than 0, so x must have a smaller **magnitude** than −2.*

Try $x = -1$: $(-1)^2 - 3(-1) - 5 = -1$

> *−1 is less than 0, so x must lie between −1 and −2.*

The solution correct to the nearest whole number is either $x = -1$ or $x = -2$. Of these, $x = -1$ gives a result closer to 0 than $x = -2$ does. So the second solution is $x = -1$.

Therefore the solutions to the equation $x^2 - 3x - 5 = 0$ are $x = 4$ and $x = -1$ (to the nearest whole number).

EXERCISE 23.4B

In this exercise use the method of
trial and improvement.

It may be helpful to use a spreadsheet.

1   One solution of the equation $x^2 - x = 7$ is between $x = 0$ and $x = 5$.
    Find this solution, giving your answer correct to one decimal place.

2   One solution of the equation $x^2 + 8x + 4 = 0$ is between $x = -3$ and $x = 0$.
    Find this solution, giving your answer correct to one decimal place.

3   One solution of the equation $x^2 + 16x + 58 = 0$ is between $x = -7$ and $x = -3$.
    Find this solution, giving your answer correct to one decimal place.

4   The equation $-x^2 + 3x = -9$ has two solutions between $x = -3$ and $x = 7$.
    Find both solutions, giving your answers correct to the nearest whole
    number.

5   The equation $-x^2 + 12x - 2 = 0$ has two solutions between $x = -5$ and $x = 20$.
    Find both solutions, giving your answers correct to the nearest whole
    number.

6   The equation $\frac{1}{2}x^3 - 5x^2 + x + 4 = 0$ has three solutions between $x = -5$ and
    $x = 20$.
    Find all three solutions, giving your answers correct to the nearest whole
    number.

Graphs from real-life situations

None of the linear equations and graphs met so far in this chapter have related
to real life. By forming and solving equations from given information, it is
possible to solve problems about real-life situations.

Worked examples

a) The exchange rate between US dollars and pounds sterling is £1 = $1.65.

    (i) Write a formula linking the number of pounds sterling (P) to the number of US dollars (D).

    (ii) Describe the relationship between the two quantities.

    (iii) Draw a graph to show the relationship between the two quantities.

    (i) £1 = $1.65, so $D = 1.65$ when $P = 1$.
        Therefore the formula is $D = 1.65P$.

    (ii) The number of dollars is directly proportional to the number of pounds.

    (iii)

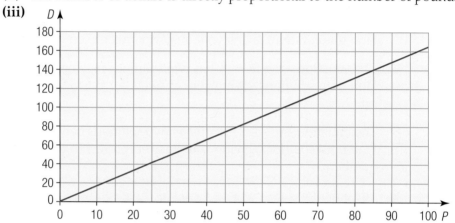

b) Two electricians have different charges for their work:
Electrician A charges a $15 call-out fee and $10.30 per hour whilst working.
Electrician B charges a $10 call-out fee and $12.20 per hour whilst working.

    (i) For each electrician, write a formula that gives the total cost ($\$y$) of a job lasting x hours.

    (ii) Draw a graph of x against y for both electricians on the same axes.

    (iii) Use the graph to estimate the number of hours at which both electricians will charge the same for a job.

    (iv) Find the exact solution to the problem, by solving the equations simultaneously.

    (i) Electrician A: $y = 10.3x + 15$
          Electrician B: $y = 12.2x + 10$

    (ii)

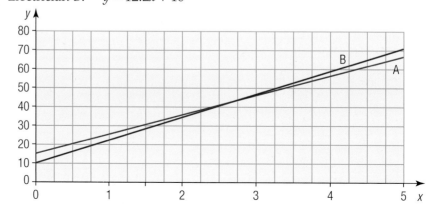

(iii) Both electricians charge the same at the point where the graphs intersect.

> *2.6 hours is 2 hours 36 minutes.*

From the graph, this is after approximately 2.6 hours.

(iv) The two equations are

$$y = 10.3x + 15 \quad \text{and} \quad y = 12.2x + 10$$

At the point of intersection:

$$12.2x + 10 = 10.3x + 15$$

$1.9x + 10 = 15$	(subtract $10.3x$ from both sides)
$1.9x = 5$	(subtract 10 from both sides)
$19x = 50$	(multiply both sides by 10)
$x = \frac{50}{19}$	
$= 2\frac{12}{19}$	

Both electricians charge exactly the same for a job lasting $2\frac{12}{19}$ hours.

EXERCISE 23.5

You will need squared paper for this exercise.

1 Cloth for making curtains is sold by length. The cost is $3.60 per metre.
   a) Write a formula for calculating the cost (C) of x metres of cloth.
   b) Draw a graph of C against x, for values of x up to 20 m.
   c) Use your graph to estimate how much cloth was bought, if the total cost was $50.
   d) Use your formula from part **a)** to calculate how much cloth was bought if the total cost was $50.
   e) Compare your answers to parts **c)** and **d)**. How close were they?

2 Fencing material is sold by length. The cost is $30.50 per metre.
   a) Write a formula for calculating the cost (T) of buying f metres of fencing.
   b) Plot a graph of T against f, for values of f up to 50 m.
   c) Use your graph to estimate how much fencing was bought, if the total cost was $1000.
   d) Use your formula from part **a)** to calculate how much fencing was bought if the total cost was $1000.
   e) Compare your answers to parts **c)** and **d)**. How close were they?

→

3 Two mobile phone companies have different tariffs for text messages:
Phone company X charges $20 per month for unlimited texts.
Phone company Y charges $5 per month and $0.05 per text.
a) For each company, write a formula that gives the total monthly charge (C) for someone who sends n texts.
b) Draw a graph of C against n for both companies on the same axes, showing the monthly charges for up to 500 texts.
c) From your graph estimate the number of texts at which both companies would have the same monthly charge.

4 Two taxi firms have different rates for carrying passengers:
Firm P charges $5 at the start and then a further $1 per kilometre travelled.
Firm Q does not have a starting charge, but charges $1.35 per kilometre travelled.
a) For each firm write a formula that shows the total fare (F) for a journey of d km.
b) Draw a graph of F against d for both firms on the same axes, showing the costs for journeys up to 20 km.
c) (i) Use your graph to estimate the length of a journey for which both firms would charge the same fare.
(ii) Estimate the fare charged for this length of journey.

5 Two cylindrical barrels contain water. Barrel A starts with water at a level of 100 cm. Barrel B starts with water at a level of 150 cm.
The taps on both barrels are opened simultaneously. The tap on barrel A causes the water level to fall at a rate of 1 cm per minute. The tap on barrel B causes the water level to fall at a rate of 2 cm per minute.
a) For each barrel, write a formula that shows the water level (L cm) after t minutes.
b) Draw a graph of L against t for both barrels on the same axes, showing the water level for times up to 100 minutes.
c) (i) Use your graph to estimate the time at which the water level in both barrels is the same.
(ii) Estimate the water level at this time.

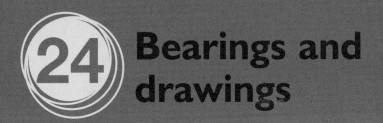

Bearings and drawings

♦ Use bearings (angles measured clockwise from the north) to solve problems involving distance and direction.
♦ Make and use scale drawings and interpret maps.
♦ Find by reasoning the locus of a point that moves at a given distance from a fixed point, or at a given distance from a fixed straight line.

Maps and scale diagrams

The scale of a map is often given as a ratio.

For example, a scale of $1:200\,000$ means that $1\,cm$ on the map is $200\,000\,cm$ or $2000\,m$ or $2\,km$ on the ground.

Plans are also drawn to a scale. These too are usually expressed as a ratio.

A plan of a house may be drawn to a scale of $1:50$. This means that $1\,cm$ on the plan is equivalent to $50\,cm$ on the ground.

EXERCISE 24.1

1 A scale plan of a room is drawn to a scale of $1:50$.
   The room is $8\,cm$ long on the plan.
   How long is the real room?

2 A plan of a playing field is drawn to a scale of $1:200$.
   A play area is $40\,cm$ long on the plan.
   How long is it on the field?

3 The plot of land for a house is shown on a plan with a scale of $1:250$.
   The plot is $27\,cm$ wide on the plan.
   How wide is the real plot of land?

4 A model car is $8.5\,cm$ long. The scale is $1:50$.
   How long is the real car?

5 The scale used to make a toy lion is $1:40$ scale. The toy is $5.2\,cm$ long.
   How long is the real lion?

In questions 6–10, give your answers in a suitable unit.

6 A map has a scale of $1:100\,000$.
How far is a journey which measures 20 cm on the map?

7 A map has a scale of $1:250\,000$.
How far is a journey which measures 5.5 cm on the map?

8 A map has a scale of $1:20\,000$.
How far is a journey which measures 40 cm on the map?

9 A map has a scale of $1:100\,000$.
How many centimetres on the map is a journey of 12 km?

10 A map has a scale of $1:250\,000$.
How many centimetres on the map is a journey of 40 km?

Bearings

In the days when travelling and exploration were carried out on the world's oceans, **compass bearings** (directions), like those shown in the diagram, were used.

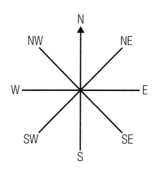

For greater accuracy, extra points were added midway between each of the existing eight points. Midway between north and north-east was north-north-east, midway between north-east and east was east-north-east, and so on. This gave the 16-point compass.

This was later extended to 32 points and even 64 points.

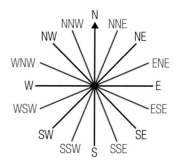

Today, however, this method of compass bearings has been replaced by a system of **three-figure bearings**. North is given a bearing of zero; 360° in a clockwise direction is one full rotation.

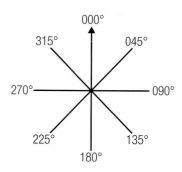

Measuring bearings

This diagram shows the positions of two boats, *A* and *B*.

To measure the bearing from *A* to *B*, follow these steps.

- As the bearing is being measured *from A*, draw a north arrow at *A*.

- Draw a straight line from *A* to *B*.

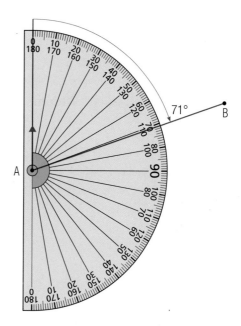

- Using a protractor or angle measurer, measure the angle from the north line at *A* to the line *AB* in a *clockwise* direction.

> *The north arrow is lined up with 0° on the protractor.*

- The bearing is the angle written as a **3-digit number**. Therefore the bearing from *A* to *B* is 071°.

EXERCISE 24.2A

Copy each of the diagrams below. On your diagram, use a protractor to measure each of the following bearings.

1 Bearing from *A* to *B*

•
B

•
A

2 Bearing from *X* to *Y*

•
Y

•
X

3 Bearing from *P* to *Q*

•
P

•
Q

4 Bearing from *M* to *N*

•
M

•
N

•
A

•
C

•
B

•
D

•
E

•
G

•
F

5 **a)** Bearing from *A* to *B*
   b) Bearing from *C* to *B*
   c) Bearing from *A* to *C*

6 **a)** Bearing from *E* to *D*
   b) Bearing from *E* to *F*
   c) Bearing from *G* to *F*
   d) Bearing from *F* to *D*

Worked example

This diagram shows two towns *M* and *N* on a map. The bearing from *M* to *N* is known to be 060°. Without measuring, work out the bearing from *N* to *M*.

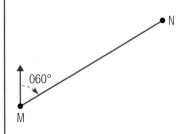

Extend the line *MN* and draw a north arrow at *N*. By using known angle relationships, you can calculate the bearing from *N* to *M*.

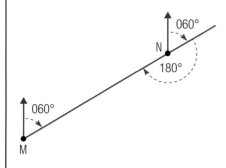

The bearing from *N* to *M* is 060° + 180° = 240°.
The bearing from *N* to *M* is known as the **back bearing**.

EXERCISE 24.2B

1 Copy this diagram.
   a) Measure the bearing from *A* to *B*.
   b) Calculate the back bearing from *B* to *A*.
   c) Measure the bearing from *C* to *D*.
   d) Calculate the back bearing from *D* to *C*.
   e) Copy and complete this table.

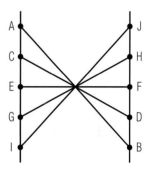

	Bearing		Back bearing
A to *B*		*B* to *A*	
C to *D*		*D* to *C*	
E to *F*		*F* to *E*	
G to *H*		*H* to *G*	
I to *J*		*J* to *I*	

   f) Describe any patterns you can see that link a bearing and its back bearing.

2 For each of these bearings, calculate the back bearing.
   a) 045°   **b)** 090°   **c)** 100°
   d) 180°   **e)** 105°   **f)** 000°
   g) 315°   **h)** 213°   **i)** 342°

3 This map shows a route through five villages labelled *A*, *B*, *C*, *D* and *E*.

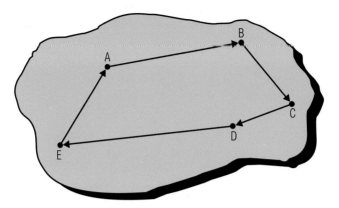

Some of the bearings needed to travel from one village to the next are given in the table below. Copy and complete the table.

Route	Bearing	Route	Back bearing
A to *B*	080°	*B* to *A*	
B to *C*	140°	*C* to *B*	
C to *D*		*D* to *C*	070°
D to *E*	264°	*E* to *D*	
E to *A*		*A* to *E*	212°

EXERCISE 24.2C

For questions 1–3, draw diagrams using a scale of 1 cm : 1 km.
Take north as a line vertically up the page.

1 **a)** A boat starts at a point *A*. It travels a distance of 7 km on a bearing of 135° to point *B*. From *B* it travels 12 km on a bearing of 250° to point *C*. Draw a diagram to show these bearings and journeys.
   b) The boat makes its way straight back from *C* to *A*. What distance does it travel and on what bearing?
   c) Another boat travels directly from *A* to *C*. What are the distance and bearing of this journey?

2 **a)** An athlete starts at a point *P*. He runs on a bearing of 225° for a distance of 6.5 km to point *Q*. From *Q* he runs on a bearing of 105° a further distance of 7.8 km to a point *R*. From *R* he runs towards a point *S* a further distance of 8.5 km and on a bearing of 090°. Draw a diagram to show these bearings and journeys.
   b) Calculate the distance and bearing the athlete has to run to get directly from *S* back to *P*.

3 a) Starting from a point *M*, a horse and rider set off on a bearing of 270°
and travel a distance of 11.2 km to a point *N*. From *N* they travel 5.8 km
on a bearing of 170° to a point *O*. Draw a diagram to show these
bearings and journeys.

b) What are the bearing and distance of *M* from *O*?

4 The map extract shows a part of Malaysia and Singapore. The scale of the
map is 1 : 4 000 000.

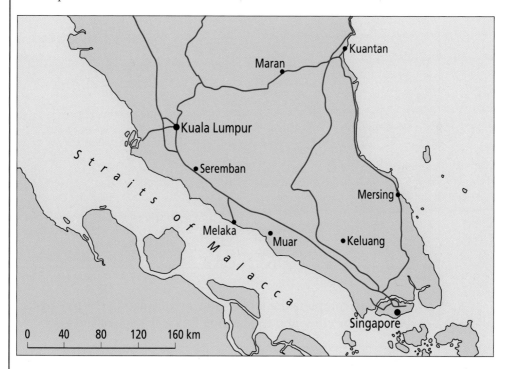

a) A tourist travels from Kuala Lumpur to Singapore. By measuring the
map with a ruler, calculate the real (direct) distance between the two
cities. Give your answer in kilometres.

b) What is the bearing from Kuala Lumpur to Singapore?

c) A traveller decides to travel from Kuala Lumpur to Singapore and then
on to Kuantan, before returning to Kuala Lumpur. Copy and complete
this table of distances and bearings.

Journey	Distance (km)	Bearing
Kuala Lumpur to Singapore		
Singapore to Kuantan		
Kuantan to Kuala Lumpur		

5 A light aeroplane flies from London to Cambridge and then on to Birmingham and Cardiff before returning to London again. The cities are shown on this 1:4 000 000 scale map of part of Britain.

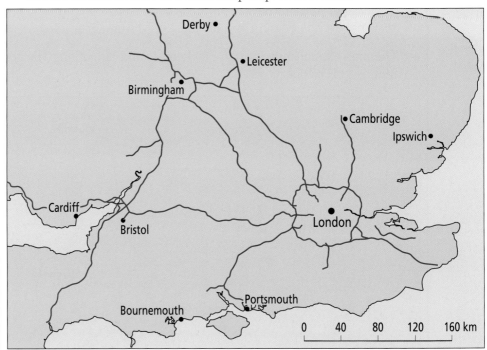

Copy and complete the table below by calculating the true distance between the cities and the bearing for each stage of the journey.

Journey	Distance (km)	Bearing
London to Cambridge		
Cambridge to Birmingham		
Birmingham to Cardiff		
Cardiff to London		

6 This 1 : 10 000 000 scale map shows part of southern Africa.

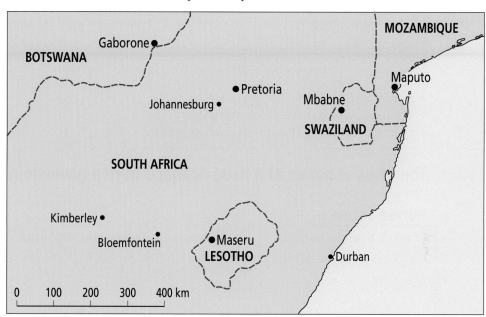

A businesswoman needs to visit the cities of Pretoria, Mbabne, Maputo, Maseru and Gaborone. The only conditions of the trip are that she must start in Pretoria and end in Maseru.

Copy the table below and plan a possible route for the businesswoman by filling in the details of the route that she takes.

Journey	Distance (km)	Bearing
Pretoria to _____		
_____ to _____		
_____ to _____		
_____ to _____		
_____ to Maseru		

Simple loci

A **locus** (plural **loci**) describes where a series of points (or a single point) lie, when the points fit a particular rule. The points can create a region, a line or both.

Most simple problems involving loci involve one of these types:

● points at a fixed distance from a given point
● points at a fixed distance from a straight line
● points at the same distance from two points.

The locus of points at a fixed distance from a given point

Worked example

Imagine a point labelled O. What is the locus of all points 5 cm from O?
The diagram below shows four points, each 5 cm from O.

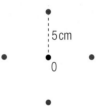

However, these are not the only points which can be plotted 5 cm from O. This diagram shows more points plotted 5 cm from O.

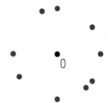

Once again, however, these are not the only points. In fact, if you draw a circle with its centre at O and with a radius of 5 cm, then every point on the circumference of the circle is 5 cm from O.

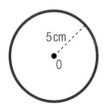

The locus of all the points 5 cm from O is therefore the circumference of this circle.

The locus of the points at a given distance from a given straight line

Worked example

Imagine a straight line *AB*. What is the locus of all the points 5 cm from *AB*?

The diagram below shows four points, all 5 cm from the line AB. Note that these distances are measured at right angles to the line.

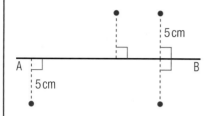

However, more points can be plotted 5 cm from *AB*, as shown in this diagram.

In fact, if you draw two lines through the points on either side of *AB*, and parallel to *AB*, then every point on the lines will be 5 cm from *AB*.

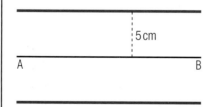

The parallel lines either side of *AB* are therefore the locus of the points 5 cm from *AB*.

However, the diagram does not include the points at the two ends of the line *AB*. If these two points are taken into account, then the locus becomes more complicated, as shown in this diagram.

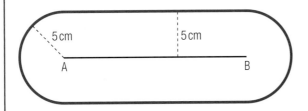

As the two ends of the line *AB* are points, the locus of the points 5 cm from each of them is part of a circle.

The locus of points equidistant from two given points

✪ Worked example

Two points *M* and *N* are shown. What is the locus of all the points that are equidistant (the same distance) from points *M* and *N*?

M ●

N ●

This diagram shows four points, all equidistant from *M* and *N*.

M ●

N ●

Once again, there are other points which are equidistant from *M* and *N*.

M ●

N ●

All the points that are equidistant from M and N in fact lie on the perpendicular bisector of MN.

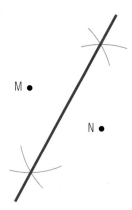

Therefore the perpendicular bisector of MN is the locus of all the points that are equidistant from points M and N.

EXERCISE 24.3A

You will need a pair of compasses and a ruler for this exercise.

1   Draw the locus of all the points that are 6 cm from a point X.

2   The points X and Y are 8 cm apart.
    Draw a scale drawing of the diagram and
    draw the locus of points that are equidistant
    from both points X and Y.

3   Draw a line CD 10 cm long. Draw the locus of all the points 4 cm from the line, including its end points.

4   Two points X and Y are 7 cm apart as shown.
    a) Copy the diagram and draw the locus of
       all the points equidistant from X and Y.
    b) A third point Z is 6 cm below X. Find the
       locus of points equidistant from points X,
       Y and Z.

5   Two points L and M are 6 cm apart. Find the locus of points 4 cm from both L and M.

So far we have only looked at cases where the locus is a line (straight or curved). The locus can, however, also be a region or area.

Worked examples

a) A garden is 10 m × 10 m. In its centre is an apple tree. Grass cannot be planted within 2 m of the tree.
   (i) Draw a scale drawing of the garden.
   (ii) Shade the locus of points where the grass can be planted.

(i) **(ii)**

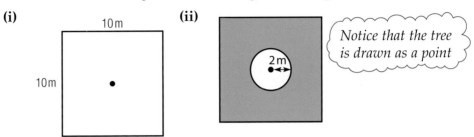

Notice that the tree is drawn as a point

b) A garden is 10 m × 15 m. Grass can only be planted where it is further than 4 m from each of the four corners of the garden.
   (i) Draw a scale drawing of the garden.
   (ii) Shade the locus of points where the grass can be planted.

(i) **(ii)**

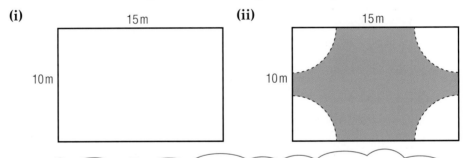

Notice that this time the boundaries are drawn as dashed lines. This is because they are not included in the locus of points, as the grass can only be planted at a distance greater than 4 m from each corner

If the boundary *is* included in the locus of points (as in example **a)** above), it is drawn as a solid line. If the boundary is *not* included in the locus of points (as in example **b)** above), it is drawn as a dashed line.

EXERCISE 24.3B

1 A goat is tied to a rail 8 m long. The rope tying the goat to the rail is 3 m in length and is free to run along the whole length of the rail.
   a) Draw a scale diagram of the rail.
   b) Construct the locus of all the points which can be reached by the goat.

2 The diagram shows a plan view of a rectangular garden 10 m × 8 m in size.
The wall of the house runs along one side of the garden.
The owner of the house wants to grow grass in the garden.
However, the grass must be *more* than 4 m from the side of the house and *at least* 2 m from the edge of the rest of the garden.

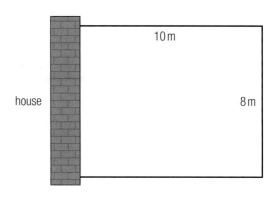

a) Draw a scale drawing of the garden.
b) Draw the locus of all the points where the grass can be grown.

3 Two radio transmitters, Amber Radio and Beacon Radio, are 50 km apart. Beacon Radio is south-east of Amber Radio.

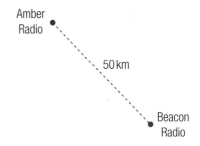

Amber Radio has a range of 40 km; Beacon Radio has a range of 30 km.
a) Draw a scale diagram of the position of the two radio transmitters.
b) Draw the locus of all the points which are within the range of Amber Radio.
c) On the same diagram, draw the locus of all the points which are within the range of Beacon Radio.
d) Shade on your diagram the region which falls within the range of both radio transmitters.

4 Three water sprinklers (*X, Y* and *Z*) are placed in a field. Their positions relative to each other are shown in the diagram.

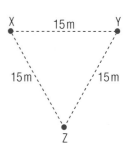

Sprinklers *X* and *Y* have a maximum range of 10 m; sprinkler *Z* has a maximum range of 15 m.
a) Draw a scale diagram of the position of the sprinklers.
b) Construct the locus of all the points that can be reached by each of the three sprinklers.
c) Shade the region that can be reached by all three sprinklers.

5 This garden is in the shape of a trapezium. A garden designer wishes to build a flower bed in the garden. The flower bed must be further than 3 m from the edge of the garden.

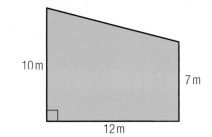

a) Draw a scale drawing of the garden.

b) Construct the locus of all the points where the flower bed can be built.

6 This diagram is a plan view of a girl standing on one side of a brick wall. The wall is taller than the girl, so she cannot see over it.

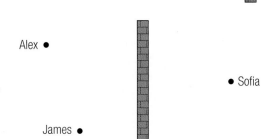

a) Copy the diagram.

b) On your diagram identify the locus of all the points that the girl cannot see.

7 Three children, Alex, James and Sofia are standing near a wall. Alex and James are on one side of the wall, Sofia on the other. None of them is able to see over the wall.

a) Draw a copy of the diagram.

b) Identify the locus of points where Sofia should stand if she wants to remain hidden from Alex and James.

c) Identify the locus of points where Sofia should stand if she wants to remain hidden from James but visible to Alex.

d) Identify the locus of points where Sofia should stand if she wants to remain hidden from Alex but visible to James.

8 A cage is in the shape of a quadrant. The perpendicular sides have a length of 6 m. A path needs to be built around the cage. It must have a constant width of 2 m.

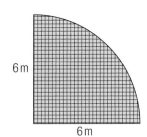

a) Draw a scale drawing of the cage.

b) Construct the locus of all the points occupied by the path.

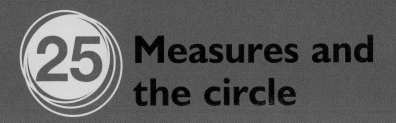

25 Measures and the circle

◆ Solve problems involving the circumference and area of circles, including by using the π key of a calculator.
◆ Calculate lengths, surface areas and volumes in right-angled prisms and cylinders.
◆ Round numbers to a given number of decimal places or significant figures; use to give solutions to problems to an appropriate degree of accuracy.

The circle

Circumference of a circle

You already know from Student's Book 2 that the circumference of any circle is given by the formula:

Circumference $= \pi \times$ **diameter**   or $C = \pi D$

As the diameter is twice the radius, the circumference of a circle can also be given as:

Circumference $= \pi \times 2 \times$ **radius**   or $C = 2\pi r$

Pi (π) is not an exact number; it has an infinite number of decimal places.
   To two decimal places, $\pi = 3.14$
   To 14 decimal places, $\pi = 3.141\,592\,653\,589\,79$

   Scientific calculators have a $\boxed{\pi}$ key. Check to see how many decimal places your calculator gives pi to.

EXERCISE 25.1A

1 Calculate the circumference of each of these circles. The diameter of each circle has been given. Give your answers correct to two decimal places.

a)

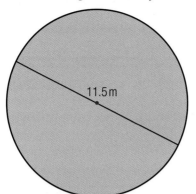

11.5 m

b)

5.2 cm

c)

32 mm

d)

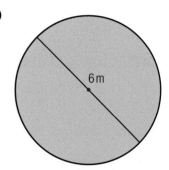

6 m

2 Calculate the circumference of each of these circles. The radius of each circle has been given. Give your answers correct to two decimal places.

a)

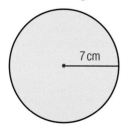

7 cm

b)

4.9 cm

c)

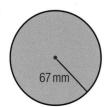

67 mm

d)

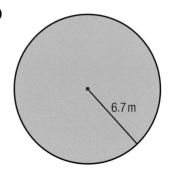

6.7 m

3 Calculate the perimeter of each of these shapes. Give your answers to a suitable degree of accuracy.

a)

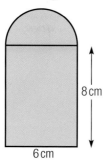

8 cm

6 cm

b)

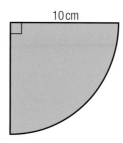

10 cm

c)

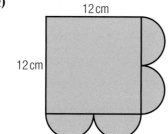

12 cm

12 cm

d)

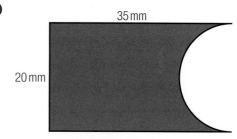

35 mm

20 mm

e)

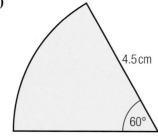

4.5 cm

60°

f)

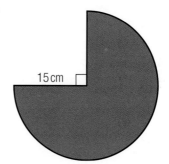

15 cm

4 A bicycle wheel has diameter 75 cm.
  a) Calculate the length of its circumference to one decimal place.
  b) How many times will the wheel rotate if a girl rides the bicycle for 1 km?

Give your answer correct to the nearest whole number.

5 A circular hole of radius 49 cm is cut from a circular metal disc of radius 50 cm, to produce a ring as shown.

How much longer is the outer circumference of the ring compared with the inner circumference?

Give your answer correct to one decimal place.

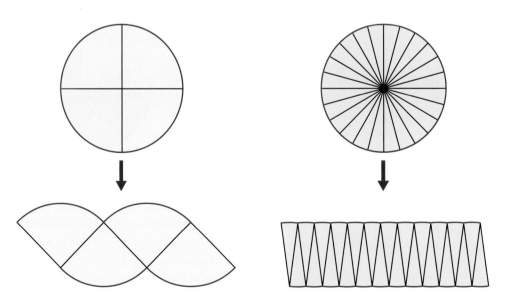

6 A school has a circular athletics track. The inner track has radius 40 m and the middle track has radius 46 m. Two friends decide to race each other. One runs on the inside track, whilst the other runs on the middle track. If both of them run a complete lap of the track, calculate the difference in the distances they have to run. Give your answer correct to two decimal places.

Area of a circle

You already know from Student's Book 2 that the area of a circle can be calculated using a formula. You saw that the formula can be deduced by splitting the circle into smaller and smaller sectors and rearranging them.

Eventually each sector is so small that the rearranged shape is a rectangle.

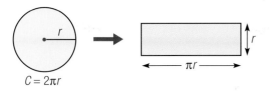

$C = 2\pi r$

Then:

Area of the circle = area of the rectangle
$$= \text{length} \times \text{width}$$
$$= \pi \times r \times r$$
$$= \pi r^2$$

Area of a circle = πr^2

EXERCISE 25.1B

1 Calculate the area of each of these circles. Give your answers correct to one decimal place.

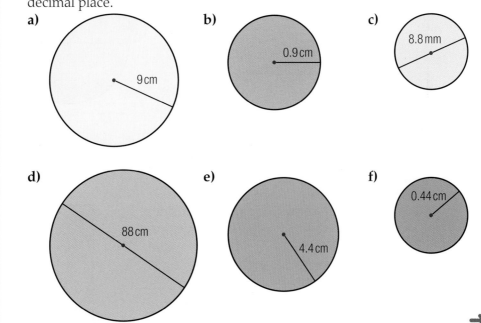

a) 9 cm

b) 0.9 cm

c) 8.8 mm

d) 88 cm

e) 4.4 cm

f) 0.44 cm

2   Calculate the area of each of these shapes. Give your answers to a suitable degree of accuracy.

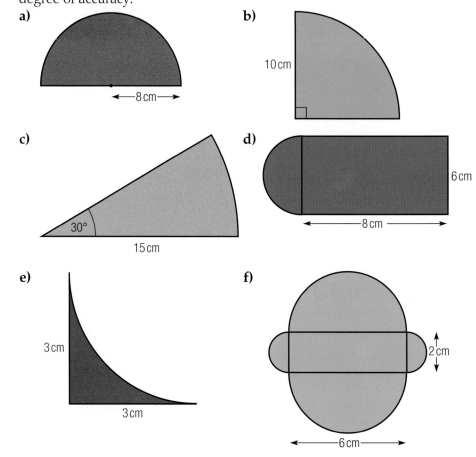

a)

b) 10 cm

c) 30° 15 cm

d) 6 cm 8 cm

e) 3 cm 3 cm

f) 2 cm 6 cm

1   This diagram shows a circular disc inside a square frame. The disc just fits inside the square. Calculate:
  a) the area of the square frame
  b) the area of the circular disc
  c) the area of the square not covered by the disc.

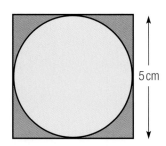

5 cm

2 This diagram shows a circular disc inside a rectangular frame. The width of the rectangle allows the disc just to fit inside the frame.

Calculate the area of the rectangle not covered by the disc.

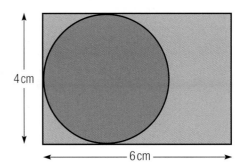

3 Four semicircular pieces of chocolate are arranged in a box as shown in the diagram. Calculate:
   a) the area occupied by the chocolate
   b) the percentage of the base of the box not covered by the chocolate.

4 This diagram shows a spiral made from five quadrants of different-sized circles, joined together. The radius of the smallest quadrant is 1 cm. The radius of adjacent quadrants doubles in size each time.

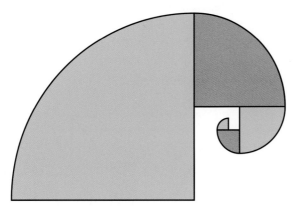

   a) Calculate the area of the spiral. Give your answer correct to the nearest whole number of square centimetres.
   b) Calculate the total perimeter of the spiral. Give your answer to the nearest whole number of centimetres.

5 A circular track has a width of 10 m. If the outer radius of the track is 100 m, calculate the area of the track. Give your answer to the nearest whole number of square metres.

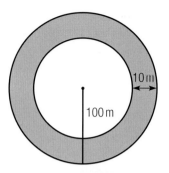

6 This diagram shows a target made from four concentric circles (circles with the same centre). The radius of the inner circle is 2 cm. The radius of the other circles increases by 2 cm each time.

Calculate the area of each of the rings numbered 1, 2 and 3. Give your answers to a suitable degree of accuracy.

Prisms

Volume of a prism

A **prism** is a three-dimensional shape which has the same **cross-sectional** area all through it, i.e. if you were to cut slices through the shape, the shape and area of each slice would be exactly the same.

Here are some examples of prisms:

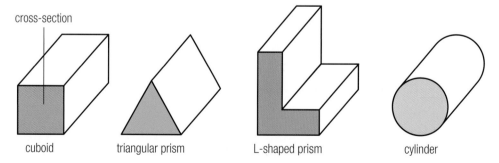

cross-section

cuboid   triangular prism   L-shaped prism   cylinder

When each of these shapes is sliced parallel to the coloured face, the **cross-section** will always look the same. This means it is easy to calculate the volume of a prism.

> **Volume of a prism = area of cross-section × length**

The cross-section of a cylinder always looks the same, so a cylinder is a prism. Its cross-section is a circle, with area πr^2. So

> **Volume of a cylinder = πr^2 × length**

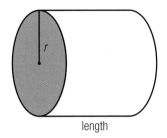

length

Worked examples

a) Calculate the volume of this cuboid.

Area of cross-section = $6 \times 4 = 24\,\text{cm}^2$
Volume = $24 \times 3 = 72\,\text{cm}^3$
In this case, because the prism is a cuboid, other cross-sections could have been used, for example:

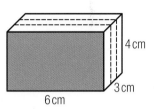

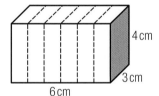

Area of cross-section = $3 \times 4 = 12\,\text{cm}^2$
Volume = $12 \times 6 = 72\,\text{cm}^3$

The volume is the same as before.

b) Calculate the volume of this cylinder. Give your answer to correct to one decimal place.

Area of cross-section = $\pi \times 5^2$
$= 78.539\,816\ldots\,\text{cm}^2$

Volume = $78.539\,816\ldots \times 10$
$= 785.4\,\text{cm}^3$ (to one decimal place)

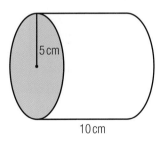

10 cm

c) Calculate the volume of this 'N'- shaped prism.

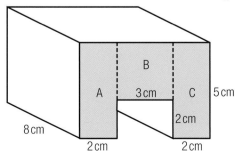

Area of cross-section =
area A + area B + area C
$= (2 \times 5) + (3 \times 3) + (2 \times 5)$
$= 10 + 9 + 10$
$= 29\,\text{cm}^2$
Volume = $29 \times 8 = 232\,\text{cm}^3$

EXERCISE 25.2A

1   Calculate the volume of each of these cuboids, where L = length, W = width and H = height.

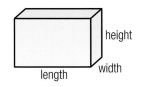

   a) $L = 8\,\text{cm}$ $W = 1\,\text{cm}$ $H = 3\,\text{cm}$
   b) $L = 10\,\text{cm}$ $W = 5\,\text{cm}$ $H = 3\,\text{cm}$
   c) $L = 20\,\text{cm}$ $W = 1\,\text{cm}$ $H = 2\,\text{cm}$
   d) $L = 20\,\text{cm}$ $W = 0.1\,\text{m}$ $H = 5\,\text{cm}$
   e) $L = 50\,\text{mm}$ $W = 30\,\text{cm}$ $H = 0.05\,\text{m}$

2   Calculate the volume of each of these cylinders, where r = radius of circle, D = diameter and L = length.
   (Use your calculator value for π.)

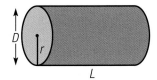

   a) $r = 3\,\text{cm}$ $L = 12\,\text{cm}$
   b) $r = 6\,\text{cm}$ $L = 25\,\text{cm}$
   c) $D = 9\,\text{cm}$ $L = 0.15\,\text{m}$
   d) $D = 58\,\text{mm}$ $L = 0.35\,\text{m}$
   e) $r = \pi\,\text{cm}$ $L = 50\,\text{mm}$

EXERCISE 25.2B

Calculate the volume of each of the prisms in questions 1–2.

1
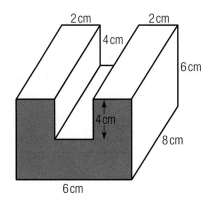

2
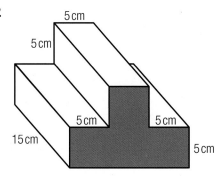

3   Part of a steel pipe is shown. The inner radius is 60 mm, the outer radius is 65 mm and the pipe is 200 m long.
   Calculate the volume of steel used in making the pipe.
   Give your answer in cm³ and correct to three significant figures.

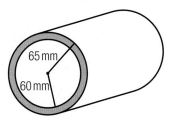

EXERCISE 25.2C

1 This cuboid has a volume of 320 cm³.
Calculate the length (in cm) of the edge marked x.

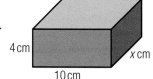

4 cm

x cm

10 cm

2 A cube has a volume of 729 cm³. Calculate:
a) the length of one side
b) its cross-sectional area.

3 A cylinder has a volume of 1540 cm³.
If the radius of the circular
cross-section is 7 cm, calculate the
cylinder's length L.
(Take $\pi = \frac{22}{7}$.)

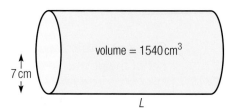

volume = 1540 cm³

7 cm

L

4 A compact disc is shown in the diagram.
It has a thickness of 1 mm. The diameter of the
disc is 12 cm.
The volume of the CD is 11.13 cm³ (to two
decimal places).
Calculate the diameter of the inner circle.
(Take $\pi = 3.14$ or use your calculator value.)

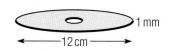

1 mm

—12 cm—

Surface area of a prism

The surface area of a prism (indeed of any three-dimensional shape) is the total
area of its faces. The surface area of a cube, therefore, is simply the area of its six
faces added together.

Worked example

Calculate the surface area of this cube.

Area of one face = $7 \times 7 = 49$ cm²
Total surface area = $6 \times 49 = 294$ cm²

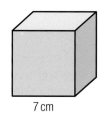

7 cm

To calculate the surface area of a **cuboid**, look at its faces. These are either
squares or rectangles. The surface area of a cuboid is the sum of the areas of its
faces. As the front is the same as the back, the top is the same as the bottom, and
the two sides are the same as each other, the areas can be worked out in pairs.

Area of top and bottom = $2 \times wl$
Area of front and back $= 2 \times lh$
Area of two sides $= 2 \times wh$
Total surface area $= 2wl + 2lh + 2wh$
$= 2(wl + lh + wh)$

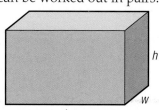

h

w

l

Worked example

Calculate the surface area of this cuboid.

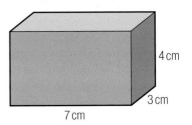

Area of top and bottom $= 2 \times 7 \times 3 = 42\,\text{cm}^2$
Area of front and back $= 2 \times 4 \times 7 = 56\,\text{cm}^2$
Area of two sides $\quad = 2 \times 4 \times 3 = 24\,\text{cm}^2$
Total surface area $\quad\ = 42 + 56 + 24 = 122\,\text{cm}^2$

One way to calculate the total surface area of a prism is to draw (or imagine) the net of the prism.

Worked example

Calculate the surface area of this cylinder.

Draw (or imagine) the net.

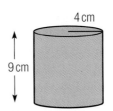

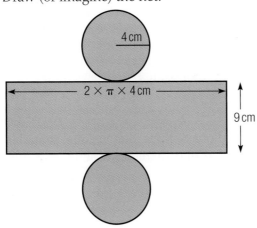

The surface area of a cylinder is made of two circles and a rectangle. The length of the rectangle is equivalent to the circumference of one of the circles.

> Write down your answers rounded to two decimal places at each stage but use the full values, not the rounded values, in the calculations.

Area of one circle $\quad = \pi \times 4^2 = 50.27...\,\text{cm}^2$
Area of both circles $= 50.27... \times 2 = 100.53...\,\text{cm}^2$
Area of rectangle $\quad = 2 \times \pi \times 4 \times 9 = 226.19...\,\text{cm}^2$
Total surface area $\quad = 226.19... + 100.53... = 326.73\,\text{cm}^2$
$\qquad\qquad\qquad\quad$ (to two decimal places)

EXERCISE 25.2D

Calculate the surface area of each of these prisms.

1

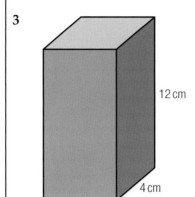

5 cm
5 cm
5 cm
5 cm

2

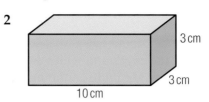

3 cm
3 cm
10 cm

3

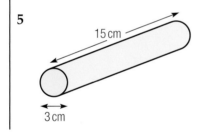

12 cm
4 cm
6 cm

4

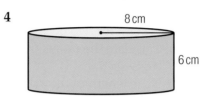

8 cm
6 cm

5

15 cm

3 cm

EXERCISE 25.2E

1 A cube has a surface area of 486 cm². Calculate the length of one of its sides.

2 This cuboid has a total surface area of 158 cm². If its length and width are as shown, calculate its height (h) in centimetres.

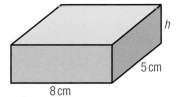

3 A cylinder has a cross-sectional area of 402.12 cm² (to two decimal places).
   a) Calculate the radius (r) of the circular cross-section.
   b) If the length of the cylinder is 20 cm, calculate its total surface area.

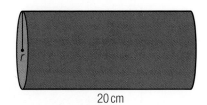

4 A rectangular piece of card has a length of 20 cm and a width of 15 cm. Its total surface area is 614 cm². Calculate its thickness (d) in mm.

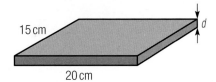

Probability

◆ Know that the sum of probabilities of all mutually exclusive outcomes is 1 and use this when solving probability problems.

◆ Find and record all outcomes for two successive events in a sample space diagram.

◆ Understand relative frequency as an estimate of probability and use this to compare outcomes of experiments in a range of contexts.

You already know from Student's Book 1 that the probability of an event happening must have a value between 0 and 1.

If the probability of an event (E) happening is 0 (i.e. P(E) = 0) then the event is impossible. If the probability of an event happening is 1 (i.e. P(E) = 1) then the event is certain.

In Student's Book 2 you found that the probability of an event happening and the probability of the event not happening are related.

If the probability of an event happening is p, then the probability of the event not happening is 1 − p.

Successive events

Successive events are events that happen one after the other. In order to work out the probability in these cases, it is necessary to know how many possible outcomes there are. One way of displaying all the possible outcomes is to use a **sample space diagram**. A sample space diagram is another name for a two-way table.

Worked example

A coin is tossed and an ordinary six-sided dice is rolled. The coin has a head (H) on one side and tails (T) on the other; the faces of the dice are numbered 1–6.

a) Show all the possible outcomes in a sample space diagram.

b) How many possible outcomes are there?

c) What is the probability of getting a head on the coin and a 3 on the dice?

d) What is the probability of not getting a head on the coin and not getting a 3 on the dice?

e) What is the probability of getting a tail on the coin and an even number on the dice?

a)

		Dice					
		1	2	3	4	5	6
Coin	H	H1	H2	H3	H4	H5	H6
	T	T1	T2	T3	T4	T5	T6

b) From the sample space diagram it can be seen that there are 12 possible outcomes.

These are H1, H2, ... , T5, T6.

c) All the possible outcomes are equally likely, so the probability of getting a head and a 3 is $\frac{1}{12}$.

We can write $P(H3) = \frac{1}{12}$

d) It is certain that one of the possible outcomes will happen, so the probabilities of all the possible outcomes must add up to 1. From part **c)**, the probability of getting a head and a 3 is $\frac{1}{12}$.

The probability of an event not happening can be found by subtracting the probability of the event happening from 1.

The probability of this *not* happening is therefore $1 - \frac{1}{12} = \frac{11}{12}$.

e) From the sample space diagram, there are three possible outcomes with a tail on the coin and an even number on the dice. Each of these has a probability of $\frac{1}{12}$.

These are T2, T4 and T6.

The probability that one of them will happen is
$$P(T2) + P(T4) + P(T6) = \frac{1}{12} + \frac{1}{12} + \frac{1}{12} = \frac{3}{12} = \frac{1}{4}$$

$Probability = \dfrac{number\ of\ successful\ outcomes}{number\ of\ possible\ outcomes}$

EXERCISE 26.1

1 A four-sided dice, numbered 1–4, is rolled and an ordinary coin is tossed.
  a) Construct a sample space diagram to show all the possible outcomes.
  b) How many possible outcomes are there?
  c) What is the probability of getting a head on the coin and a 2 on the dice, i.e. P(H2)?
  d) What is the probability of not getting a head on the coin nor a 2 on the dice?

2 Two four-sided dice, each numbered 1–4, are rolled. The scores on the two dice are added together.
   a) Copy and complete the sample space diagram to show the possible outcomes.

		Dice A			
		1	2	3	4
Dice B	1				
	2		4		
	3			7	
	4				

   b) How many possible outcomes are there?
   c) What is the probability of getting a total score of 6?
   d) What is the probability of not getting a total score of 6?
   e) How many times more likely is a total score of 5 than a total score of 3?

3 Two ordinary six-sided dice, each numbered 1–6, are rolled. The scores on the two dice are added together.
   a) Copy and complete the sample space diagram to show the possible outcomes.

		Dice A					
		1	2	3	4	5	6
Dice B	1						
	2		4				
	3			7			
	4						
	5						
	6						

   b) How many possible outcomes are there?
   c) (i)   Which total score is the most likely outcome?
      (ii)   What is the probability of getting the most likely outcome?
      (iii) What is the probability of not getting the most likely outcome?
   d) What is the probability of getting a total that is an even number?
   e) How many times more likely is a total score of 6 than a total score of 3?

4 The diagram shows two spinners.

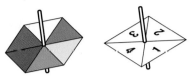

   a) Construct a sample space diagram to show all the possible outcomes for these two spinners.
   b) How many possible outcomes are there?
   c) Calculate the probability of spinning a yellow and a 2.
   d) Calculate the probability of not spinning a yellow and a 2.
   e) Calculate the probability of spinning a yellow *or* a 2.

Relative frequency and probability

So far all the probabilities dealt with have been **theoretical probabilities**, i.e. what you would expect to happen in theory. But, because probability is based on chance, what should happen in theory does not necessarily happen in practice. There are also cases in real life when the theoretical probability of an event happening is not known, for example when you have a biased coin or dice.

In these cases, experiments are conducted to find the **experimental probability** of the event happening. If a biased coin is spun ten times and you get a head seven times, the experimental probability of getting a head with this coin is $\frac{7}{10}$.

Another name for the experimental probability is **relative frequency**.

$$\text{Relative frequency} = \frac{\textbf{number of successful trials}}{\textbf{total number of trials}}$$

You know from Student's Book 2 that generally, the more times an experiment is carried out (i.e. the larger the total number of trials), the closer the experimental probability gets to the theoretical probability.

Worked examples

a) Here is a spinner made out of card.
   To check whether it is biased, it is spun 20 times and the results are recorded.

The table shows the results.

Colour	Red	Blue	Yellow	Green
Frequency	3	2	8	7

(i)   Use these results to decide whether the spinner is biased or not.
(ii) From these results, what is the experimental probability of getting a red?

(i)   An unbiased spinner would land on each colour approximately the same number of times. The frequencies for this spinner differ quite a lot. The spinner is likely to be biased.
(ii) Red occurred 3 times out of 20 spins, so the experimental probability is
    $$P(\text{Red}) = \tfrac{3}{20}$$

b) The same spinner is spun 80 more times and the results are added to the table.

Colour	Red	Blue	Yellow	Green
Frequency	23	24	27	26

(i)   What do these results say about the bias of the spinner?
(ii) Which set of results is likely to be more accurate?

(i)   These results show that the spinner landed on each colour approximately the same number of times. The spinner does not appear to be biased.
(ii) The more times an experiment is repeated, the more reliable the results. Therefore the results from the 100 spins are likely to be more accurate.

EXERCISE 26.2

1 A six-sided dice is suspected of being biased.
   a) If a fair dice is rolled 60 times, approximately how many times would you expect each number to come up?
   b) The dice is rolled 60 times. The table shows the results.

Number	1	2	3	4	5	6
Frequency	9	10	6	18	5	2

   From these results, is the dice likely to be biased? Justify your answer.
   c) From these results, is the dice definitely biased? Justify your answer.
   d) Assuming that the results in the table are representative, calculate the probability of rolling a 6 with this dice.

→

2 When toast is dropped it always lands 'butter side down' – or so it seems!
To test this theory, 50 slices of toast are buttered and dropped.
The table shows the results.

How the toast landed	Butter side up	Butter side down
Frequency	8	42

a) From these results, what is the probability of toast landing 'butter side
down'?

b) Comment on the statement 'Toast always lands butter side down' in the
light of these results.

3 Some red, blue and yellow discs are put in a bag. The number of each
colour is not known. One disc is taken out at random and its colour is
recorded. Then it is put back in the bag. This is done 100 times.
The table shows the number of times each colour was picked.

Colour	Red	Blue	Yellow
Frequency	36	48	16

a) What is the experimental probability of picking a blue disc?

b) There are 25 discs in the bag altogether.
How many discs of each colour would you expect there to be?

4 A consumer magazine compares two types of light bulb, A and B.
It claims that type A bulbs have a $\frac{1}{50}$ chance of being faulty, whilst type B
bulbs have a $\frac{1}{75}$ chance of being faulty.

The survey was carried out on 150 bulbs of each type.

a) How many bulbs of type A were faulty when tested?

b) How many bulbs of type B were faulty when tested?

Another consumer magazine carries out a similar test on the same light
bulbs. This time 750 bulbs of each type were tested. It claimed that type A
bulbs have a $\frac{1}{100}$ chance of being faulty, whilst type B bulbs have a $\frac{1}{20}$ chance
of being faulty.

c) Which set of results is likely to be more accurate? Justify your answer.

d) Which type of light bulb is likely to be more reliable? Justify your
answer.

5 A pharmaceutical company is conducting a trial on a new drug. 100 patients with the same condition are given the new drug and 100 patients are given a placebo.

A placebo is a pretend drug, but the patients believe they are being given the real drug.

The results of the trial are shown in the tables.

Real drug

Patient condition after treatment	Got better	Stayed the same	Got worse
Frequency	37	55	8

Placebo

Patient condition after treatment	Got better	Stayed the same	Got worse
Frequency	38	40	22

a) What is the experimental probability of a patient getting better if they are given the real drug?

b) What is the experimental probability of a patient staying the same if they are given the placebo?

c) The pharmaceutical company claims that the results show that the drug works. Comment on this statement in the light of the results.

27 Calculations and mental strategies 4

◆ Consolidate use of the rules of arithmetic and inverse operations to simplify calculations.
◆ Recognise the effects of multiplying and dividing by numbers between 0 and 1.

The order of operations

You already know that the order of priority in calculations is:

> **B**rackets
> **I**ndices
> **D**ivision and/or **M**ultiplication
> **A**ddition and/or **S**ubtraction

You can use the shorthand **BIDMAS** to help you remember this.

Worked examples

a) Calculate $7 + 9 \div 3$.

$$7 + 9 \div 3$$

The division is done first ($9 \div 3 = 3$) ...

$$= 7 + 3$$

$$= 10$$

... then the addition.

b) Calculate $(8 + 12) \div 4$.

$$(8 + 12) \div 4$$

The brackets are done first ($8 + 12 = 20$) ...

$$= 20 \div 4$$

$$= 5$$

... then the division.

EXERCISE 27.1A

Work out these calculations without using a calculator.
You may make jottings if necessary.

1	$12 \times 4 - 4$	**2**	$8 \times 8 + 6$
3	$4 + 10 \times 6$	**4**	$16 - 8 \div 8$
5	$44 - 24 \div 12$	**6**	$12 \times 6 \div 36$
7	$3 \times 3 + 4 \times 4$	**8**	$(8 + 3) \times 2 - 5$
9	$(9 - 6) \div 3 + 4$	**10**	$20 \div 5 \times (12 - 8)$
11	$(36 - 18) \div (15 + 3) + 4$	**12**	$(5 + 7) \times 2 \div 4 - 5$
13	$(4 + 1) \times 3 + 4$	**14**	$6 \times (8 - 5) - 17$
15	$(24 - 6) \div (6 + 3)$	**16**	$(3 + 2) \times (12 - 5)$
17	$4 - 1 + 3 \times 4 + 2$	**18**	$6 \times (3 + 5) \div 8 - 5$
19	$8 \times (9 - 3) \div 12$	**20**	$16 \div 8 + (2 + 6) \div 8$

EXERCISE 27.1B

Work out these calculations without using a calculator.
You may make jottings if necessary.

1 $\dfrac{(9 + 7)}{2^3}$ $\qquad$ **2** $\dfrac{(9 + 18)}{3^3}$

3 $\dfrac{(6 \times 12) + (4 \times 7)}{5^2}$ $\qquad$ **4** $\dfrac{(2 + 30)}{2^4}$

5 $\dfrac{(8 + 4)}{3} + (3^2 + 1)$ $\qquad$ **6** $2^2 + 8 \times 2 - \dfrac{36}{(11 - 2)}$

7 $25 + \dfrac{(15 + 6)}{(11 - 4)} - 5^2$ $\qquad$ **8** $15 - \dfrac{18}{6} + 2^3$

9 $2 + \dfrac{(25 - 9)}{4} + (12 - 3^2)$ $\qquad$ **10** $\dfrac{6^3}{(16 + 2)} + (5 + 2^2)$

Multiplying and dividing by numbers between 0 and 1

Multiplying

Worked example

Estimate the answer to each of these multiplications.

a) 83×2.9 **b)** 83×0.29 **c)** 83×0.029

a)   A good estimate would be $80 \times 3 = 240$.
b)   A good estimate would be $80 \times 0.3 = 240 \div 10 = 24$.
c)   A good estimate would be $80 \times 0.03 = 240 \div 100 = 2.4$.

You can see that:

- **multiplying by a number greater than 1 increases the value**
- **multiplying by a number less than 1 decreases the value.**

EXERCISE 27.2A

Estimate the answer to each of these multiplications.
In each question, use your estimate from part **a)** to estimate the answers to parts **b)** and **c)**.

1   **a)** 29.5×5 **b)** 29.5×0.5 **c)** 29.5×0.05

2   **a)** 3.8×6 **b)** 3.8×0.6 **c)** 3.8×0.06

3   **a)** 9.4×3 **b)** 9.4×0.3 **c)** 9.4×0.03

4   **a)** 7.93×4 **b)** 7.93×0.4 **c)** 7.93×0.04

5   **a)** 8.92×5 **b)** 8.92×0.5 **c)** 8.92×0.05

6   **a)** 12.39×6 **b)** 12.39×0.6 **c)** 12.39×0.06

7   **a)** 77.44×9 **b)** 77.44×0.9 **c)** 77.44×0.09

8   **a)** 42.12×8 **b)** 42.12×0.8 **c)** 42.12×0.08

9   **a)** 91.03×9 **b)** 91.03×0.9 **c)** 91.03×0.09

10   **a)** 0.93×2 **b)** 0.93×0.2 **c)** 0.93×0.02

Dividing

Worked example

Estimate the answer to each of these divisions.

a) $8.73 \div 3$ **b)** $8.73 \div 0.3$ **c)** $8.73 \div 0.03$

a) A good estimate would be $9 \div 3 = 3$.

b) $8.73 \div 0.3 = 8.73 \div \frac{3}{10} = 8.73 \times \frac{10}{3}$

A good estimate would be $9 \times \frac{10}{3} = 3 \times 10 = 30$.

c) $8.73 \div 0.03 = 8.73 \div \frac{3}{100} = 8.73 \times \frac{100}{3}$

A good estimate would be $9 \times \frac{100}{3} = 3 \times 100 = 300$.

EXERCISE 27.2B

Estimate the answer to each of these divisions.
In each question, use your estimate from part **a)** to estimate the answers to parts **b)** and **c)**.

1	**a)** $37 \div 3$	**b)** $37 \div 0.3$	**c)** $37 \div 0.03$
2	**a)** $7.7 \div 2$	**b)** $7.7 \div 0.2$	**c)** $7.7 \div 0.02$
3	**a)** $29 \div 3$	**b)** $29 \div 0.3$	**c)** $29 \div 0.03$
4	**a)** $8.1 \div 4$	**b)** $8.1 \div 0.4$	**c)** $8.1 \div 0.04$
5	**a)** $37.65 \div 5$	**b)** $37.65 \div 0.5$	**c)** $37.65 \div 0.05$
6	**a)** $17.72 \div 6$	**b)** $17.72 \div 0.6$	**c)** $17.72 \div 0.06$
7	**a)** $42.19 \div 7$	**b)** $42.19 \div 0.7$	**c)** $42.19 \div 0.07$
8	**a)** $87.56 \div 8$	**b)** $87.56 \div 0.8$	**c)** $87.56 \div 0.08$
9	**a)** $18.36 \div 9$	**b)** $18.36 \div 0.9$	**c)** $18.36 \div 0.09$
10	**a)** $50.86 \div 3$	**b)** $50.86 \div 0.3$	**c)** $50.86 \div 0.03$

You can see that:

● **dividing by a number greater than 1 decreases the value**
● **dividing by a number less than 1 increases the value; the closer the number is to 0, the greater the increase is.**

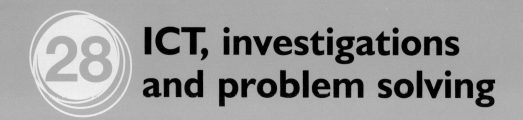

28 ICT, investigations and problem solving

1 Packaging

Manufacturers of packaging often try to reduce their costs and therefore maximise their profits by minimising the surface area of packaging needed for a given volume.

a) Collect a range of different prism-shaped packaging.
b) For each packet:
    (i) calculate its volume and its surface area
    (ii) write the ratio of volume to surface area in the form $1:n$.
c) Which packets have the most efficient volume:surface area ratio?
d) Can you think of some examples when a manufacturer might *not* be trying to minimise this ratio?

2 Scattering leaves

Scientists and environmentalists keep a lot of data on living things in order to increase their understanding of the world and to monitor changes that occur.

    You will be collecting data on a leaf variety of your choice.
  a) Collect about 30 leaves of the same type. Avoid picking them directly from the tree or bush; try to pick them from the ground.

b) Measure the length and width of each leaf. You will need to decide beforehand what you consider to be the length and the width of a leaf. (For example, does the length include the stalk?) Record your results in a table.

c) Plot graphs to display your data clearly (this could be done using a spreadsheet). For example, you could plot a scatter graph.

d) Do leaves of the same variety have different sizes depending on the location of the tree?

e) Write a short report on your findings.

Review 4A

1 Copy and complete these so that the ratios in each pair are equivalent (in proportion).

a) $3:7$ and _____$:28$ **b)** $8:$_____$:$ and $56:42$

2 **a)** Manuel walks 15 km in 3 hours.
    How long does it take him to walk 22 km at the same rate?

    b) A bricklayer lays 120 bricks in 50 minutes.
    How many bricks will he lay in 1 hour 35 minutes, if he continues to lay them at the same rate?

3 For each of the following equations:
    (i) re-write the equation in explicit form, making y the subject
    (ii) produce a table of values giving the coordinates of at least three points on the line
    (iii) draw the straight line on a coordinate grid.

    a) $2y - x = 8$ **b)** $y + \frac{1}{2}x - 3 = 0$

4 Calculate the gradient of the line passing through each of these pairs of points.

    a) $(1, 4)$ and $(3, 14)$ **b)** $(2, 7)$ and $(6, -7)$

5 For each of the following graphs:
    (i) work out the equation of the straight line
    (ii) calculate the gradient of the straight line
    (iii) give the value of the y intercept.

a)

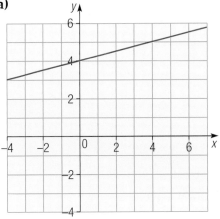

b)

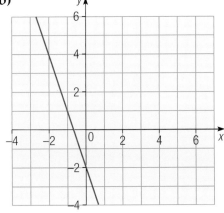

6 a) On the same coordinate grid, draw the straight lines represented by the following equations.
$$y = -3x - 1 \quad \text{and} \quad y = \tfrac{1}{2}x - 2$$

b) Use the coordinates of the point of intersection to find an approximate solution to the simultaneous equations.

7 A map has a scale $1:50\,000$.
a) How far is a journey which measures $42\,\text{cm}$ on the map? Give your answer in kilometres.
b) How many centimetres on the map is a distance of $3.8\,\text{km}$?

8 a) A small plane starts at a point X. It travels a distance of $50\,\text{km}$ on a bearing of $245°$ to point Y. From Y it travels $80\,\text{km}$ on a bearing of $015°$ to point Z.
Draw a diagram to show these bearings and journeys, using a scale of $1\,\text{cm}:10\,\text{km}$ and taking north as a line vertically up the page.
b) Use your diagram to work out the bearing and distance of X from Z.

9 For each of the following circles, calculate:
(i) the circumference   **(ii)** the area.
Give your answers in terms of π.

a)

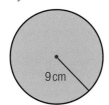

9 cm

b)

45 mm

10 Water is stored in a large tank in the shape of a cylinder.
a) Calculate the area of the top of the cylinder.
b) Calculate the circumference of the top of the cylinder.
c) Calculate the curved surface area of the cylinder.

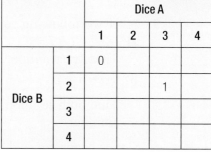

2 m

9 m

11 Two four-sided dice, numbered 1–4, are rolled. The smaller score is subtracted from the larger score.
a) Copy and complete the sample space diagram to show all the possible outcomes.
b) How many possible outcomes are there?
c) What is the probability of getting a score of 3?

		Dice A			
		1	2	3	4
Dice B	1	0			
	2			1	
	3				
	4				

d) (i) Which outcome has the greatest probability of occurring?
(ii) What is the probability of getting the most likely outcome?

12 Copy the following calculations, writing in any brackets which are needed to make the answer correct.
a) $4 + 6 \times 3 - 1 = 29$ **b)** $4 + 6 \times 3 - 1 = 16$ **c)** $4 + 6 \times 3 - 1 = 21$

Review 4B

1   In 2011 the exchange rates for US dollars were:
$1 = 0.70 euros
$1 = 0.61 pounds sterling
$1 = 81 Japanese yen
$1 = 6.9 South African rand.
   a) How many pounds would you get for 5000 yen?
   b) How many rand would you get for 1200 euros?

2   **a)** A boy scored 45 marks out of 83 in a test.
      What is his percentage score?
   b) 27 students out of the 35 students in a class come to school by car.
      What percentage of the students do not come to school by car?
   c) 65% of a woman's monthly income is $630.
      What is her monthly income?

3   For the straight line represented by each of these equations, find the value of
the gradient and the y intercept.
   a) $y = -3x + 4$ **b)** $y + \frac{1}{3}x = 6$
   c) $4y = 2x + 4$ **d)** $-2y + 5x - 4 = 0$

4   Find the inverse of each of the following functions.
   a) $f(x) = 2x - 6$ **b)** $f(x) = \frac{x+4}{2}$
   c) $f(x) = \frac{1}{3}x + 1$ **d)** $f(x) = -\frac{3}{4}x + 2$

5   Solve the following equations using the method of trial and improvement.
   a) $-2x^2 + x + 7 = 0$
      Find one solution, giving your answer correct to one decimal place.
   b) $\frac{1}{2}x^2 = 5 - 4x$

      Find both solutions, giving your answers correct to the nearest whole
      number.

6   Coffee beans are sold by weight. The cost is $2.30 per kilogram.
   a) Write a formula for calculating the cost (C) of x kg of coffee beans.
   b) Draw a graph of C against x, for values of x up to 15 kg.
   c) Use your graph to estimate how much coffee was bought, if the total
      cost was $25.

7 For each of these bearings, calculate the back bearing.
a) 074°   b) 312°   c) 179°

8 The points A and B are as shown. Copy the diagram and construct the locus of points that are equidistant from points A and B.

9 The diagram is a plan view of a rectangular room. The dimensions of the room and the positions of the windows are given. A girl is standing at point O.

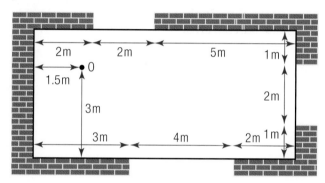

a) Draw a scale diagram of the room, using a scale of 1 cm : 1 m.
b) Using a ruler for your construction, mark on your copy of the diagram the locus of all the points outside the room which the girl can see.

10 A circular ring is cut from a sheet of metal. The cross-section is as shown.
a) The outer radius is 18 cm and the inner radius is 15 cm.
Calculate the cross-sectional area. Give your answer correct to one decimal place.
b) How much longer is the outer circumference of the ring compared with the inner circumference?
Give your answer to a suitable degree of accuracy.

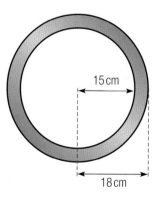

11 *Without using a calculator*, work out the value of x in each of the following. You may make jottings if necessary.

a) $\dfrac{(5-x)}{3^3} = -2$

b) $2(x^2 - 5) + 4^2 = 56$

Index